पुरातत्त्व
PURĀTATTVA

Bulletin of the Indian Archaeological Society

No. 16 1985-86

Editor
S.P. Gupta

D.K. Printworld (P) Ltd.
New Delhi

Cataloging in Publication Data — DK
[Courtesy : D.K. Agencies (P) Ltd. <docinfo@dkagencies.com>]

Purātattva : bulletin of the Indian Archaeological Society, no. 16, 1985-86 / editor, S.P. Gupta.
p. cm.
Includes bibliographical references.
ISBN 8124602913

1. Archaeology — India — Periodicals. 2. India — Antiquities — Periodicals. 3. India — Civilization — Periodicals. I. Gupta, S.P. (Swarajya Prakash), 1931 - II. Indian Archaeological Society.

DDC 934 21

First Published in 1987
First Reprinted in 2005
ISBN 81-246-0291-3
Price for volume 16 (1985-86): Rs. 800 US $ 40

Reprint authorised by
Indian Archaeological Society
New Delhi - 110 016

The Editors are not responsible for the opinions expressed by the Contributors.

Purātattva is published annually.

Manuscripts (whether in the form of articles or notes or book reviews) offered for publication should be sent to the Editor, Purātattva, Indian Archaeological Society, B-17, Qutab Institutional Area, New Delhi - 110 016.

Published and printed by:
D.K. Printworld (P) Ltd.
'*Srikunj*,' F-52, Bali Nagar
New Delhi - 110015
Phone : (011) 2545 3975, 2546 6019 Fax : (011) 2546 5926
E-mail : dkprintworld@vsnl.net
www. dkprintworld.com

PURATATTVA

CONTENTS

NOTES AND NEWS

BOOK REVIEWS

PURATATTVA

NUMBER 16 **1985-86**

Editorial

Puratattva No. 16 contains research papers presented to the annual conference and seminar of the Indian Archaeological Society held from 3rd January through 5th January 1986 at the National Museum, Janpath, New Delhi. The seminar was hosted by the National Museum as a major event of the year long Silver Jubilee celebrations of its foundation in the present building. We thank Dr. L.P. Sihare its Director, for the kind invitation he extended to us.

The entire expenditure incurred on its publication was very kindly provided by the Department of Culture, Ministry of Human Resource Development, Govt. of of India, through the National Museum. We are extremely grateful to them for these most timely grants-in-aid. We are also thankful to the ICHR for giving us a small grant by way of financial assistance to organize the seminar. The ICHR, as well as the National Museum however, are not responsible for any views expressed by the contributors, these are their personal views.

Plates have been numbered according to the serial number of the article. For example, Pl. 4. IV refers to article no. 4, plate no. IV.

In editing and seeing this number of the *Puratattva* through the press, I have received all possible help from Sri K.S. Ramachandran and Sri S. Ganesh Rao. Sri Amarendra Nath helped us in proof reading. To all of them of my hearty thanks..

New Delhi. —S.P. GUPTA

OBITUARY

PROFESSOR D.P. SINGHAL (1925-1986)

DAMODAR PRASAD SINGHAL hailed from Khair near Aligarh in Uttar Pradesh, India. He graduated from Panjab University in 1946 and obtained his M.A. in Political Science from East Panjab University in 1949. He married Devahuti in 1950. They both obtained their Ph.D. in history from the University of London respectively in 1955 and 1956. During this period Mr. Singhal also worked as a political commentator for the B.B.C. In 1956 they moved to Singapore where Dr. Singhal was appointed lecturer at the University of Malaya. His interest in the South-East Asian region dates back to this period. In 1961 Dr. Singhal joined the University of Queensland, Brisbane, where he became Reader in 1964 and Professor in 1969. In 1975 he was awarded a Doctor of Letters from the University of Queensland for his distinguished contribution to the study of Indian history, particularly his major 2 volume work on India's interaction with world civilizations.

Professor Singhal served the Queensland University with distinction, serving on various academic and administrative committees.

Professor Singhal was a keen traveller and together the couple visited the sites of all the major civilisations from Egypt, Greece and Rome to China and Peru. They also travelled widely through other parts of the world reinforcing their historical interests with personal experiences. In the Indian subcontinent Professor Singhal participated in several conferences and symposia in connection with diplomatic and cultural history. He spent his sabbatical leave in 1981 as Visiting Professor at the Jawaharlal Nehru University in Delhi.

Professor Singhal was a Fellow of the Royal Historical Society and the Royal Asiatic Society. He was the Chairman of the Indian History and Cultural Society, Delhi from 1982-85. In January 1986, he was honoured with the presidentship of the Centre for Research and Training in History, Archaeology and Palaeo-environment of which he laid the foundation stone in New Delhi.

Professor Singhal was a scholar of eminence, a perceptive analyst of historical processes, a fine speaker, and a warm and generous person. He was known for his wit and humour which were matched only by his deep observations on human nature. He wrote many books and he wrote well. Some of his publications are listed below:

1. *The Annexation of Upper Burma*, Eastern Universities Press, Singapore, 1960.
   British Diplomacy and the Annexation of Upper Burma, 2nd ed., South Asian Publishers, New Delhi, Madras 1981.
2. *India and Afghanistan : A Study in Diplomatic Relations* 1897-1907, University of Queensland Press, 1963.
3. *Nationalism in India and Other Historical Essays*, Munshiram Manoharlal, Delhi, 1967.
4. *India and World Civilizations*, Vols. I and II, Michigan State University Press, 1969; Sidgwick and Jackson, London, 1972; Rupa, Delhi 1974,

5. *Pakistan*, Prentice-Hall, New Jersy, 1972.
6. A Hindi translation of *India and World Civilization*, Vols. I and II by Meenakshi Prakashan, Meerut, 1979.
7. *Modern Indian Society and Culture*, Meenakshi Prakashan, Meerut, 1980.
8. *Gypsies : Indians in Exile*, Folklore Institute, Meerut, 1982.
9. *A History of the Indian People*, Methuen, Great Britain, 1983.
10. *Buddhism in East Asia*, Books and Books, New Delhi, 1984.

Professor Singhal's character and mission are well summed up in a dedication to him by his old friend and colleague, Professor Hugh Tinker in his book *The Banyan Tree* : "A true son of India and a citizen of the *world*".

PROF. G.R. SHARMA (13-8-1919 — 11-11-1986)

GOVERDHAN RAI SHARMA, the eminent archaeologist of Allahabad University, is no more. His earthly sojourn came to a peaceful close on 11 November, 1986. The torch of learning he lit about four decades back and handed over to his students recently continues to burn brightly and illumine every nook and corner of Indian archaeology.

Prof. Sharma's is a story of the poor lad going from an obscure hamlet to a big city and achieving success by his indomitable will, indefeatigable industry and incessant perseverance. He chose the city of Allahabad and its University for his advancement. The career he preferred was archaeology—in those days an exclusive preserve of the British and a handful of alumni of Calcutta University. His erudition and dedication impressed Sir Mortimer Wheeler, the colossus of Indian Archaeology, in the forties, who initiated him in the intricacies of field archaeology on the bank fo the River Ravi at Harappa. Sharmaji also secured a licence, the first one ever to be granted to a university, for Allahabad University to conduct excavations at Kausambi. Prof. Sharma's archaeological studies spread from Kausambi and ultimately embraced the whole of Gangetic basin and adjoining sites in the Vindhyan region.

Prof. Sharma was a brilliant teacher. Even such a dull subject like Copper Hoards, became almost revetting when Prof. Sharma expatiated on it. He was a visiting Professor of the Oxford and Cambridge Universities.

Prof. Sharma was an extraordinary organiser. In the early fifties, when Pandit Jawahar Lal Nehru visited Kausambi, Prof. Sharma arranged a special exhibition at Kausambi for him. It was so impressive that even today his students are able to recall from memory every single detail connected with it. He was instrumental in the inception of the fullfledged Department of Ancient Indian History, Culture and Archaeology, and its departmental museum in the Allahabad University. Prof. Sharma's crowning achievement as an organiser was the Silver Jubilee Function of the Department and, Seminar on Indian archaeology, he arranged on the eve of his superannuation.

Prof. Sharma never forgot his traditional roots. He eschewed sartorial elegance. At home he was clad in Dhoti and Kurta. His professional attire was Churidar Pyjamas, Kurta and Nehru Jacket with Gandhi cap —all of Khaddar.

His spartan simplicity was reflected in his writings. His, the *Excavation of Kausambi* (1957-59), *Kushana Studies*, etc. are a marvel of simplicity, clarity and economy of expression.

Above all, he had great humane qualities. He could never tolerate injustice. Legend has it that he once cowed down a bully in his village and in the process fractured his hand. He was ever ready to recommend his students for furthering their careers. He always helped people going out of his way, both administratively and financially. Today his students adorn directorial and professorial chairs in many state and central government offices, research institutes, universities and museums. One of his students is currently India's ambassador to Yugoslavia.

Prof. Sharma was a unique, warm human being, the like of him are rarely seen.

SHRI KAILASH CHANDRA VARMA (11-9-1907—31-8-1986)

THE world of traditional Indian scholarship and Indian archaeology has lost a great champion and stalwart in the passing away of Shri Kailash Chandra Varma of Ghaziabad on the last day of August, 1986 at the age of 78 years. He died at New Delhi after a brief illness at his son's, Commander S. Varma's, place.

Shri K.C. Varma was born on 11th September, 1907 in Allahabad. He was the only son of Shri S.P. Varma, CSI, CIE, a well-known family of Zamindars of Uttar Pradesh. He had his initial education at Kanpur and his higher studies at Allahabad, where he graduated in B.Sc. (Agriculture) in 1928.

He joined the Remington Rand Co. (India) Ltd. in 1933 and by dint of his own merit and perseverance, rose to the rank of General Manager (Sales) for India and retired in 1967. Married to Sumitra Srivastava in 1933, they were blessed with two illustrious sons.

He settled at Ghaziabad in 1968 and had his abode to his desire where he continued his brilliant academic pursuits vigorously almost to the last.

A great and erudite scholar to the core, he belonged to that world of scholarship which has imbibed the true spirit of tradition coupled with restless modern scientific temper, thereby arriving at conclusions, whether acceptable or not to the academics working on those problems. One of his main facets of equiry is the astronomical basis of the Vedic and Early Vedic times, including the period of Epics, the Kaliyuga Era, the famous Bharata War *vis-a-vis* the chronology of the contemporary cultures prevalent in Middle East, South Asia and extending to Egypt and Asia Minor. For nearly two decades he laboured hard on these intellectual domains and brought to bear his researches in various annual sessions of the academic bodies of the country. Another of his main intellectual pre-occupations included his study of Western Indologists and Indian civilization which neatly reveals his great sagacity and acumen to dissect the trivial from the ordinary and extraordinary and also excels in the quality of his judgement.

One of his absorbing fields of interest was the Military History in general and it was fascinating to hear his glint of admiration of the logistics and tactical nuances of the great conquerors of the world, be they Napoleon Bonaparte, Alexander the Great or Nadir Shah.

He was a great and voracious reader and a discriminating lover of books which is glimpsed by his rich and vast collection of valuable and rare books which occupy his whole house. Each and every inch of space is packed to capacity. His breadth of scholarship is revealed by his collections which include Ancient Indian History, Archaeology, Zoology, Anthropology, English literature, fiction, poetry, ornithology, Military History, and so on.

During the last decade and a half, his abode became a sylvan retreat for the aged and young scholars, his impassioned and absorbing discussion caught those who were near to him, so much that it became a venerable place beaming with people for most of the day. He gave an institutional base by founding a Society for Indic Studies in 1985 at his own place and as fitting tribute of its beginning by assuming the Editorship of a Felicitation Volume to the great Sanskrit and Vedic scholar and octogenarian Acharya Udayavira Shastri, aptly named *Rtambhara—Studies in Indology* and released the volume to the galaxy of scholars of the Indian Archaeological Society attending the Annual Session in New Delhi during the first week of January, 1986. The enormous labour put forth by him in the previous months in 1985 taxed his health too much.

He was a rare combination of simple habits and great wisdom and his place was open at all time of day to all scholars, or one who reaches in search of knowledge. Among his other great qualities that he possessed was his photographic memory and quick to heels to recapitulate whole pages, date, year, including footnotes. He seldom forgot what he once read.

He knew Tulsidas's *Ramayana* almost by heart and freely recited major portions of the *Mahabharata,* the *Ramayana* and the *Gita.*

He was member of various academic bodies such as All India Oriental Conference, Indian History Congress, Indian Archaeological Society, etc. He was seldom found missing from any one of them and evoked great interest by his new revelations of astronomical data on the vast array of ancient Indian literature.

There can be no doubt that he has not only made a lasting contribution to the field of ancient Indian Astronomy, but also as a non-professional how much he could bring to bear upon the Indian scholarship his overbearing influence and also succeed in convincing them of his convictions. Verily his passing away is a great loss and the void will be felt for many years to come.

1

Microlithic Industry of Damdama—Pratapgarh, U.P.: A Preliminary Analysis

J.N. Pal

The discovery of Mesolithic sites in the Gangetic plain has added a completely new chapter to the prehistoric studies of India. Since 1973 a large number of sites have been discovered and some of these have been excavated: quite a good number of material related to these cultures has been studied[1] and published. The excavated sites of the region, viz. Sarai-Nahar-Rai, Mahadaha and Damdama are our main source of information about the different facets of the Mesolithic culture of the Ganga Valley. Among these sites, Damdama has greater significance due to the fact that it has thickest occupational deposit in a better preserved habitation mound.

The excavations at Damdama[2] have revealed ten phases of Mesolithic associated to ten different layers. Many new information e.g. crouched burial, burials in prone position, twin burials placed opposite each other in north-south and south-north direction respectively, double burials of males and triple burials, etc. have been revealed by the excavations at Damdama.

A good number of artefacts associated with different phases of the culture has been recovered—animal bones, bone objects, burnt clay lumps, querns, mullers, hammer stone-*cum*-anvils and microliths.

Microliths have been largely the main determining point of a Mesolithic site and often the Mesolithic industry. In the following pages an attempt has been made to present the nature of the microlithic industry recovered from the excavations at Damdama upto 1985.

The result of the excavations of 1982-1984 has already been published[3]. The excavation in the lower levels was comparatively in smaller area, therefore, we have a vague idea about the cultural assemblage of earlier levels. In 1985 some more squares were opened in about 19 sq. m area. We excavated the lower levels of occupation and hearths and burials of earlier levels were exposed. Microliths from earlier levels were also recovered in good quantity.

The nature of raw material, very bad quality of nodules of chalcedony, chert, quartz, etc. poses a question whether really these were brought from the Vindhyas crossing a vast territory of nearly hundred fifty kilometres. Besides the raw material, there are also laterite nodules which were often used as source of pigment, but these also are of very bad quality. Generally the import is done of superior quality of material. The nature of raw material forces us to investigate in the Gangetic plain itself for the source of raw material. There is a possibility that the Pleistocene and Holocene deposits might have brought with their alluvium the gravels and chalcedony, chert nodules from the hills and the Mesolithic man in the Ganga Valley collected them from these deposits. But still we have to locate those spots of the source of raw material.

The microlithic artefacts of Damdama have been divided mainly into two categories: (1) unmodified waste, and (2) finished and utilized artefacts. The unmodified waste includes blades (0.950%), blade fragments (6.082%), flakes (8.037%), flake fragments (80.885%), cores (2.688%), core trimming flakes (0.841%) and core rejuvenating flakes (0.515%). These are the unretouched and unutilized artefacts. Table 1 shows the layerwise distribution of unmodified waste.

The finished tools and utilized artefacts (Figs. 1 & 2), showing layerwise distribution of this category of artefacts indicates, include utilized blades/blade fragments (2.249%), normal retouched blades/blade fragments (10.429%), inversely retouched blades/blade fragments (3.271%), normal and inversely retouched blades/blade fragments (0.817%), Quchlata retouched blades/blade fragments (2.044%), straight backed blades/blade fragments (15.337%), convex backed blades/blade fragments (12.883%), concave backed blades (0.408%), partly backed and retouched blades/

TABLE 1. DISTRIBUTION OF UNMODIFIED WASTE

					Core								
Artefact type / Layer	Blade	Blade Frag.	Flake	Flake Frag.	Exhausted	Frag.	Single platform	Double platform	Flake	Total	Core Trimming Flake	Core Rejuvenating Flake	Total
1	19	157	199	1752	20	20	9	6	9	64	13	8	2212
2	5	18	34	352	4	5	2	3	1	15	5	4	433
3	3	10	7	178	1	1	1	1		4	3		205
4	3	8	20	110	3	2				5		3	149
5		5	8	150	3	2				5	4		172
6	1	6	6	90				1		1	1		105
7		7	9	74	1	2				3	3	4	100
8	4	4	4	150							1		163
9		8	4	78	1			1		2			92
		1	5	45							1		52
Total %	35 0.950%	224 6.082%	296 8.073%	2979 80.885%						99 2.688%	31 0.841%	19 0.515%	3683 100%

TABLE 2. DISTRIBUTION OF RAW MATERIAL

Layer	Chalcedony	Chert	Quartz	Agate	Carnelian	Total
1	1737	750	53	41	7	2588
2	339	97	9	8	2	455
3	159	61		3		223
4	135	22		2		159
5	169	15	1	1		186
6	99	16	2	3		120
7	92	17	1	1	2	113
8	145	47	4		1	197
9	81	12	3	1	1	98
10	49	7	1	1		48
Total	2995	1044	74	61	13	4187
%	71.531%	24.934%	1.76%	1.457%	0.310%	100%

blade fragments (1.431%) double backed blades/blade fragments (1.022%), backed and truncated blades/blade fragments (4.294%), truncated blades/blade fragments (1.635%), scalene triangles (7.361%), isoceles triangles (10.020%), trapezoid (0.613%), trapezes (1.022 %), lunates (8.793%), percoirs (2.658%), drills (1.840%), transverse arrow heads (0.817%), tip of triangles/misc. (0.613%), utilized flakes (1.431%), normal scrapers (1.226%), concave scrapers (1.022%), convex scrapers (0.613%), notch scrapers (0.613%) and micro-burins (1.635%),

The unmodified waste is 88.279% while the finished tools and utilized artefacts are only 11.721%. The analysis of the artefacts shows (Table 2) that the most popular raw material was chalcedony represented by 71.531%, followed by chert (24.934%), quartz (1.76%) agate (1.457%) and carnelian (0.310%').

The lunates and backed blades start coming from he lowest layer, i.e. layer (10) and scalene and isoceles triangles and percoir from layer (9). The trapeze first appears in layer (5).

REFERENCES

1. Sharma, G.R. Mesolithic Lake Culture in the Ganga Valley, *Proceedings of the Prehistoric Society* Vol. XXXIX, 1973; Sharma, G.R., Misra, V.D. and Pal, J.N. *Excavations at Mahadaha*, Allahabad, 1980; Misra, V.D. *Some aspects of Indian Archaeology*, Allahabad, 1977; Varma. R.K. The Mesolithic Culture of India, *Puratattva*, No. 13 and 14, 1984; Pandey, J.N. Settlement Pattern and Life in the Mesolithic Period in Uttar Pradesh., D. Phil. Thesis, University of Allahabad, 1985; Banerjee, T., Studies in the Lithic Industries of Southern Uttar Pradesh (from the Upper Palaeolithic to Mesolithic), D. Phil. Thesis, University of Allahabad, 1985; and Pal, J.N., Some New Light on the Mesolithic Burial Practices of the Ganga Valley: Evidence from Mahadaha, Pratapgarh, Uttar Pradesh, *Man and Environment*, Vol. IX, 1985;

2. Varma, R.K., Misra, V.D., Pandey, J.N., Pal, J.N. A Preliminary Report on the Excavations at Damdama, *Man and Environment*, Vol. IX, 1985.

3. *Ibid.*

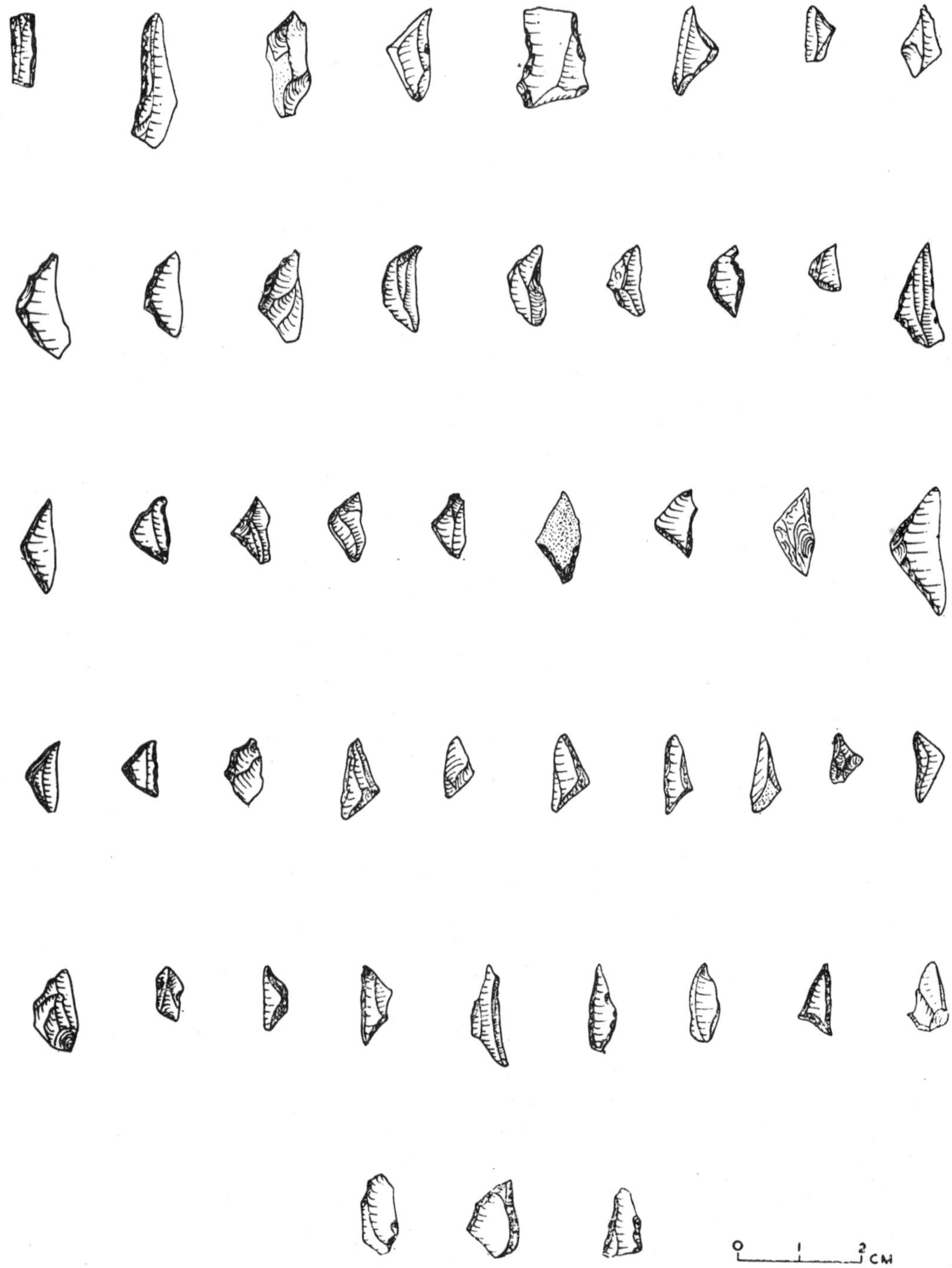

FIG. 1

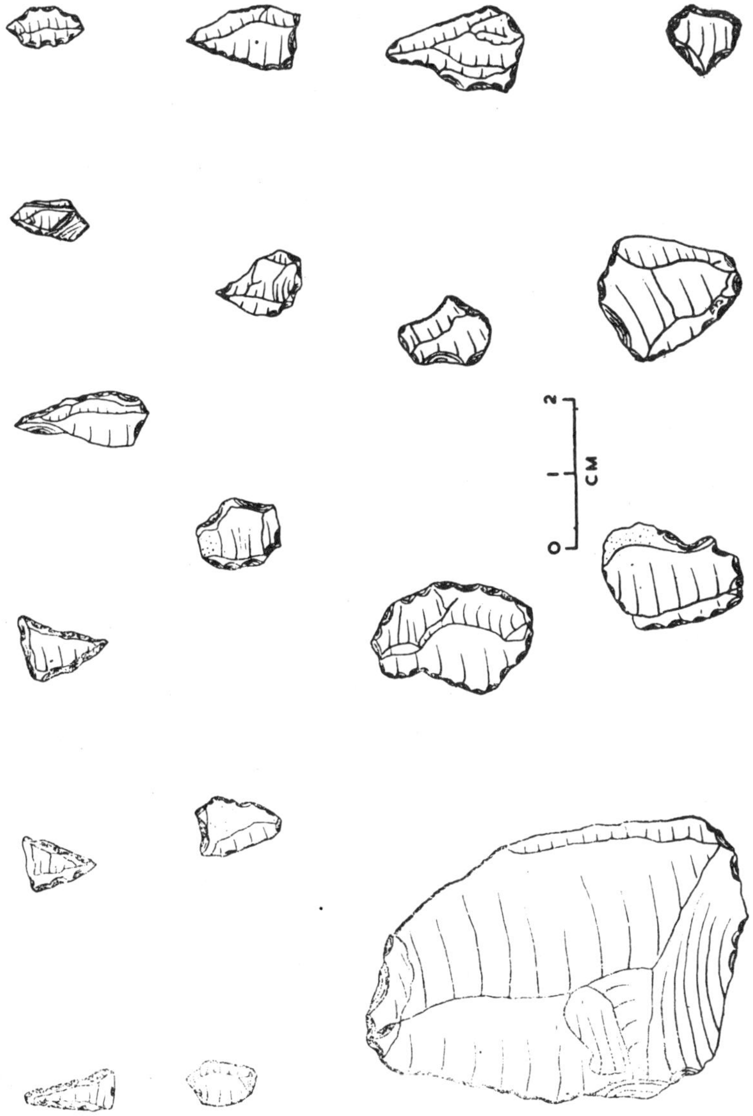

Fig. 2

2

Lady of Beasts—The Harappan Goddess

Shubhangana Atre

Female terracotta figurines supposedly of a Mother Goddess found at Mohenjodaro and Harappa are well-known to scholars and it is generally accepted that, though all the female figurines found at these sites may not have a claim to divinity yet a certain type does represent the Mother Goddess. This type is usually denoted by the figurines who wear a typical fan-shaped head-dress, sometimes with cup-shaped attachments. They are shown standing with arms hanging straight at their sides. They wear a short skirt which is tied with broad girdle and they wear one or more necklaces (Fig.1). Wheeler observed that these Mother Goddess figurines differ from the widespread type of nude figurines as "there is no emphasis on the generative organs such as normal to Mother Goddess cults".[1] There are very few figurines where pregnancy seems to be the focal point in their making. This fact is no doubt, peculiar if viewed against the background of the ancient Mother Goddess cults where, "she and her organs and attributes have been the life giving symbols *par excellence* ever since their first appearance in the Middle East and Europe at the begininng of the Upper Palaeolithic."[2] Not only the nudity but also the obesity had become synonymous with the concept of female fecundity and thus with abundance, right from the palaeolithic times.

Is it then a disregard that is reflected by the Harappan female figurines for this basic 'mother-symbolism' of plenty ? The breasts and hips lack the extraordinary opulence of the more common type and the emphasis on sexuality is removed by the skirt worn by the Harappan figurines. They fit neither into the nude, heavy-bosomed types nor into the abstract fiddle-shaped forms. At the same time they are not so thin as to suggest an under-developed body. The round breasts, prominent hips and the attenuated waist are indicative of a mature maiden. The clothing around her waist probably confirms her virginity.

The notion that these female figurines represent a Mother Goddess is so deeply entrenched in the minds of scholars that the immediate possibility which strikes the mind, under the circumstances is that of a virgin Goddess. It is evident that throughout the ancient world, wherever the Mother Goddess reigned supreme, she was also recognized as eternal 'virgin' emphasizing her independence of the male principle. She was deemed as being able to procreate without male participation, a phenomenon basic to the concept of 'parthenogenesis'. If at all the male element was to play any part, it was as a subordinate tool to activate her for procreation. The concept of an eternal 'virgin' is mainly associated with the Mother Earth and the ever renewing cycle of her vegetal fertility. Every year she sends forth fresh vegetation and yet remains unaberrated just ready for fructification like a 'virgin'.

Is the Harappan Goddess to be identified with the Virgin Earth ? A possibility that cannot be overlooked, but needs further investigation. Such an attempt, however, anticipates a better understanding of Harappan iconographic standards which were then existent. This should help us in determining the exact function of the type of female terracotta figurines which are unquesti onably presumed to be the true representations of a Mother Goddess. If they could have been employed for some other function, then the question arises in what form was the Mother Goddess represented ?

Our present understanding of the Harappan pantheon is based on Marshall's work.[3] He identified a certain type of terracotta female figurine as representative of a Mother Goddess, a seated figure occurring on the seals as proto-Siva and certain types of stone objects as phallic objects. Unfortunately, further attempts to interpret Harappan religion got entangled in the web of Aryan-Dravidian dichotomy and the possibility of an altogether radical and more rational interpretation became remote. In the initial enthusiasm surged by the apparent proof of the antiquity of Brahamanic deities as well as their non-Aryan origin, the basic fallacies in Marshall's interpretation escaped detection.

The first and foremost lacuna in Marshall's interpretation is that he compared the religious phenomenon of an extinct society with modern Hinduism, including its various folk-cults, although this civilization had left no direct links in the succeeding cultures. This perhaps caused his expounding an oversimplified and scattered view of a complex and more organized phenomenon. Modern Hinduism has emerged as a result of an age-long process of assimilation of various diverse elements and it is doubtful to what extent the modern parallels, in this case, should be stretched back to understand the ancient religious life. Most of the earlier attempts to interpret any of the Harappan religious elements are based in superficial similarities, as for example the idea of phallic worship. The particular shape of the stone objects was considered to be sufficient to identify their phallic nature oblivious of their contextual associations.

Secondly, Marshall's interpretation was largely based on the findings at Mohenjodaro and the data available from the excavations at Harappa were only used where it served to support the observations based on the evidence from Mohenjodaro.

It is noteworthy that Marshall's methodology of identifying the iconological value of the artefacts was not uniform. He recognized the image of the Mother Goddess in the terracotta female figures while the male figurines were almost neglected. To identify a male divinity he searched the figures occurring on seals. It is strange that he should have imagined that the Harappans would choose a diverse media to represent the two divinities which were according to him of equal central importance.

He also erroneously compared the *purusha* and *prakriti;* the basic elements on which the highly philosophical system like Sankhya is based, with Saktism and phallic worship. In reality these three systems are very tenuously connected with each other and represent three entirely different planes, albeit within the bounds of modern Hinduism.

Now, we may again turn to the problem whether the terracotta female figurines with a fan-shaped head-dress which have pannier-shaped appendages and wearing a short skrit, ornaments, etc. could be treated as Mother Goddess figurines. It has been already pointed out that these Harappan female figurines distinctly stand apart as a type from the rest of their kind found at ancient as well as contemporary archaeological sites. In some instances soot marks were observed inside the pannier-shaped appendages and hence Mackay felt that perhaps people used to burn incense in them so that their plea should reach the goddess.[4] It, however, remains to be explained as to why people should use the images of a principal deity to burn incense.

Another important factor which should be decisive in determining the exact nature of these terracotta figurines is the context in which they were found. Most of them were found in damaged condition and in the heaps of debris. None of them bore evidence of being elaborately worshipped. Whether they were mutilated on purpose is, however, a matter of guess, at least at the present moment.

The last and the most important factor is that the inconography of these figurines is not even in a single instance repeated on the seals and sealings which are equally important as a source for the study of Harappan religion. There are various kinds of figures occurring on them which are identified with various Vedic or proto-Hindu deities by different scholars. It is incomprehensible that if the terracotta figurines are really images of the Mother Goddess who was supposed to be the central deity of the Harappan pantheon, why her representations should not recur on the seals in the same form as that of the figurines?

Thus, we form a hypothesis that the terracotta female figurines which are invariably presumed to be the Mother Goddess figurines were not so in practice and they probably served a different function. It will be our aim to identify their true function. We should also be able to trace the representation of the Goddess on the seal motifs.

To begin with we may cite the famous Pasupati motif on the seals found at Mohenjodaro (Fig. 2). The figure on this seal was identified, as a male divinity by Marshall which he named as proto-Siva or Pasupati and on this basis he postulated the practice of *linga-worship,* in the Indus Valley. There were other scholars who differ in the identification of this but almost all agreed upon its being a male, with the sole exception of Sullivan. K.N. Shastri could detect the combination of various animals in this deity.[5] Dorothy Srinivasan also agrees that the deity is a male, half-human, half-animal and represented a deity of fertility and abundance.[6] Scholars like B.A. Saletore preferred to identify it with the Vedic Agni.[7] Only Sullivan deviated from the mainstream of the prevalent notions in insisting that this was a female deity—a goddess of fertility, a 'Mistress of animals'. He thought that actually the ends of the knotted waist band were erroneously interpreted as an erect phallus by Marshall which led him to identify the deity as ithyphallic.[8] It is strange that Sullivan's view did not receive sufficient attention and scholars continued to nurse the idea of a Harappan *Siva* and phallic workship. Iconographically, the curious face of the deity appears to be not human and the idea of ithyphallicism put forward by Marshall was not acceptable to many. Sullivan expressed a possibility that even the arms which look as if they were decked with a number of armlets were in fact insect like, accentuating the combined form of the Great Goddess. The fact that the limbs in her iconography were not human, becomes clear when other seals and sealings are compared together. Often the deity has hoof-like ends on its limbs.

There are other seals where the same deity appears in the same sitting posture but without the surrounding animals (Fig. 3) making it clear that beasts are only a part of the regime of this deity while there must have been other aspects equally important. The feminity of this deity was suggested by Sullivan and it is vaguely supported by some other seals where the rounded curves of the body appear more feminine than masculine. Although the other seals do not provide very positive evidence in this regard there is one seal which helps to dissolve all suspicions about the sex deity (Fig.4). It proves that it is a female deity no other than the great 'Lady of the Beasts'. She appears to have a complete hold over the animal world. The basic characteristic of her iconography is her horned head-dress with a foliage or plume sprouting from the centre. This attribute recurs in all her representations even though other details like her posture or the degree of emphasis on the feminine attributes vary.

On some seals the "Lady of Beasts" appears standing between two branches or under an arch formed of two branches of Pipal (*Ficus religiosa*). Doubtless, this is the goddess whom Harappans worshipped.

There are some sealings which are probably of narrative type related to some rituals. All rituals cannot be identified in the present state of our knowledge of the Harappan Civilization but the scenes on two seals, if arranged in proper order reveal very interesting information perhaps about a major ritual. On one of these the scene is divided into two registers (Fig.5). In the upper register we see the goddess standing between two branches and in front of her is a kneeling figure attired in the same head-dress. An enormous goat or a goat-like animal, which has a human face (Fig.6) is seen standing. It appears as if it is watching the proceedings very keenly. In the lower register stand seven human figures, all clothed in an uniform style and having lone plaits and plumed head-dress. The seal is well-known and has been variously interpreted. Unfortunately another seal which seems to depict a similar scene has been overlooked so far. If scrutinized closely it becomes apparent the second seal differs from the former in order of these figures, though the figures themselves do not change. Now the standing figures in the lower register on the former seal are shifted to the upper register and there are only six of them. In the lower register the human-faced goat occurs between the goddess and the kneeling figure.

We will not be wrong if we infer that the scene on the second seal is the sequel of the scene appearing on the earlier one. The two seals, if interpreted together and in a right order, reveal the complete process of an important ritual.

In the former seal the human-faced goat is shown standing behind the kneeling figure, most probably a priestess, who is about to be replaced by a new one. This guess is supported by the fact that in the second seal there are only six figures standing. Perhaps one amongst them has been chosen to assume the role of the high priestess. The human-faced goat, perhaps a genie who is standing between the goddess and the new aspirant, seems to be presenting her to the goddess by way of consecration and that is why its position is shifted to the middle. In the former seal the fact, that the seven figures (probably seven virgins) are seen standing in the lower register, in all likehood indicates that they are either standing with their backs towards the scene of the older priestess retiring or they are proceeding towards the spot where the ritual is to take place. On the latter seal six of them appear in the upper register obviously watching the consecration of their fellow-virgins.

The number seven is very signficant in this regard. The semblance of seven mothers or seven water nymphs, etc., have been pointed out by some scholars. The concept of seven mothers, though more apt in the Indian context, cannot be stretched back beyond the historical period. Besides, we should accept now that it is more appropriate if we free Harappan Civilization, or to be more precise Harappan religion, from the narrow frame of either the Vedic of the later-day Hinduism. As we proceed urther in antiquity the distinction between different cults begins to diminish and it can be observed that the basic religiosity of mankind was bound together by more common concepts and subsequently similar religious practices. The prehistoric goddess cults of different cultures were commonly associated with fire and water. This feature was more prominent when the goddess was worshipped in her wilder form as the 'Lady of the Beasts'. She weilded power over the fertility of animals, vegetation as well as of human beings. Her original form was retained even in many of the agricultural and civilized societies. For example, the cult of Diana, a goddess of fertility, was originally known as 'Diana of the wood.' James Frazer, while describing the mode of her worship states that "from the votive offerings which have been found on the site, it appears that she was conceived of especially as a huntress, and further as blessing men and women with offspring, and granting expectant mothers an easy delivery. Again fire seems to have played a foremost part in her ritual. Further, the title of Vesta borne by Diana at Nemi points clearly to the maintenance of a perpetual holy fire in her sanctuary. . . Here the sacred fire would seem to have been tended by vestal virgins, for the head of a vestal in terracotta was found on the spot, and the worship of a perpetual fire cared for by holy maidens, appears to have been common in Latium from the earliest to the latest times".[9] Numbers of these vestal virgins was originally four but later on it was increased to six. It is not unlikely that in the Harappan context it was probably increased to seven due to the importance attached to this number.

The following points are to be noted for understanding what we are driving at :

(1) Firstly, it is important that though the cult of Diana was more firmly instituted at Nemi in Italy around 495 B.C., she was originally an eastern goddess known as Tauric Diana. At Nemi a god by name Virbius was associated with her but probably in her original form as Tauric Diana she was not associated with any male partner. Frazer has suggested that, "in his character of the founder of the sacred grove and first king of Nemi, Virbius is clearly the mythical predecessor or archetype of the line of the priests who served Diana under the title of Kings of the wood. . "[10].

(2) Fire and water formed the main elements of her cult. Among her main titles she bore the title of Vesta. It is significant that a goddess of woods should bear the title of *Vesta*—divine presonification of hearth-fire, symbol chastity. Vesta or Hestia which was supposed to be the centre of the universe and thus Earth-Goddess was also identified with the Vesta thus combining the Huntress, the Earth and the domestic hearth together though some may feel it to be an unseeming combination. It is also noteworthy that there was never an image or a temple of Vesta; the hearth, with its fire itself was the object of worship. However, a terracotta head of a Vesta was discovered at Nemi, indicating that it must be purely votive in nature.

The cult of Diana or Vesta in the west are no doubt much later than the Harappan but strangely enough Harappan religion seems to have been characterised by many features similar to these cults. It is believed now that Harappan cults displayed certain regional variations. For example in Sind and Punjab the terracotta female figurines were very common but they become conspicuous by their absence in Gujarat, Saurashtra and Rajasthan. At sites like Kalibangan the importances of sacred fire is very obvious by the presence of fire-altars at public ritual-complex as well as in residential structures. However, there is reason to believe that the sacred fire and its preservation was equally important at Mohenjodaro and Harappa. Only the external form of the procedure was different. It may be recalled that some of the so called Mother Goddess figurines were reported to have soot marks inside the cup-shaped attachments of their head-dress. We strongly feel that these figurines represented the vestal virgins or maidens and the sacred fire was preserved by keeping it constantly burning inside those cup-shaped appendages, whereas it was preserved at Kalibangan in the domestic fire altars. Probably these figurines were replaced periodically by new ones. The old ones were discarded probably after mutilating them as a token of scrifice.

A cylinder seal suggestive of virgin sacrifice has been discovered from Kalibangan (Fig. 7).It bears a horned half-human, half-animal figure which also occurred on a seal from Mohenjodaro (Fig. 8). The figure certainly represents a manifestation of the goddess whose forequarters are completely human with the same three-pronged head-dress and the long plait. The forequarters are otherwise complete and the hind portion of the body seems to be attached to the frontal body just like an appendage. Both arms of the goddess are similar to the figure which is popularly known as Pasupati but is in fact the Lady of Beasts as indicated earlier. Behind this strange figure is seen a tree, probably a stylized *acacia*, and another faint figure with raised arms. In the left corner a scene depicts a shorter figure with a long plait in the centre flanked by two taller figures wielding spear-like weapons which meet just above the head of the central figure. The hair style of all the three figures are notable. The taller figures, who appear to be nude, wear their hair in a style which is similar to that of the male heads of limestone found at Mohenjodaro (Fig.9). However, the central figure, clothed below the waist, wears her hair in a long plait. It may be recalled that at Harappa and Mohenjodaro it is always the female figurines which are clothed without exception while the male figurines are invariably nude. The hair styles are also indicative of the sex of the respective figures. The stone heads of male statues confirm that the fashion of long plaits was not in vogue among the Harappan men but they combed their hair into a bun with the help of a fillet that went around the head. The taller figures holding spears in their hands wear their hair exactly in the same style. Furthemore, the physical height may also help distinguish the sex. If the scene is allusive of human sacrifice, it is significant that another scene on a sealing from Harappa which also suggests human sacrifice is closely associated with vegetal goddess (Fig.10). It is therefore highly likely that human sacrifice was in vogue in the Harappan religion. Moreover, the victims offered were in all likelihood females, especially virgins.

We may safely conclude that the Harappans worshipped the Great Goddess basically in her primitive form as the 'Lady of Beasts' but modified her rituals to the needs of a society which depended on agriculture and trade. The same process perhaps occurred in many civilized societies and the cult of Diana can be cited as an example though not as an exact model.

If the primitive goddess of the woods and the Earth

were to be treated on par or simply as the manifestations of one and the same principle it is natural that agricultural symbolism should appear hand in hand with the animal symbolism of the primitive goddess, perhaps in a very innovative and a unique way because Harappans were adept at displaying individuality of their culture in every possible way. This we witness in the unique motif of 'unicorn'.

Various attempts have been made to identify this animal and two distinct groups of opinion exist on this matter. Initially, it was thought that the animal is a fabulous one but later on some scholars suggested that perhaps the animal represents a real species and has been depicted with a single horn as a result of its being positioned in profile. However, a close scrutiny reveals that the composition of the animal varies in its features and morphological characters in many instances which should not happen if a real species is being the subject of the carving; especially in a civilization in which in all other motifs such strict standardization exists when the animal belongs to reality. Besides there are examples of two horns being shown very skillfully even when the animal is in profile and there is no satisfactory reason why the artists should make an exception only in the case of unicorn, unless there is some symbolic meaning behind it. That means this animal was meant to be understood as having only a single horn. This fact leads us to a question: What can be the significance of this single-horned, fabulous creature with a very conspicuous emphasis on its male member, within the paraphernalia of the goddess cult? The concept of fertility and that too of the virgin Earth, can be the keynote of the whole symbolism.

It is supposed that "the work of food gathering, maintained. . . . by the women led to cultivation of seeds in the vicinity of the tribal settlement, and accordingly garden tillage is almost universally women's work"[11]. It is obvious that initially a hoe or a simple hand-plough similar to the digging stick must have been used by the female gatherers-*cum*-farmers. These digging sticks or hand-ploughs were shaped out of a forked branch mostly out of some pointed bones for durability. When the question of durability arises antlers prove to be the toughest material which was used in prehistoric times for mining flint in Europe.[12] An implement known as *Kudavana* really a hand-pick was in use among the hill tribes of Maharashtra." "They use it on steep places where it is possible to grow varieties of coarse millet. One form is also used in rice growing districts to dig up the fine soil for covering the rab (*sic*) material in the preparation of rice-seed beds. It will be noticed that the form of the pick is practically that of the plough. In some instances, it is provided with a long shaft, so that all that is necessary to make into an actual plough is to add a handle, supply a yoke, and attach a pair of diminutive bullocks."[13] These hand-picks and hand ploughs clearly seem to have been derived from a forked branch or forked antler. Such antlers have been found at the chalcolithic site of Inamagon in Maharashtra where they are identified as hand-ploughs.[14] It proves that Moti Chandra very rightly conjectured that "the antelope horn at some distant past was used for tillage and therefore it symbolised a good harvest bringing wealth in its turn". The horn motif has been developed around antlers at Harappan towns. The Harappan unicorn which was no doubt a composite and a mythical animal, displays a single antler on forehead. In the sacrificial pit of Kalibangan antlers were found along with bovine bones.[14] There is sufficient corroborative evidence to support unicorn's phallic importance and its association with the virgin goddess and the phallic value of a plough-share is well known which is associated with the virgin Earth.[15]

A question may be raised regarding the occurrence of ploughshare at Harappa and Mohenjodaro. Unfortunately, we do not have the record of such a find in the respective excavation reports, except one stray find recorded by Mackay. He casually suggests that this might have been a ploughshare.[16] It is an implement made of chert, in shape like the metal blade-axe but very much thicker. Mackay's suggestion does not call for serious consideration because he himself suggests alternatives for his own proposition. However, it is reported that "the antlers of both Kashmir stag and the sambar deer have been found in the ruins of Mohenjodaro, the horns of the latter being very common indeed". Owing to the absence of other skeletal remains of these animals, Col. Sewell, the then Director of Zoological Survey, has suggested that "these horns were imported for their medicinal properties as at the present day."[17] A different but more convincing explanation may be suggested for this phenomenon. Antlers, if imported, were important not only for their medicinal properties but for a more practical use such as a hand-plough or plough-shares, as the hardest material in the absence of iron and also an easily available material. Perhaps people collected only those antlers which were shed. That is why antlers have been reported in abundance but no plough or plough-shares in a form as the excavators anticipated them to be. The fact that antlers were very rarely used for making handles appears intriguing to Mackay and he ponders over the thought as to "why it was not more extensively used for this purpose."[18] Expensiveness of the material cannot be the only explanation as it may not keep people from using fancy things, at least occasionally. Harappans probably preferred to reserve the material for the exclusive function of ploughing and it fits in with the hard core practicality of those who regularly traded a material like lapis lazuli but were rarely tempted to keep it for personal use.

Whether the Harappans shaped antlers specially to serve as ploughshares is diffcult to know, but there is a curious object which is a "part of the horn of a deer or antelope 15.36 cm long, with a groove cut round it near the broader end". Mackay thinks it to be "rather short for a tent-peg, it was more probably used as a hook to which to tie something."[19] The picture of this object as originally given, if reversed resembles exactly the unicorn's horn—a straight pointed bone, slightly curved at the tip, and there is no reason why one should not identify this object as a ploughshare. Randhawa mentions a terracotta toy plough 7cmx19.7 cm from Mohenjodaro. At present it is kept in the Prince of Wales Museum, Bombay. "There is a longish beam and the plough breasts terminate in a rectangular manner. There is no indication that it has a handle (munna) for a ploughman to hold."[20] The same object has been illustrated by Mackay but he described it as a strigil.[21] He himself, however, admits that the strigils in this shape are rather uncommon but maintains the same explanation for want for a better one. However, Randhawa's identification is quite convincing and is further supported now by recent finds of models of terracotta ploughs at Banawali. The antler with groove at it border and as described earlier is exactly identical in its shape to the longish beam of the terracotta toy plough described by Randhawa.

Thus it is evident that the unicorn, a fabulous animal, was closely associated with the concept of fertility. Its horn, an antler to be precise, which might have been used as either a hand-plough or more likely as ploughshare formed the basis of the animal's symbolic composition. We are of the opinion that the cult of the primitive goddess who ruled the world of wild animals was modified to suit a prospering society, sustained basically by a combination of agriculture, animal husbandry and trade. It becomes obvious then that the modified symbolism should be guided by phallic value. Hence the antler by virtue of its being used as a plough-share becomes the basic phallic symbol in the context of the virgin earth which is to be opened for sowing seeds. The ploughshare is the basic instrument to stimulate her latent powers of reproduction. A digging stick or a pointed bone carried a phallic value even among the pre-agricultural people.[22] It is very significant that the Harappan chose a composite animal—a combination of 'ruminants'—to bear the antler on its forehead clearly illuminating the awareness of the interdependence of agriculture and animal husbandry.[23] Only a highly civilized people like the Harappans who demonstrate a fascination for composite forms could have devised such a motif. This fascination for com posite forms is evident through many other motifs of which the 'composite monster' in only one example. Hence, we may state that the primitive 'Lady of Beasts' was elevated by the advanced Harappans to the status of the Supreme deity controlling the overall fertility, expanding the range of her symbolism which encompassed a vast range of motifs - primitive as well as agricultural. The ingenuity of Harappans added new symbols in a perfectly novel manner. Addition of ploughshare and the domestic fire which was regarded holy is sufficient to demonstrate the enhanced position of the primitive goddess. This process of modification and alternation seems to have reached its culmination at Kalibangan resulting in the 'Vestal fire' attaining the supreme importance as indicated by the presence of public as well as residential fire-altars.

REFERENCES

1. Wheeler, R.E.M. *The Indus Civilization* (3rd Ed.) Supplementary volume to the Cambridge History of India, Cambridge, Cambridge University Press, 1968, p. 91.
2. James, E.O. *Prehistoric Religion*, Thames and Hudson, London, 1957, pp. 152-53.
3. Marshall, John *Mohenjo-daro and the Indus Civilization*, vol. I, London, 1948, pp. 48-78.
4. Mackay, E.J.H. *Early Indus Civilization* (2nd Ed.), Luzac and Co., London, 1948, p. 53.
5. Shastri, K.N. *New Light on the Indus Civilization: Religion and Chronology*, vol. I, Atma Ram and Sons, Delhi, 1957, p. 8.
6. Srinivasan, D. The so-called Proto-Siva Seal from Mohenjo daro. An Iconological Assessment, *Archives of Asian Art*, 1976-77, pp. 47-58.
7. Saletore, B.A. Identification of a Mohenjodaro Figure, *The New Review*, 10, 1939, pp. 28-35.
8. Sullivan, H.P. A Re-examination of the Religion of the Indus Civilization, *History of Religion*, Chicago, 1964, 4(i), pp. 15-23.
9. Frazer, James. *Golden Bough. A Study in Magic and Religion* (abr. eds.) Macmillan and Co, London, 1933, p. 3.
10. *Ibid.*, p. 8.
11. Bhattacharya, N.N., *Indian Mother Goddess*, Calcutta, 1971, p. 4.
12. Clarke, Grahame *Pre-historic Europe : The Economic Basic*, Methuen, London, 1952, p. 117.
13. Wallace, Robort *India in 1887*, Edinbourgh, 1888, p. 168.
14. Lal, B.B. Some reflections on the structural remains at Kalibangan in Lal, B.B. and S.P. Gupta (Ed.) *Frontiers of the Indus Civilization*, Books & Books, Delhi. 1984, pp. 52-62.
15. Atre, Shubhangana The Harappan Riddle of 'Unicorn', *Bulletin of Deccan College Research Institute*, Pune, 1985, pp. 44. 1-10.
16. Mackay, *Further Excavations at Mohenjo daro*, Vol. 1, New Delhi, 1938, p. 397.
17. *Ibid.*, p. 424.
18. *Ibid.*,
19. *Ibid.*, 434.
20. Randhawa, M.S. *A History of Agriculture in India*, vol. 1, New Delhi, 1980, p. 156.
21. Mackay, *op. cit.*, p. 416.
22. Campbell Joseph. *Primitive Mythology : The Masks of God*, 1982, pp. 300-04.
23. Atre, *op. cit.*

FIG. 1—4

Fig. 5—10

5

6

7

8

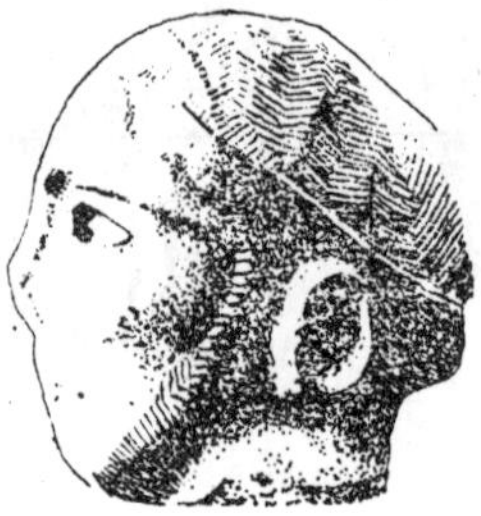

9

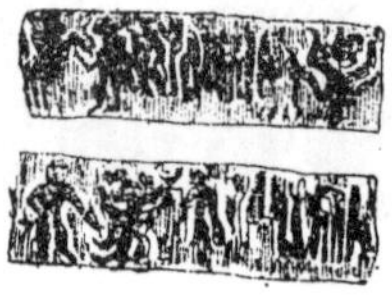

10

3

The Indus Civilization—Echoes in Later Literature

Y. B. Singh

It is generally believed that the Indus Civilization was completely forgotten in later years and thus there are no references to that epoch of Indian civilization in Sanskrit texts except few allusions like Hariyūpūyā in early Vedic hymns.[1] Contrary to this a reminiscence of that great civilization is found in *Kathāsaritsagara* of Somadeva.[2] One of the several reasons put forth for the decline of Mohenjodaro is the theory of recurring floods which assumed abnormality and turned vast areas into lakes.[3] Though several other factors contributing to the decline and decay of that place are equally cogent, the flood theory on the basis of archaeological finds seems to have the strongest case[4]. Such floods may have combined with tectonic movements to which the areas are now suggested to be prone in those days.

That such floods which continued to ravage vast areas of lower Panjab and Sindh were remembered and associated with time immemorial is revealed by a narration incorporated in that fabulous story collection of eleventh century A.D. cited above.[5] It relates that the mighty Indus which could at times be tremendously powerful and impossible to check had flooded and ravaged a large part of Sindh country.[6] This forced most of its habitants, few of whom followed the Saivite faith, to flee in all directions.[7] Accordingly, the region is portrayed as an urban centre predominantly a seat of Vedic studies in spite of the fact that the lower Indus region is never mentioned as an area having dominance of Vedic way of life in later literature. And, therefore, this suggests that the nucleus of the story belongs to an early period—the days of Mohenjodaro. The hero, as the theory has it, in distress migrated to Varanasi which is described as a city dominated by the Saivites.[8] Strangely at this point we are told that the hero originally belonged to Varanasi region and had moved to Sindh in search of fortune.[9] Still more we are also informed that his kith and kin were Saivas and have had firm faith in left-handed practices.[10]

The description when juxtaposed with the theory associating Aryans with pre-Harappan Culture and the details about Rudra-Siva from *Veda-Purana* traditions lures us to conjecture certain possibilities of great awakening of unorthodox nature.[11] For, the Great Bath at Mohenjodaro, conspicuous because of the particular care shown in its construction and *yoni-linga* symbols have already been analysed and suggestive of yogic religious rituals known to the people of that place.[12] Interestingly, the *apsaras* are associated with lakes, rivers, etc. in Vedic literature and through *mantras* they are requested to remain at lakes, ponds and rivers without causing unhappiness to human beings by their bewitching beauty.[13]

Rudra-Siva is a god of myriad character. When we trace the genesis of his cult, *Vedas* talk about Rudra who was in possession of brown coloured body, light brown (*pita*—literally yellowish and poetically golden brown) braided hair along with immense vigour.[14] He was capable to punish as well as to heal. He is also described as the protector of cattle.[15] He is addressed as Siva meaning *Kalyanakari* (benevolent), cause of happiness, etc.[16] Later texts describe him as one whose *griva* (neck) is blue and who is lord of beasts.[17] Among his many wives the most important was Uma, the daughter of Himavana.[18] Rudra, however, was denied his lawful share from the sacrificial offerings and had a quarrel with Prajapati about this.[19] Ultimately as a compromise he was promised the latest portion from the said type of offerings as his residue.[20] In later version of this story, Siva is taken as the son-in-law of Daksha Prajapati.[21] As the legend runs, Siva was humilitated for his unusual living and as a consequence of this his wife Sati committed suicide. In an act of retaliation Siva is said to have destroyed the *yagna* (sacrifice) and punished all those who were party to that religious ceremony.[22]

If we analyse the said story in the light of the aforesaid what appears most probable is that when the urban centre of Mohenjodaro was at its peak the adjoining rural areas were inhabited by the people known to us from Vedic literature. And, that ups and downs of various gods found in the *Samhitas*, etc., was due to change in the status of their devotees. Thus, the gods worshipped by the successful people used to command higher status in comparison with the gods of unsuccessful *janas*.

Rudra-Siva when viewed in this light appears to be an ambitious person who after loosing ground among his own fold started developing contacts with people whose life and living conditions were different from the people of the *Vedas*. In this context, it should also be taken into consideration that whenever such things happen it is the unrecognised or defeated but ambitious people with a zeal to do something new who go for adjustments and readjustments helpful in nature. Rudra-Siva was a person of the above type and, therefore, with the passage of time he became popular among the masses and later deified. Possibly when his wife Sati, the daughter of Daksha-Prajapati, a conservative Aryan noble, died he married Uma, offspring of mountain chief Himavana who was probably closely connected with urban settlements of the Indus region. Combination of the Rudra's military skill and material possessions of Himavana and the people of Mohenjodaro brought popularity to socio-religious system reflected in the Saiva literature of the later years. And, it is the old nucleus of such literature because of which even the authors of eleventh century A.D. remembered Siva as a blond, a concept known to early Vedic hymns alone.[23] Popularity of Saivism in north-western India even during the days of Kushanas in spite of the royal patronage given to Buddhism by rulers like Asoka is a positive proof, in this regard.[24]

Further, the story proves that the Indus cities remained alive among the folk-memory and traces of their culture can still be had from the tales of later years.

NOTES AND REFERENCES

1. Wheeler, R.E.M., *The Indus Civilization*, p. 27.
2. In the absence of a critical edition and other factors I have consulted the following translations and books related with *Kathasaritsagara:* (a) *Kathasaritsagara* of Somadevabhatta, Sanskrit text and its translation by Kedarnath Sharma Sarsvata; Tawny, C.H., *Ocean of Stories* an English translation of *Kathasaritsagara;* (c) Agarwal, Neelam, *Brihatkatha* of Gunadhya, Hindi translation; and (d) Buitenen, J.A.B., *Tales of Ancient India*, English translation.
3. Wheeler, *op. cit.*, pp. 127 ff. See also Fagan, B.M., *People of the Earth*, pp. 276-81.
4. *Ibid.*
5. Buitenen, *op. cit.*, pp. 199 ff.
6. *Ibid.*
7. *Ibid.*
8. *Ibid.*, pp. 125-26
9. *Ibid.*
10. *Ibid.*
11. Gaur, R.C. The Aryans—A fresh Appraisal, *Puratattva*, Bulletin of the Indian Archaeological Society, No. 12, 1980-81, pp. 133 ff; Chakravarti, M. The concept of *Rudra-Siva* (for details of Rudra-Siva concept).
12. Kosambi, D.D., *The Culture and Civilization of Ancient India in historical outline*, p. 68.
13. Macdonell, A.A. *Vedic Mythology* (Hindi translation by Ram Kumar Rai), p. 255.
14. *Ibid.*, pp. 140-45; Keith, A.S. *The Religion and Philosophy of the Vedas*, Harvard Oriental Series, pp. 142-50.
15. Macdonell, *op. cit.*, p. 145.
16. Keith, *op. cit.*, p. 149; Macdonell, *op. cit.*, p. 145.
17. Keith, *op. cit.*, p. 142.
18. *Ibid.*, p. 144.
19. Chakravarti, *op. cit.*, p. 51.
20. *Ibid.*
21. Sarasvata, K.S. *op. cit.*, 1st *lambaka* and 1st *taranga sloka*, p. 37; see also Chakravarti, *op. cit.*, p. 51.
22. Sarsvata, K.S., *op. cit*, 1st *lambaka* and 1st *taranga* slokas 37-39; Chakravarti, *op. cit.*, p. 51.
23. Sarsvata, K.S., *op. cit.*, 4th *lambaka*, 3rd *taranga* sloka, 4; Agarwal, *op. cit.*, p. 2.
24. Chattopadhyaya, S.C. *Early History of North India*, p.70 ff. Kujul's titles show Buddhist leanings; Puri, B.N., *India under the Kushanas*, p. 139. Coins of Kings from Wema onward reflect Saivism.

4

Recent Exploration in the Valley of Khari and Mansi Rivers Rajasthan : With Special Reference to the Chalcolithic Sites

B. R. Meena

The archaeological explorations and excavations were carried out in the past in south-eastern Rajasthan to know the potentialities of the region and assess the expansion of the Banas culture. The type-sites, Gilund and Ahar which are the excavated sites in the region, are well-known for the Banasian culture. In order to assess the importance of the black-and-red ware with a deposit as thick as 7 m. at Ahar, an extensive exploration in the valleys of Banas and Berach in south-eastern Rajasthan was undertaken earlier by K.M. Srivastava of the Survey in the years 1956-57, 1957-58 and 1958-59[1], which brought to light more than 20 sites having the same cutural assemblage as at Ahar.

Further, the region was also explored by the Excavation Branch of the Archaeological Survey of India and the Deccan College, Pune, along the Chambal-Banas Valley. The thrust was from the southern Indore-Ratlam region upto Chitorgarh along the Chambal and Banas rivers and from Udaipur and Beawar to the south-east of Ajmer. This brought out more than 100 sites right from palaeolithic to post-Aharian cultures. Against this background, the recent explorations covering an area of 3400 sq. km along the upper reaches of the rivers Khari and Mansi, the tributaries of the Banas, in the districts of Ajmer, Bhilwara and Udaipur of Central Rajasthan was carried out by the author during the months of February and March 1985, with the purpose to tap the archaeological potentialities of the region and also to know the southern and south-western extension of Ahar culture. Fifty-five sites ranging from palaeolithic through chalcolithic, early historic and medieval periods were brought to light (Fig. 1 and Pl. 4. I).

After thorough study of the explored material, an attempt has been made here to lay stress on the important discoveries. Although the cultural assemblage ranges from the early palaeolithic to the late medieval period, the chalcolithic period stands out as unique, since this exploration has provided new information regarding the extent of the Aharian culture reaching as far as south-west of and nearer to Ajmer which was earlier thought to be improbable.

Chalcolithic sites like Reach Mahal, Ojena, Dantri, Unkhalia and Junikheda have yielded pottery such as the black-and-red, white-painted black-and-red, red, burnished grey, grey and incised red wares, and antiquities like bangles, animal figurines, clay wheels, ringstones, quartzite balls, etc. which speak of their affinity with Ahar. But the incised and plain red ware from Reach Mahal indicates a distant cultural affinity with the incised pottery of the Ganeshwar and other chalcolithic cultures of north Rajasthan.

A detailed examination of the chalcolithic sites in the light of the above is given below:

1. OJENA, TEH. ASIND, DIST. BHILWARA (Lat. 25°52'N, Long. 74°22' E)[2]

This site is situated 11 km north-east of Badnor on Badnor-Beawar road. The River Khari flows about 14 km south of the site. The ancient site lies on the slope of a small hill situated towards north-west of the present village. The height of the hillock is about 50 m but the occupational deposit seems to rise upto 8 to 10 m from the surrounding ground level.

The ceramic industry is represented by chalcolithic black-and-red, red, grey, and burnished black wares. The black-and-red ware consists of three sub-varieties viz. white painted black-and-red ware, with both the surfaces burnished; unburnished painted black-and-red ware; and plain black-and-red ware, medium to thin in thickness. The painting on black surface has very limited range in designs, usually, lines and dots. The shapes are bowls of several varieties.

Most of the red ware is found to be hand-made and sometimes incised externally. The shapes include vases, bowls, basins, large storage jars and dish-on-stand with ribbed stem. The red ware also indicates many varieties, viz. dull red, red with painting in black, thick slipped with white paintings, and the micaceous variety without slip. In a few cases the rim portion of the red slipped vase is found to be fluted. The painted designs executed on the external surface are simple horizontal black-bands and oblique strokes and dots in white. The large jars show applique designs or ribs on external surface.

Besides these wares, a few sherds of burnished grey, plain grey, grey with chocolate or brown slip, externally painted in white and burnished black ware were also present. A few sherds show applique designs and nail impressions.

Antiquities include terracotta bulls and other animal figurines and quartzite hammer stones or balls (Pl. 4. II).

2. REACH MAHAL, TEH. BEAWAR, DIST. AJMER (Lat. 25°58'N, Long. 74°24'E)

This site is situated 2 km west of village Devas on Vijayanagar-Beawar road and approachable by a kuchcha road from Devas. It is comparatively a large hillock about 70 to 80 m in height, having numerous rock shelters and surrounded by fertile low land. It seems that the slopes of the hillock and rock shelters on it were occupied by ancient inhabitants.

The site has yielded black-and-red ware, sometimes painted in white, white painted black slipped ware, burnished grey ware, black slipped ware, plain grey ware and plain and incised red ware. The shapes in black-and-red ware and black slipped wares are miniature vases and bowls with white paintings, dishes of black and red ware. In red ware the shapes included vases, large jars, *handi*, bowls, basins and dish-on-stand.

Among the antiquities a terracotta wheel, bangle, terracotta bead, ring-stone and quartzite balls were collected.

3. UNKHALIA, TEH. HURRA, DIST. BHILWARA (Lat. 25°47'N, Long. 74°32'E)

This site is situated to the north of the village on the left bank of the River Mansi, 12 km south-west of Rupaheli Railway station and approachable by a metalled road. It is approximately 400 x 400 m in dimension with a height of 3 to 4 m. It has yielded pottery of the chalcolithic and early medieval period.

The chalcolithic period is represented by black-and-red, burnished grey and associated red wares. The main shapes included vases, jars, bowls of red ware and dishes of black-and-red ware. The pottery is medium to coarse in fabric.

The early medieval ceramic industry is represented by red and associated grey wares.

4. JUNIKHEDA, TEH. ASIND, DIST. BHILWARA (Lat. 25°37'N, Long. 74°32'E)

The site lies on the right bank of the River Mansi, 1 km north-west of village Ganglon and 7 km north-west of Lambia Railway station which is connected by a kuchcha road.

The site which has a thin deposit of 15 to 20 cm has yielded chalcolithic black-and-red ware. In the black-and-red ware, the main shapes are bowls.

Pot sherds of medieval period were also collected.

5. DANTRI, TEH. BEAWAR, DIST. AJMER (Lat. 25°56'N, Long. 74°32'E)

This site is 11 km west of Vijayanagar on Vijaynagar-Beawar road, approachable by a metalled road. It is a small hillock whose slope was occupied by ancient inhabitants. The River Khari flows 2 km away from the site.

The site has yielded chalcolithic black-and-red, red and burnished grey wares.

The shapes include dishes, bowls of black-and-red and vases and bowls and jars of red ware. Quartzite balls were the only antiquities collected.

Apart from the chalcolithic sites, the remaining fifty sites are ranging from early historic to late medieval periods. The early historic Lachchura has yielded red, grey, black slipped and associated N.B.P. wares and ring-wells, etc. Barasani has yielded Sunga-Kushana wares comprising vases and bowls of red ware. At Junagaon some megalithic tombs—like menhirs and cairn-circles were noticed while Mataji-ki-Mangri has produced a typical red pottery decorated with human figurines which betray Gupta style.

A significant find is a stray Vishnu image of 8th-9th century A.D. from Antali village.

Among the remains of medieval and late medieval periods, forts, step-wells, temples, coins are noteworthy.

INSCRIPTIONS

Besides, a few Nagari inscriptions were also met with which are dealt with below:

1. KATAR, TEH. ASIND, DIST. BHILWARA (Lat. 25°41'N, Long. 74°15'E)

(a) A ten-lined inscription in Nagari script on a hero stone which depicts a hero collapsing from his horse. It also refers to the village Katar, in the third line. Palaeographically this can be ascribed to 16-17th Century A.D.

(b) An inscription in Nagari script dated to V.S. 1771 (i.e. A.D. 1714) is lying in a field to the north-east of the village which is possibly a hero-stone (*Veerpatthar*), dedicated to a hero slain during a battle for the protection of cows, since a cow is depicted on the top.

2. DARWAT, TEH. ASIND, DIST. BHILWARA (Lat. 25°46'N, Long. 74°21'E)

A four line inscription in Devanagari on a pillar base in the Devanarayana temple is dated to V. Samvat 1778 (i.e. A.D. 1721).

3. ANTALI, TEH. ASIND, DIST. BHILWARA (Lat. 25°52'N, Long. 74°28'E)

A three lined inscription dated to V.S. 1175 (i.e. A.D. 1118) in Nagari script was noticed on the left side of the lintel of *mandapa* of the Siva temple.

4. LAMBIAKALA, TEH. BANERA, DIST. BHILWARA (Lat. 25°36'N, Long. 74°37'E)

An inscription on a pillar was noticed at the entrance of the *baoli* (step-well) towards the east of the present village.

Conclusion :

The Aharian culture spread mainly in south-eastern Rajasthan sheltered by the Aravallis and wateied by Banas and its tributaries. Though the centre of this culture was south-eastern Rajasthan comprising the districts of Udaipur, Chitorgarh and Bhilwara, it also extended up to Nagda, located on River Chambal in Dist. Ujjain of Madhya Pradesh in the north-east and Navdatoli on Narmada in the south. Kayatha on River Kali Sindh in Dist. Ujjain and Eran on River Bina in Sagar district, both in Madhya Pradesh, are the other sites with similar characteristics. The fundamental difference amongst all these sites is the variation in the quantity of black-and-red ware. The black-and-red ware constituted one of the chief ceramic industries at Ahar, Gilund and other related sites. K.V. Soundara Rajan, however, believes that the Banas culture, represented mainly by the black-and-red ware, owed its origin to the 'Dravidians'. He says that the present day disposition of Dravidian communities in India and the viscissitudes they have been taken as having gone through in early times indicate that at one stage they were widely distributed over many parts of Central India and Rajasthan".[3]

The present exploration of chalcolithic sites of south east Rajasthan has provided new information regarding the Aharian expansion in this region and its further extension towards north, near Ajmer. It will not be a surprise if the future field work extends the Aharian expansion further north which may throw ample light on cultural relationship between Aharian and chalcolithic cultures of north Rajasthan.

Comparison with the Ahar (Banas) Culture :

The 'Banas culture' is named after the River Banas on whose banks the Banasian sites were found. Ahar is also one of them, located near Udaipur Railway station on the left bank of River Ahar, and it was first brought to light by R.C. Agrawal during the year 1954-55. Ahar is a big mound anciently known as Tambavati (city of copper). The most characteristic feature of this culture is a typical pottery known as the black-and-red ware painted in white on the exterior. Motifs are usually geometric, parallel or oblique lines, circles and spirals. Thin incised lines on the necks of bowls are very characteristic features of this cultuie. The common shapes are bowls and dishes. The red slipped ware is another fine burnished, wheel made pottery with the colour of the slip ranging from tan, orange to chocolate. There are also hand-made coarse red and grey storage jars with applique decoration, basins, dish-on-stand, etc., associated with the Red slipped ware; also a buff, cream slipped ware made of kaolin mixed with clay.

Among the terracottas only a few bull figurines are reported from Ahar.

The recent exploration of the chalcolithic sites also exhibit the same cultural features as at Ahar. The chalcolithic sites like Reach Mahal, Ojena, Dantri, Unkhalia and Junikheda have represented the ceramic industry of black-and-red, white painted black-and-red, red, burnished grey, grey, incised red, burnished black wares. The painting on black surface indicates very limited range of designs, usually lines and dots. The shapes in black and red and black slipped wares are miniature vases, bowls with white paintings and dishes.

The red ware also indicates many varieties like, dull red, red with painting in black, thick slipped with white paintings and micaceous variety without slip. The painted designs are simple horizontal black bands and oblique strokes and dots in white. Applique designs and ribs on external surface of the pots are noteworthy. The shapes include vases, bowls, dishes, basins, large storage jars, *handi* and dish-on-stand with ribbed stem (Figs. 2 and 3).

Among the antiquities, terracotta bulls and animal figurines, bangles, beads, clay wheel, ring stones, quartzite balls were collected. All the above finds speak of their affinity to Ahar. The thick sturdy grey ware bearing incised and applique decoration of the chalcolithic sites is comparable with Ahar IB[4].

The material cultures of the Reach Mahal site indicate that this region might have been a contact-zone between Aharians and chalcolithic cultures of north Rajasthan, as the ceramic industries speak of their affinity with Ahar and a typo-technological resemblance with the chalcolithic cultures of north Rajasthan.

At least three sherds of coarse and light red ware found in the ceramic assemblage of Reach Mahal bear striking semblance with a similar pottery which is present as an exotic ware in the corpus of the post-Harappan period at Banawali.[5] Many sturdy red ware sherds which now appear ochreous in look and feel due to insufficient firing also indicate some sort of fabric-nearness with some of the pottery groups of post-Harappan times of Haryana.

As far as the structural activities and the settlement pattern are concerned it is observed that the chalcolithic people of this region generally preferred hillocks and rock-shelters usually skirted by low lying fertile land, since the explored sites share similarities.

Chronology :

The chalcolithic cultures in India make their first appearance at the turn of the second millennium B.C. and are eventually replaced by the iron using cultures.[6]

The black-and-red ware industry being an important component of many a chalcolithic culture has played a significant role. This ware has been classified into six regions by K.M. Srivastava, based broadly on the associated cultural complex and the representative shapes and show distinct regional identities. The sites under discussion fall within south-eastern Rajasthan which forms Region "B" of Srivastava. He has dated the culture here to circa 2000 B.C. to 800 B.C.[7]

On the basis of 14 C dates, D.P. Agarwal has suggested a time bracket of 2000-1400 B.C. for the Banas culture. He further holds that the copper age of Ahar culture emerges sometime in the 18th century B.C., at time when Harappan Culture came to an end.[8]

The excavator of Ahar contends that several 14 C determinations enable him to place the Ahar culture between c. 1900 B.C.-1200 B.C.[9] Some indirect data on the dating of Ahar's chalcolithic have come from the excavations at Kayatha. Period II (Circa 1900 B.C.—1600 B.C.) at Kayatha witnessed the arrival of an entirely new set of people who used the characteristic white-painted black-and-red ware, similar to that from the Banas Val ey.

In their recent work,[10] the Allchins contend that the Aharians were contemporaries of the Harappans and survived even beyond the Harappan civilization, since the three phases (IA, B and C) at Ahar have been dated to a time bracket of 2580 B.C. to 1500 B.C., based on radiocarbon dates.

The chalcolithic culture represented at Gilund is also important in the region. In the absence of radiocarbon dates for Gilund, relative dating has been attempted on the basis of certain comparative features noticed in respect of potteries from chalcolithic Navdatoli, the chalcolithic levels of which have already been dated by radiocarbon tests to *circa* 1500-1000 B.C. Thus, the chalcolithic period of Gilund may roughly be placed around 1500 B.C. with a couple of centuries on either side.

Since Ahar and Gilund are comfortably dated, we may now attempt to relative dating of our chalcolithic sites. The excavator of Ahar has proposed tentatively *circa* 1200 B.C. as the lower limit and 1900 B.C. as the upper limit for the protohistoric horizons. The 14C datess given by D.P. Agarwal suggests A.C. 2000—1400 B.C. bracket for the Banas culture. Thus these chalcolithic sites may roughly be placed in the tentative time bracket between c. 1900 B.C.—1200 B.C.

Acknowledgement

I am extremely grateful to Shri R.S. Bisht, Shri S. Ananda Sastry and Shri C.B. Mishra of the Archaeological Survey of India for their valuable suggestions and encouragement to give a shape to the present study. My sincere thanks are due to my colleagues S/Shri R.S. Kulkarni, Laxmikant Rao, Y.S. Rawat, M.G. Vyas, V.H. Parmar and Shri N.A. Saiyad, who actively assisted me and also helped in classifying the material, preparation of drawings and photographs for this paper and Shri K. Bahuleyan for typing out the script.

REFERENCES

1. *Indian Archaeology—A Review* 1956-57, 1957-58 and 1958-59.
2. Information about this site was gathered from the Department of Archaeology and Museums, Rajasthan.
3. Soundara Rajan, K.V., Community-movements in protohistoric India—An Archaeological Perspective, *Journal of the Oriental Institute*, vol. XII, No. 1, 1962, pp. 74-75.
4. Sankalia, H.D., *Excavations at Ahar*, 1969, Fig. 128.
5. Personal communication by Shri R.S. Bisht.
6. Agrawal, D.P., *The Archaeology of India*, 1984.
7. Srivastava, K.M., *Community Movements in Proto-historic India*, 1980.
8. Agrawal, D.P. "C^{14} Dates, Banas Culture and the Aryans"—*Current Science*, 1966.
9. Sankalia, 1969, *op. cit.*
10. Allchin, Bridget and Raymond. *The Rise of Civilization in India and Pakistan*, 1983.

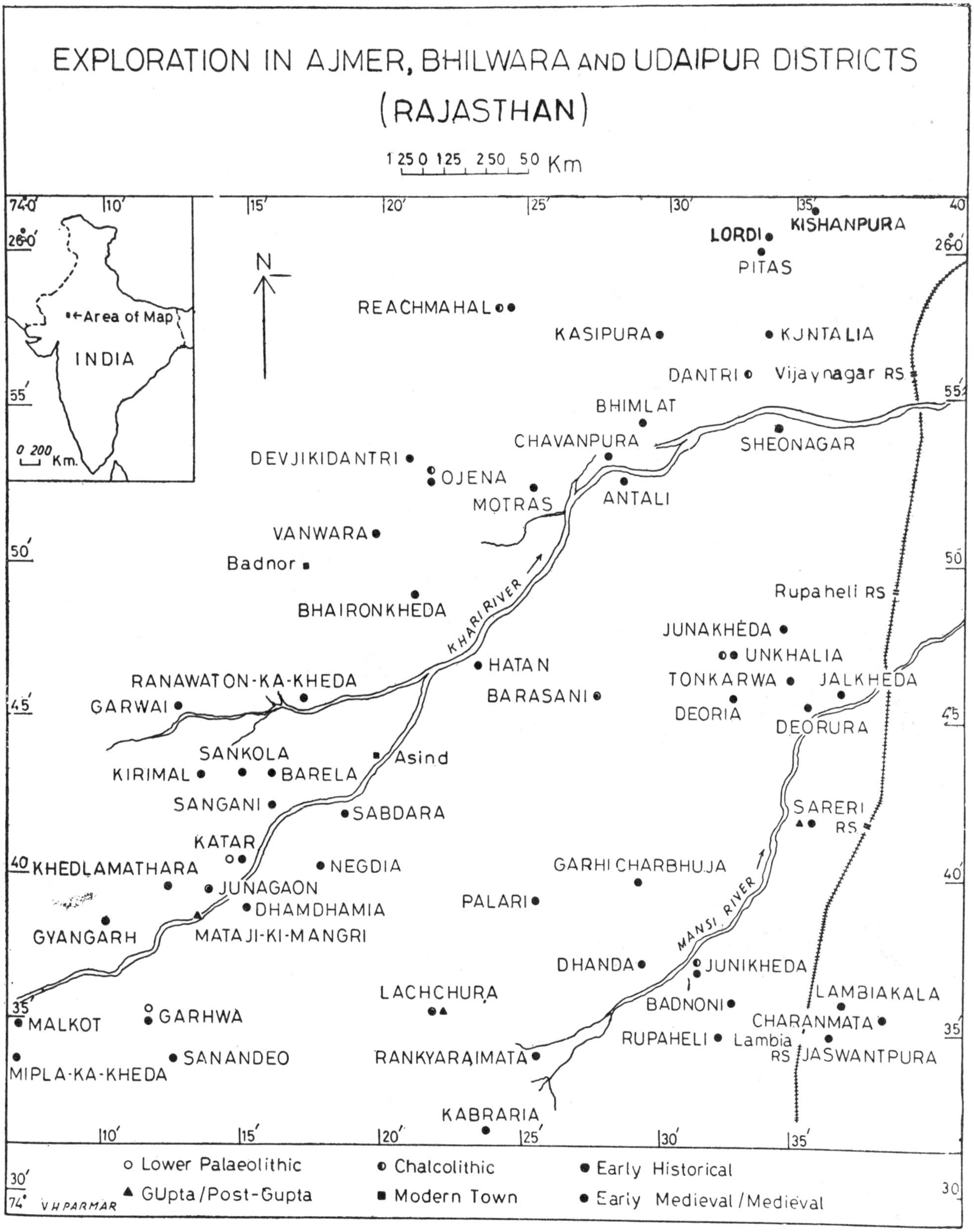
EXPLORATION IN AJMER, BHILWARA AND UDAIPUR DISTRICTS
(RAJASTHAN)
12.5 0 12.5 25.0 50 Km
74° 0′
26° 0′
10′
15′
20′
25′
30′
35′
40
55′
50′
45′
40′
35′
30′
74°
Area of Map
INDIA
0 200 Km.
N
LORDI
KISHANPURA
PITAS
REACHMAHAL
KASIPURA
KUNTALIA
DANTRI
Vijaynagar RS
BHIMLAT
SHEONAGAR
CHAVANPURA
DEVJIKIDANTRI
OJENA
MOTRAS
ANTALI
VANWARA
Badnor
Rupaheli RS
BHAIRONKHEDA
KHARI RIVER
JUNAKHEDA
UNKHALIA
HATAN
TONKARWA
JALKHEDA
RANAWATON-KA-KHEDA
BARASANI
DEORIA
DEORURA
GARWAI
SANKOLA
Asind
KIRIMAL
BARELA
SANGANI
SABDARA
SARERI RS
KATAR
KHEDLAMATHARA
NEGDIA
GARHI CHARBHUJA
JUNAGAON
DHAMDHAMIA
PALARI
GYANGARH
MATAJI-KI-MANGRI
MANSI RIVER
DHANDA
JUNIKHEDA
LACHCHURA
LAMBIAKALA
MALKOT
GARHWA
BADNONI
CHARANMATA
RUPAHELI
Lambia RS
JASWANTPURA
MIPLA-KA-KHEDA
SANANDEO
RANKYARAIMATA
KABRARIA
Lower Palaeolithic
GUpta/Post-Gupta
Chalcolithic
Modern Town
Early Historical
Early Medieval/Medieval
V H PARMAR

FIG. 1

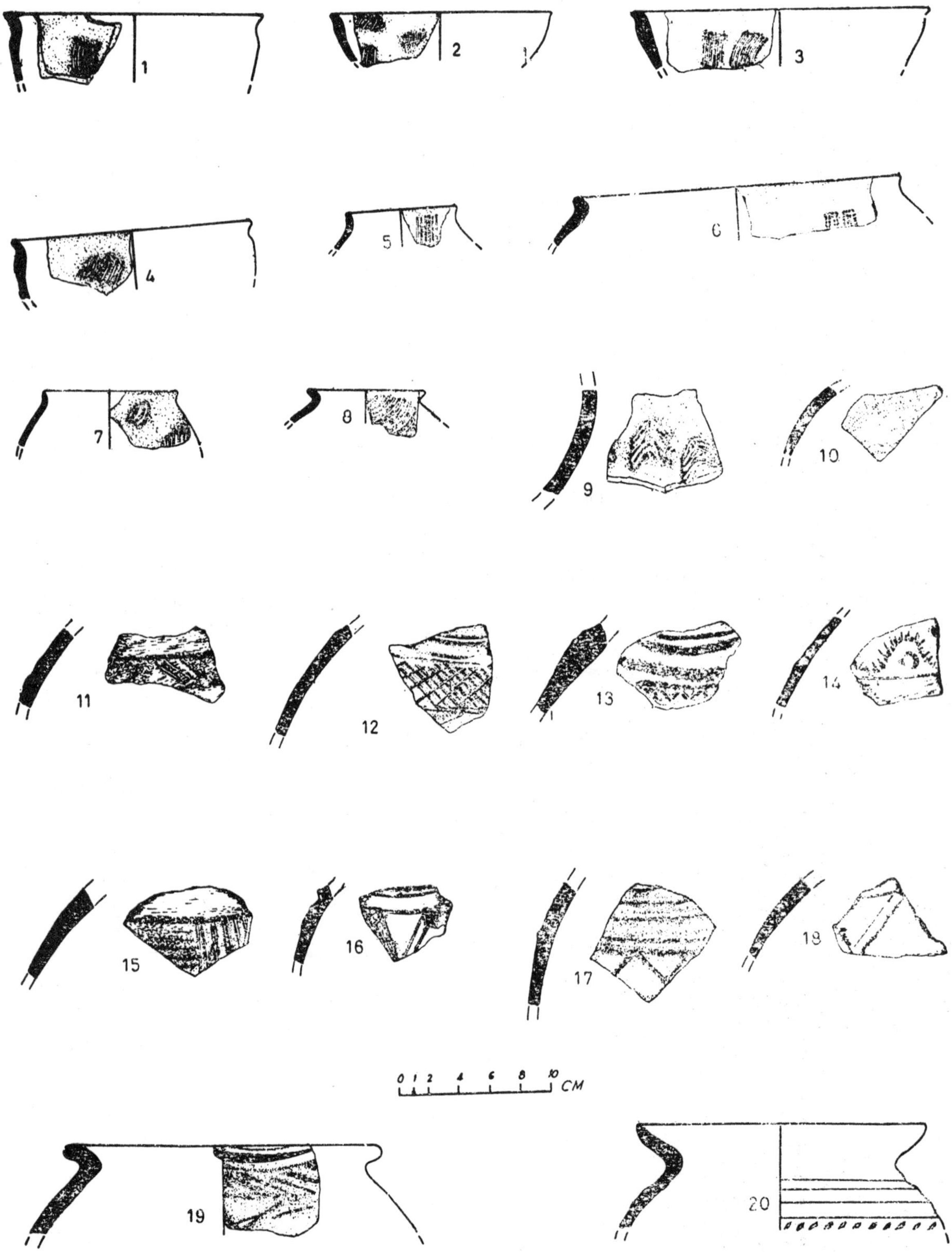

FIG. 2

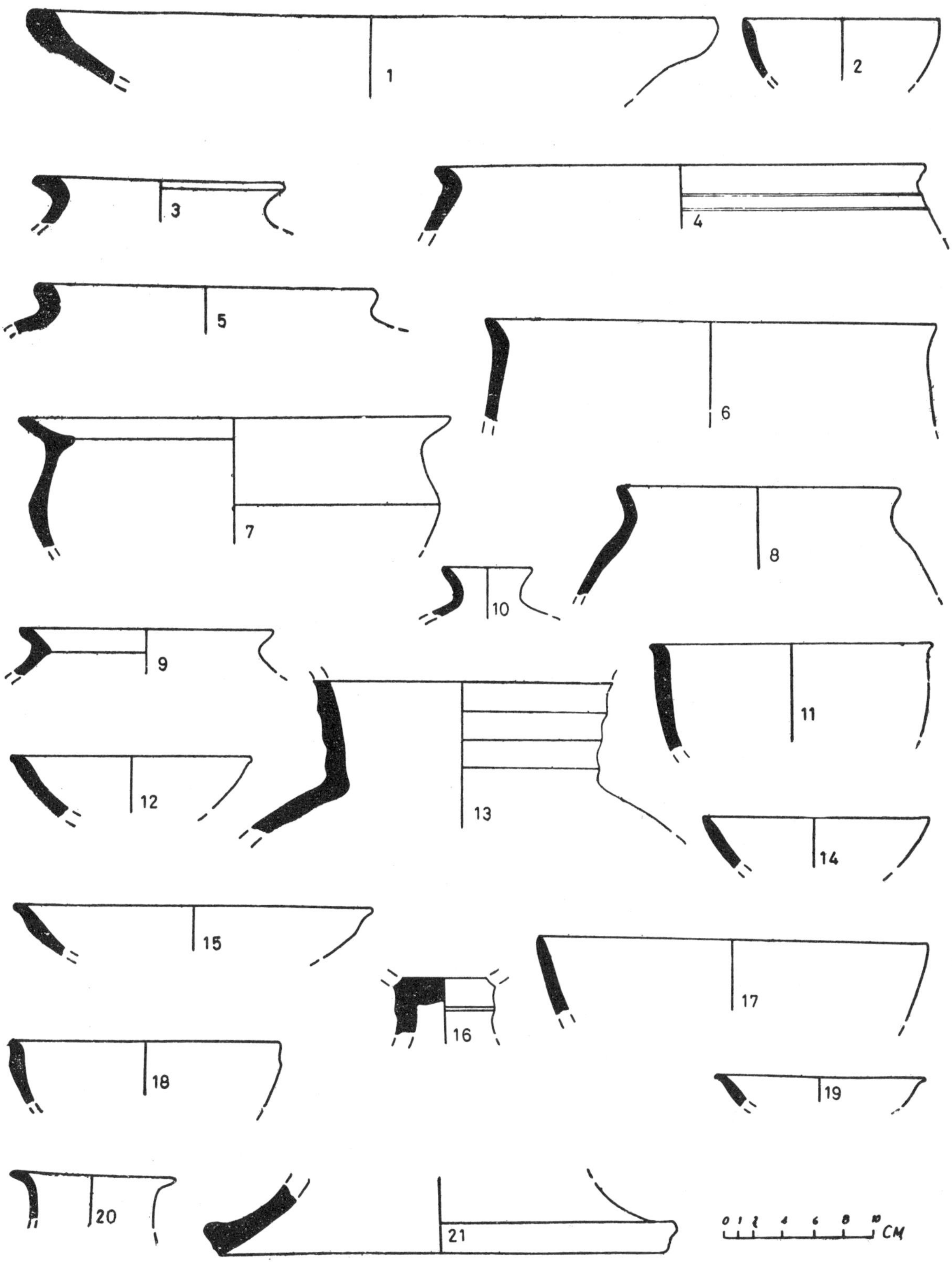

FIG. 3

5

Dots, Cup-Marks and PITS Vis-a-Vis the Megaliths—New Evidences from Kumaon[1]

Maheshwar P. Joshi

Introduction :

More than a century ago, in fact, in 1856, Henwood reported the presence of 'Rock basons' at Devidhura, district Pithorgarh, U.P.[2] Later it was Carnac who, around Dwarahat, district Almora, U.P., discovered a number of graves (?) and 'cup marks'—the characteristic features associated with the European megaliths.[3] Yet, no systematic and scientific study of these was ever undertaken by any of the archaeologists, although scholars like Wheeler[4] recognised their presence. However, at one time, he remarked: "An earlier observer found small granite and 'slate' cromlechs at Deodhoora, 18 miles south-east of Almora in northern U.P., but they were mostly if not entirely used as shrines and, on the evidence, may be discounted."

In recent years, M.C. Joshi of the Archaeological Survey of India examined the Devodura site and noticed deep and shallow depressions on the rocks as well as 'walled heaps (platforms)' of rubble which were being used in some cases as shrines of local deities.[5] These heaps, according to him, could be compared with some almost similar remains extant at Satmas near Agra.[6]

The present author also discovered similar depressions elsewhere in Kumaon more than a decade ago which prompted him to undertake extensive and intensive archaeological explorations in Kumaon in order to determine the extent of this culture. However, it was only during the last five field seasons that fruitful results were obtained in this regard when a large number of dots, cup-marks and pits of different dimensions were found in a wide area covering Pithoragarh, Almora and Nainital districts of U.P. with the Jaskot, Banadidevi mountain range as its major zone of concentration.

The Depressions—a brief description :

Typologically these depressions can be divided into the following varieties :

1. *Dot-like depressions:* These dots—tiny and shallow (approximately 0.5 cm to 1 cm in size)—are made on the surface of the rocks or stray boulders in one to four rows looking like beaded string(s) or in conglomeration. Such dot-like depressions have also been found in Central India. According to some archaeologists these may have been intended for some game.[7] We do not agree with this suggestion for if these dots were related to any game there should have been some sort of schematic uniformity in their representation such as is found in case of chess or *chaupada.*
2. *Smaller holes :* The smaller holes measure 2 cm to 8 cm in diameter and 1 cm to 10 cm in depth—the average size being 7 cm in diameter and 8 cm in depth. These depressions are also found on the surface of rocks or stray boulders either in conglomeration or in a scattered manner. Nothing can be said about their alignment, although in a few examples these are found along with the larger depressions as well.
3. *The common variety* ('Cup-marks') : This is the most common and widely distributed variety. It is found in different sizes ranging from 9 cm to 27 cm in diameter and 3 cm to 55 cm in depth, the average size being 15 cm in diameter and 32 cm in depth. With a few exceptions this variety is very neatly executed. It is also found on the rocky surface or on large boulders either singly or in pairs and occasionally in multiples. In some cases some sort of alignment is also noticeable.

Apart from these three types there are the following uncommon and peculiar varieties :

4. *Rectangular depressions :* There are a few eamples showing a group of two to five smaller rectangular depressions measuring 5 cm to 10 cm on the sides and 2 cm to 10 cm in depth. These are aligned with one another by way of channel-like depressed lines.

5. *Snake-like depressions :* A few examples show a smaller depression (variety 2 above) having zig zag channel-like depressed line added to it, thus giving a snake-like appearance. Its close parallel is to be found in the central device of the Almora coins datable to from c. 2nd century B.C. onwards.[8]
6. There is a solitary example showing an outline of a cat-like animal carved on the flat surface of the rock together with dotted depressions. Whether the animal and the dots are interrelated cannot be said in the present state of our knowledge.
7. *Pits :* The most remarkable variety among these depressions is that of the pear-shaped pits which have been excavated into the rock surface of the hills. Each of the mouths of these pits have an opening ranging from 40 cm to 50 cm in diameter which is cut down vertically almost straight, to a depth of about 22 cm and gradually widened upto a diameter of approximately 1.20 m at a depth of about 1.30 m. Below this point, all of the pits are filled with rubble, so that their exact depth and diameter could not be measured. It is also to be noted that there are many smaller holes measuring approximately 5 cm in diameter made in the inner walls of each of these pits. These holes are found at intervals in both the sides facing one another at the same level. If a bar-like object is inserted horizontally in these holes it can serve the purpose of a ladder. Around the mouth of each of the pits there is an outer depressed ring measuring 0.80 m to 1.10 m in diameter and 20 cm in depth. These pits are excavated at a distance of about 1.20 m to 1.50 m apart from one another externally, forming a triangular alignment. It is also to be noted that around these pits several smaller depressions (varieties 2 and 3above) are also made.

That these pits are also made in different sizes is seen from the fact that at one place two pits of two different sizes were found together. Of the two, the larger one measured over 2 m in depth and diameter, and the smaller one, a little less than 1 m in depth and diameter. About a hundred metres away from these pits there is one more pit of considerably large size as evidenced from the fact that sometime ago a buffalo is said to have fallen into it and the villagers had filled it with earth and rubble.

The notable sites where these depressions are found are as under :

Pithoragarh district, U.P.

Devidhura and adjoining area : Dots and pits (varieties 1, 2, 3, and 7 above); temple of goddess Varahi (a Vallabhi style structure of c. nineth century A.D.) amid assemblage of undressed stone rubble some of which are dedicated to local deities, particularly Aidi. The site is noted for the Bagavali Fair which is held on full moon day of *Savan*. On this occasion two traditional rival groups led respectively by Maharas and Fartiyals assemble at the temple ground and hold stone-throwing (Bhagval) mock fight. It is believed that formerly this occasion was celebrated by offering human sacrifice to the goddess, but later on with the consent of the goddess (?) it was resolved that the people should offer as much of human blood as a human body contains. It is for this reason that this stone-throwing mock fight takes place which continues for about an hour till sufficient human blood is shed in the course of fighting. It is interesting to note that some of the stones are specially prepared from the flakes called *phiphara* and the shield is made up of cane and leaves. The festival has a hoary past. Could it be a survival of the Stone Age practice? If that is so, we can say that it is an excellent example bearing on ethno-archaeology.

Almora District :

a. *Khaikhan :* depressions of common variety (variety 3 above) traces of rubble heap; fragment of a terracotta bangle mould together with melted piece of glass and fragments of glass bangles.
b. *Jaskot :* Dots and depressions (varieties 1, 2, 3 and 7); shrine dedicated to Aidi; rubble heap.
c. *Guna* : depressions (variety 3 above); traces of circular course of undressed stone masonry. The site used to be cremation ground and is still called *samasan*.
d. *Simalti :* depressions (varieties 1, 2, 3, 4 and 6).
e. *Dyoli-danda :* depressions (varieties 1, 2, and 5 above); traces of rubble heap and shrine of Aidi.
f. *Kalamati :* depressions (variety 3 above); trench-like cuttings.
g. *Naugaon :* depressions (varieties 2 and 3 above). About two hundred metres away fragments of grey coloured pottery with incised lines in triangular orientation made by a comb like-instrument.
h. *Bagwali Pokhar :* a large pits (variety 7 above). Two of these pits have been cut off by a local villager who has constructed a house close by. However, one can still see parts of the inner sections of both the pits.

Allied Problems :

So far as we have explored no covering has been

noticed on any of these depressions. However, taking into account the sharp edged mouths (rims) of many of these cup-marks (variety 3 above) it may be suggested that originally they might have been provided with some kind of covering; otherwise the sharpness of the edges of their mouths would have weathered by materials rolling over them during the rains. Prominent chisel marks seen on a number of these depressions and pits make it clear that a chisel like instrument was one of the tools used in making these monuments. The authors of these monuments seem to have also used a parallel sided sharp instrument to drill amazingly circular depressions with an almost 'U' like section, while the 'V' like section noticed in many examples may have been produced by a similar but triangular tool. Most of these depressions are found on the surface of the rocks or stray boulders. In several places the rocks bearing these pits are hewn out in trench like gaps with depressions on the higher level. In the present state of our knowledge nothing can be said about the nature of the tools employed in making these monuments. However, it is to be noted that without the use of metal tools it is difficult to dig the larger pits (variety 7 above) in the rocky surface, although it is not improbable that these pits were made without any metal tools, for the rocks bearing these pits are not very hard. Such a likelihood does not lie within realm of mere surmise. It seems to be substantiated by the fact that in Malta, for example, the neolithic people have also made rock-cut graves.[9]

All the varieties of these depressions are interconnected as is evident at Jaskot, district Almora, U.P., a site situated in a forest some 10 km east of Almora on a mountain ridge running north-south. Towards the northern slope almost at the end of the ridge, the rocky surface is cut down, more or less, vertically at a number of places.[10] At two such spots there are approximately 10 m long trench-like gaps measuring 4 m to 5 m in width and 2 m to 4 m in depth, partly hewn out in the rocky ridge in east-west direction. Close to the eastern end of one of the trenches is found a cluster of 37 circular pits of different sizes ranging from 2.5 cm to 55 cm in depth and 6 cm to 27 cm in diameter. No perfect alignment of these depressions could be noticed. However, some of the depressions seem to form triangles; whether they are intentional or coincidental cannot be said.

Still more interesting objects are the three pear-shaped pits (variety 7 above) together with the smaller depressions of different sizes (varieties 1,2, and 3 above). These pits are excavated into the higher level of the ridge towards north of these trenches. It is interesting to note that close by these trenches many heaps of rubble—looking like cairns—have also been noticed.

Associated Material :

In some of these pits small pieces of quartz and rolled flat and circular or oval shaped micaceous pebbles have been found. The latter seem to have been brought from a place situated some one kilometre away towards south where one can still find them in abundance on the surface. According to the villagers, fragments of red pottery and a small piece of bangle made of glass-like material were also found in one of these depression (variety 3 above). However, their relationship remains to be established. It may be noted that these objects were found at Jaskot only. In this connection, it is to be noted that the so called glass-like material is indeed glass. As noted above, at Khaikhan a factory site(?) of these glass bangles was discovered by the present author in the field season of 1980-81. From the surface of this site a fragment of a bangle mould of terracotta, broken and unfinished pieces of bangles in black, ash and orange colours and hardened semi or completely melted pieces of raw material were picked up. The site is situated some 8 km away towards south-east of Jaskot.

At Bagwali Pokhar the villager who cut off two of the larger pits (variety 7 above) found two *handi*-like pots of 'red-coloured' pottery inside the larger pit which were broken since then. Close by, in the section of the smaller pit (measuring a little less than a metre in depth and diameter) which was also cut off, the present author noticed rolled fragments of pottery which were undoubtedly brought down by the rainy water from the upper reaches of the hill where these are found in abundance. However, at this stage, it would be premature to establish any relationship between the pits and the pottery.

Identification of the depressions and their authors:

The identification of these depressions is an enigmatic problem. The brief account of different notable sites given above makes it clear that all the varieties are interconnected. Therefore, it would appear that different varieties had different functional use. Accordingly some of them, particularly varieties 1, 2, 4, 5 and 6 may have been used for some kind of ritualistic purpose. Variety 3 may be taken as sepulchral in nature. If this is accepted, their authors may be associated with megalithic culture for, elsewhere in India[11] as also in Europe 'cup-marks' are associated with burials.[12] In this connection the evidence of village Guna is interesting, because, it is here that this variety is associated with crematorium and is still called *samasan*. However, it is to be noted that to the best of our knowledge these depressions do not have any hitherto known parallel in India.[13] As regards the pear-shaped pits (with almost flat bottom as evidenced at Bagwali Pokhar), taking into account their large size there is a possibility that they were used as dwelling pits. In that case the smaller variety of depressions (variety 2 and 3 above) may have served as the post-holes to support a roof, as these depressions are found around the larger pits at Jaskot. However, the exact nature of these pits can be assessed only after the clearance of rubble.

But for the pits (variety 7 above) no traces of any material bearing on the settlement associated with these depressions tempts us to suggest that their authors lived a sport of nomadic life. However, the larger pits as also the cluster of 37 depressions (variety 3 above) at Jaskot and larger pits as Bagwali Pokhar do suggest a 'communal or group activities' and therefore, we can tentatively identify their society as 'group-oriented'.[14] Could their ethnic survival be identified with the local tribal group known as the Rajis or the Bhotiyas? The former is a nomadic tribe and the latter a pastoral. It is also interesting to note that in case of the Bhotiyas (who call themselves Shaukas) we know that after cremation they used to bury a charred bone of the deceased in an iron or tin box on the ground where a hole was dug for this purpose.[15] The casing of iron or tin box may have been a later introduction.

Before we conclude, it would not be out of place to add in passing that the Kumaoni society affords an interesting field for ethno-archeological studies. The low tradition in Kumaon has retained many such traits which seem to have a hoary antiquity. In this connection two deities, namely Aidi and Goril are interesting. Association of the shrines dedicated to Aidi with the depressions and rubble heaps has already been mentioned above. The Goril shrines are equally interesting as they are, in most cases, set up near the big boulders which are besmeared with vermilion. In this connection Carlleyle's comments are worth quoting :

> "We learn from the writings of Sir John Malcom that the genuine Bhils raised cairns to the memory of their chiefs when they died and poured oil on the top of the cairns afterwards, to which they added red-lead; which reminds us of the fact mentioned in the Bible, that Jacob poured oil on the stones which he raised."[16]

NOTES AND REFERENCES

1. The author gratefully acknowledges the financial assistance from the Kumaun University. Sarvashri R.C. Gaururani, N.K. Joshi and T.N. Tiwari helped him the field study. The photographs are through the courtsey of the Department of History, Kumaun University Campus, Almora.

2. Henwood, W.J., Notice of the Rock Basons at Doodhoora near Almora in Upper India, *Edinburgh New Philosophical Journal*, New Series IV, 1856, pp. 204-06.

3. Rivett-Carnac, Rough Notes on Some Ancient Sculptures on Rocks in Kumaon similar to those found in Monoliths and rocks in Europe, *Journal of Asiatic Society of Bengal*, XLVI (1) 1877, pp. 1-15.

4. Wheeler, R.E.M., *Early India and Pakistan*, London, 1960, pp. 159-60.

5. Wheeler, R.E.M., Brahmagiri and Chandravalli, 1947: Megalithic and other Cultures in Chitaldrug District, Mysore State, *Ancient India* No. 4, 1947-48, p. 302.

6. Carllele, A.C.L., *Archaeological Survey of India Report of a Tour in Eastern Rajputana*, Vol. VI, 1878, pp. 33-39.

7. Information from Dr. N.R. Banerjee.

8. Allan, J. *Catalogue of the coins of Ancient India*, Reprint 1975, plate 7,8,9.

9. Renfrew, Colin. Beyond a Subsistence Economy: The Evolution of Social Organization in Prehistoric Europe in Moore C.B. (Ed.), *Bulletin of the American School of Oriental Research*, Supplement No. 20, 1974; *Reconstructing Complex Societies An Archaeological Colloquium*, April 29-30, 1972 (MIT) 1972, p. 76.

10. At Kalamati (District Almora) also asimilar trench together with the common variety (number 3) of depressions have been noticed.

11. Recently Sri R.P. Rao, a research student in the Department of Ancient Indian History and Archaeology, Nagpur University, has also discovered some "cup marks" associated with megaliths in Deccan. Prof. A.M. Shastry very kindly sent me a detailed account of these 'cup marks', some of which may be compared with the third variety. Shri J.P. Joshi, Addl. Director General, Archaeological Survey of India, also informed me that cup marks are also found in Central India.

12. Carnac, *op. cit.*, Fox, Cyril, *Life and Death in Bronze Age*, London, 1959, p. 84, pl. 229.

13. Childe, V.G. Megaliths, *Ancient India* No. 4, 1947-48, pp. 5-13, Wheeler, 1947-48, *op. cit.*, pp. 181-310, Krishnaswami, V.D. Megalithic types of South India, *Ancient India*, No. 5, pp. 35-45; Sundara, A., Typology of Megaliths in South India, in Agrawal D.P. and D.K. Chakrabarti (eds.), *Essays in Indian Protohistory*, Delhi, 1979, pp. 239-251; Sarkar, H., Some Aspects of Megalithic Culture in India, *Puratattva*, 1. pp. 49-55, and Narain, A.K. (ed.) *Seminar Papers on the Problems of Megaliths in India*, Varanasi, 1969.

14. Renfrew, *op. cit.*, pp. 74-78.

15. Sherring, C.A., *Western Tibet and the British Borderland*, London, 1956, p. 125.

16. Carnac *op. cit.*

6
Excavations at Manjhi 1983-85 : A Preliminary Report

T.N. Roy

The excavation work at Manjhi was conducted for two season's from 1984. The work was very limited in scope but in view of the absence of a suitably documented report on any Black slipped Culture site in Bihar, this work, however limited, deserves publication. The purpose of this paper is to present the basic documentation of the archaeological material brought out from this small scale excavation. There is, however, ample scope for a regular horizontal excavation of this site.

Here only the basic field data including the site and the periodisation has been set forth. The results of technical studies on animal bones, iron and copper objects and radiocarbon dates, etc. will be published when these results are known.

The Site

Falling in the Saran district of Bihar, Manjhi is 19 km west of the district headquarters, Saran (bearing also the name of Chapra) which lies on the Allahabad—Sonepur metre gauge section of the North-Eastern Railway and from there a regular bus and trekker (Four wheeler) operates right upto Manjhi. One intending to visit the site from Varanasi by rail may do so via Ballia; the journey being a little over 191 km in the north-east direction. The ancient site, sprawling along the left bank of the Ghaghra, lies in the revenue limits of Manjhi, a small village occupying a sizeable part of the site.

As one approaches Manjhi village, a huge mound nearly 14 metres in height from the ground level, strikes the eye. From the top of the mound one can have a glimpse of the River Ghaghra (Sarayu), which flows just near the mound from north-east to south-west direction. As has been the case with most of the ancient sites, Manjhi also seems to have flourished more along the bank of the river. This is obvious by the extent of the mound which is about 526 m from north to south but only about 390 m from east to west. These dimensions, however, may not represent the overall area covered by the ancient people, since as the excavation has revealed, the ancient people had once removed a substantial portion of older settlement for the construction of a huge fortification wall and a moat. This construction has resulted in the division of an older habitation into two clear blocks of the mound.

So, as seen today there are two main blocks of the mound, separated by a moat, which is fairly wide on the south-east direction but narrows down towards other sides. The main mound locally known as *Manhi-Ka-Tila* (herein named as Mound-1) has a rain-gully running south-north which on the southern extreme towards the river gives the impression of an ancient opening (pl. 6 I). The main mound, as it appears today, is dish-shaped. It slopes down on either sides. While the highest contour on the top is 68 m above Mean Seal Level that on the inner side is 66 m, a difference of about 2 meters which accounts for the absence of regular strata of late occupational debris at the site. This inner slope and the absence of regular late deposit all over the mound is due to extensive ploughing and cultivation which is going on at the site since long. The outer slope of the mound, making a rough circle on plan, is well marked throughout its circuit of approximately 1500 m and gives an impression of a huge fortification of baked bricks. This defence wall is completely obliterated by the accumulation of occupational debris of later period but exposed at several points due to robbing of baked bricks and mud by the local villagers. On the south-eastern top of the mound stands a recent small baked-brick building known as *Mauni-Baba-Ki-Pakki-Kuti*.

To the east of the main mound, across the ancient moat,. is another small mound called here for the sake of convenience as Mound 2. This is comparatively very low in height but one can pick up ancient pottery on it. This tends to suggest that while the main settlement may have been on the main mound (Mound 1), stray ancient dwellings also existed on this part of the area. On this mound recently a couple of residential buildings have been constructed along with a temple dedicated to Kali. There is very little area in which a probe for ancient remains could be made on this part of the mound.

It appears that in ancient times these two mounds formed one continuous unit, and it is the construction of the ancient defence wall and the moat which has resulted in giving the site its present shape.

The Cuttings

Two small trenches MJH—1 and MJH—2, were laid on the main Mound 1. It was on the south-eastern area of this mound between *Mauni-Baba-Ki-Pakki-Kuti* (Hanuman Mandir) and rain-gully, a huge concentration of Northern Black Polished Ware was observed. It was thought that this portion of the site could be suitable for laying a trench across the inner slope of the city defence wall which, besides, throwing light on the defence may also give clues regarding the antiquity of the site. MJH—1 was, therefore laid at this point. This had an added advantage. With more funds and time at our disposal this trench could be easily extended on the outer area of the defences. This will enable us to find out the basal width of the defences, its vertical extant height and outer slope, if any, during future excavation. Similarly MJH—2 was laid on the north-eastern side of the mound with almost the same objective, i.e. finding out the occupational strata within the defences and the antiquity of the site. This had an advantage of exposing within our means the minimum possible occupational deposit. Primarily it was, therefore, to confirm the findings of MJH—1. The alignment of both these trenches was along the cardinal direction.

The sequence of Cultures

MJH—1 provides the sequence of cultures from about the beginning of the first millennium B.C. upto the early medieval times and the culture contents of the various periods in brief are as follows:

Period I (Black-Slipped Ware Culture)

This period having an average deposit of about two metres above the natural soil, belongs to the black slipped ware Culture. It is characterized by black slipped ware, black and red ware and associated red ware. Of these in the black slipped ware the principal ceramic industry of this period, bowls and dishes predominated. Amongst the bowls, the shapes available were the sub-ovaloid, straight sided, carinated, hemispherical, convex-sided and round-sided. The black and red ware was marked by bowls with everted and featureless rim, platters, and dish-on-stand. Of interest in the red ware was one almost complete dish-on-stand. No other antiquity was recovered from this period except pottery discs and two fragments of stone of indeterminate use. Remnants of burnt earth with red-impression indicate that the hutments of this period were constructed of wattle-and-daub. The use of copper and stone tools were not at all attested. Iron was also not recorded from the lowest levels. But we were fully satisfied that iron was found from the middle strata of this period. In later levels, this period distinctively overlapped with the NBPW period (Period II). Such a situation would however suggest three stages for the black slipped ware (BSW) occupation at Manjhi:

(1) A few layers where the BSW is not associated with iron and it is quite likely that this deposit may represent an earlier stage in the history of BSW.
(2) The second stage appears to be the time when it comes to be associated with iron.
(3) The third stage was when there was an overlap between the BSW and the NBPW.

While the first stage may go back to about the beginning of the first millennium B.C., the third is unlikely to be later than middle of the first millennium B.C. Since the evidence is very meagre and confined to a small area, it would not be proper to pronounce a final word on the nature of this deposit.

Period II (NBPW period—600 B.C. to 50 B.C.)

Without any break of occupation from Period I, Period II, with a thickness from 5.43 to 3.92 m, was mainly characterized by the introduction of the Northern Black Polished Ware (NBP) and greater use of iron. With so much of thick deposit belonging to NBP period, it is now possible to divide this period into three Sub-periods II A, II B and II C. A notable industry requiring closer attention in Sub-period II A is the plain grey ware. The distinctive feature of this ware is its superior quality and an apparently smoothened dark grey surface. Special mention may be made of a few sherds in this fabric which were painted in black over dark grey surface with a simple and elementary horizontal rim band. Although dissimilar in fabric from the well-known Painted Grey Ware (PGW), its occurrence in Sub-period II A does show the contact and interrelationship between PGW and NBP. In Sub-period II B, Ahichchhatra 10A type and miniature bowl in red ware made their appearance. In Sub-period II C, the dominant industry was a coarse NBP (Fabric E), but top-graded NBP (Fabric A) also continued. The introduction of carinated *handi* and incurved bowls was a noteworthy feature of this sub-period. Of the thirteen iron objects recovered from this period, two came from Sub-period II A, three from Sub-period II B and the remaining six from Sub-period II C. The miscellany of objects included both tools and weapons like, arrow-head, nails, dagger, hammer knife-blades, etc. The limited number of small pieces of iron slag which we found in this period and in the core of the defences suggest that there was an element of iron-smelting at the site right from the earliest levels although it was only in the upper level of period II, it became more popular. The use of copper remained subordinate to iron. Of the four objects obtained from the excavation, as many as three came from Sub-period II C and one from Sub-period II B. These included tools and broken fragments of objects of indeterminate use. Thirteen beads, variously of agate, glass and terracotta were recovered from this period. Of these, one long barrel-shaped bead of banded agate from Sub-period II A and one twenty-four faceted green bead of glass from Sub-period II C are particularly noteworthy for workmanship. Among the terracotta beads the most common shape was the vase-shaped or *ghata*-shaped circular bead, and this shape is available in all the three sub-periods. Grinding-stones or querns along with pestles and sharpeners, formed the kitchen equipment. A circular steatite casket with a knobbed lid is one of the unique finds from Sub-period II C (Pl. 6. II).

It is significant to note that bone industry was an integral part of this Iron Age culture. Of the thirty-eight objects obtained from period II, three came from Sub-period II A, six from Sub-period II B and as many as twenty-one from Subperiod II C. These included bone points, arrow-heads, bangles and unfinished tools. Of these, the bone points formed an overwhelming majority (Pl. 6. III). These were manufactured out of splintered bones, revealing distinct cut marks and attempts to prepare a working point either at one or both the ends. In several cases, the whole body of these bone points is highly polished and the working edge is so well defined and pointed that one wonders if some metal implements were used in their manufacture. Vertically they show, in frequency, a consistent increase from bottom upwards, indicating that the industry became more popular as the occupation advanced from early, middle to late phases of the Iron Age. These bone points must have been used for various purposes. Among the lesser miscellany of finds were an ivory arrow-head from Sub-period IIB and unidentified tool of bone from Sub-period IIA.

Amongst other finds, mention may be made of: pottery-discs form all the sub-periods, two terracotta animal figurines from Sub-period II C, and toy-cart wheel, mould, balls, cone stoppers, bangles all of terracotta, from Sub-period II C. Of terracotta objects from the period, a boat-shaped object and a mould with five deep concentric circles both from Sub-period II B are noteworthy (Pl. 6. IV). A heavily-corroded cast coin of copper and two inscribed sealings of terracotta, recovered from Sub-period II C bear witness to the prevalence of coinage and of writing during the late levels of this period.

No house-remains were encountered throughout the strata of Sub-periods II A and II B. The presence of one piece of not well baked small lump of terracotta in the deposit belonging to Sub-period II B gives the impression of the beginning of baked brick activity. But in view of the very restricted area of the dig, this phenomenon, however, remains doubtful. The houses during Sub-period II C were made of baked bricks, the size of which averaged 50 x 25 x 9 cm. While complete plans were out of question because of the limited extent of the dig, interesting evidence in this respect was obtained. In MJH-1, there was a floor made of earth and brickbats, on which was found brick debris of a collapsed house of a bone-tool maker. In the structural debris were found several bone points, both finished as well unfinished. In the vicinity, a long pit along with several broken fragments of terracotta ring-well shows that the practice of constructing ring-wells was a common feature during this sub-period (Pl. 6. V). Ascribable to the late levels of this sub-period was a massive baked brick fortification. It was observed to be directly constructed over the deposit of Sub-period II C after levelling the ground (Pl. 6. VI). The antiquities recovered from the core of the defences were essentially the material from Sub-periods II A and II B indicating that the defences could not be associated with the early and middle phases of the NBP period. The other details, like its various stages of construction, vertical extant height, basal width and its relation with the habitation area still remain to be ascertained. It is, therefore, clear that neither the finds recovered from the core of the defences nor its present stratigraphical sequence as revealed in the two seasons' excavations are able to pronounce any final verdict on it.

Period III (50 B.C. to A.D. 300)

Perhaps there was no appreciable time gap between the end of period II and the beginning of Period III. The cultural equipment of this period showed marked contrast with that of the preceding one. NBP was completely absent. The coarse NBP of sub-period II C with its characteristic shapes like, bowls, dishes, carinated *handis*, lipped bowls, etc., were also no more to be seen now. The notable feature of this period was its exclusive red ware industry.

Among the most important tapes of this period red ware industry, mention may be made of bowls with incurved rim, ink-pot lids, buttom-knobbed lids, spouted basins and bottlenecked sprinklers. Baked brick structures ascribable to two structural phases were noticed. While complete plan was out of question because of limited area excavated, both in MJH—1 and MJH—2, several walls were noted in which the size of baked bricks were not at all uniform. In this connection particular mention may be made of a structural complex lined with gravel which, however, could not be completely traced.

This period yielded the largest number of antiquities. Mention may be made of large number of terracotta human figurines, both male and female (Pl. 6. VII); terrocotta animal figurines including horse, monkey and camel; stone and terracotta pestles (Pl. 6. VIII); and stoppers, gamesmen, ear-ornaments, pendent, wheel and decorated discs of terracotta. From the early deposit of this period, a decorated scale of ivory is also noteworthy find (Pl. 6. IX). An inscribed terracotta sealing which on the basis of palaeography can be assigned to 2nd-3rd centuries A.D. was an important find of this period.

Period IV

After a considerable lapse of time, a new settlement cropped at the site, the deposits of which were noticed in a very limited area. It appears that though the city was deserted, a small group of people belonging to Medieval age settled over the earlier ruins though sporadically in very small area. As is to be expected the pottery was now entirely different from what it used to be in Period III. It was made of medium to coarse grained clay, wheel-turned and dull red in colour. Superficial dusting of mica was the usual feature of the pots. The pots were decorated with stamped, incised and applique designs. Among the noteworthy types in red ware mention may be made of knife-edged bowls, carinated *handis* with soot marks, knobbed lids, sturdy basins and shallow plates. Apart from the ordinary red ware, a few pieces of the glazed ware were also reported mainly from the late levels of the site.

Significance of the results

(1) Manjhi for the first time, provides an insight into the various stages of the BSW culture deposit in this part of the Middle Ganga Plan. Possibly, it has cast doubts on an iron-free chalcolithic horizon in this category of sites in Bihar. One finished object of iron which we found in the middle levels of the BSW deposit cannot be ignored. It is, of course, possible that the intial occupation of the BSW culture started at the site after iron was already introduced elsewhere in the region. However, this point can be settled only with more work at the site.

(2) This BSW culture of period I is characterized by unpainted ceramic tradition, possibly belonging to some non-Aryan ethnic group. It has a sizeable deposit of about two metres, so far not reported from any site of the Middle Ganga Plain. It clearly overlaps with the early phase of NBP period.

(3) With the occupational strata of NBP period (Period II) ranging in thickness from 4.40 m to 3.92 m, it is now possible to sub-divide this NBP period into three sub-periods, viz., II A, II B and II C. Unlike other sites NBP has a longer duration at Manjhi. It continued to be in use upto 50 B.C.

(4) The present evidence shows that the site was not urbanized before 400-300 B.C. The process of urbanization set in only during the late phase of the NBP period. The baked brick fortification wall and the moat belongs to the late phase of the NBP period and if worked out in detail (as suggested in the foregoing pages) is likely to throw light on the defence system of the township during the period.

(5) Absence of Gupta period occupation, so well known from historical records, is yet another feature to be noted.

(6) With so much of thick deposit belonging to BSW *Ware* and NBP periods along with a huge baked brick fortification of about 1500 m in circuit, it is now possible to say that this is one of the key-sites for the Iron Age archaeology of the Middle Ganga Plain. More so when Manjhi is unknown from ancient Indian texts.

Acknowledgement

The excavations were carried under the auspices of the Department of Ancient Indian History, Culture and Archaeology under my direction during season's 1983-84 and 1984-85. Throughout the work, I was assisted by Sri Satyendra Kumar Singh (one of my research scholars) and Sri Jawahir Singh Yadav, who, besides helping me in multifarious works, also supervised the trenches, indexed each antiquity carefully and pieced potsherds to resurrect them into recognisable shapes. Mention may also be made of Sri Jairem Singh and Sri Rambadan, who formed the rest of the excavation team. The photographs of the site and the antiquities were taken entirely by Sri O.P. Khaneja. I am deeply beholden to Prof. Lallanjee Gopal, Dean, Faculty of Arts and Head of the Department for his full cooperation during the work, I am also obliged to the Director General of Archaeological Survey in India for granting me license to excavate this protected site for three years. However, work during (1985-86) could not be continued for want of adequate funds.

7

Archaeological Findings from Durvasa

B.C. Shukla

The ancient mound at Durvasa, situated at a distance of 10 kilometres south-east of Allahabad city, Uttar Pradesh, is an important archaeological site. Located on the bank of the River Ganga, the site has become important from the religious and economic points of view. Archaeological remains exposed due to erosion lie scattered the between two villages—Kakara-Kotawa in the north-east and Tiwaripura in the west.

The present site covers approximately an area of 1700 x 1000 square metres. As the site is not protected, under any relevant Act, it is being converted partly into agricultural field and partly into habitational area. A time would come when no trace of any archaeological vestige would be available.

The ancient trade route from Sravasti (Sahet-Mahet, U.P.) passed through Alavi (Ranki, Pratapgarh, U.P.)[1] Bihar (Pratapgarh, U.P.)[2] and Phulpura (Allahabad, U.P.)[3] before reaching to Durvasa. From here, after crossing the River Ganga this route led to Vidisha via Bharhut (Satna, M.P.). The people of Durvasa and its surroundings still use this route to reach Karama and Sohagi-ghat (Vindhyan hill near Chakghat, a place on the border of U.P. and M.P.). The recent discovery of Aśokan stupas at Deour-Kothar,[4] 4 km. south-west from Sohagi, confirms that this place might have been of some importance. The ancient remains at Kasarawal-dih,[5] Mahanai-dih,[6] Durvasa, Manaiyadiha[7] (opposite to Durvasa on the other bank of the Ganga), Pandevara, Karma indicate that this route was in regular use for trade purposes and Durvasa was probably a regular ferry crossing. Between Varanasi and Allahabad many sites like Purani-Kasi,[8] Semaradhinath,[9] Sitamarhi,[10] Lakshagiri,[11] Chhatanaga,[12] etc. are found. These sites have yielded numerous vestiges of temples and images. Materials obtained from Durvasa in a brief surface exploration are presented here for the first time.

Pottery

The earliest pottery available on the site is the Painted Grey Ware. The quantity being limited it is difficult to ascertain the shapes and fabric of this ware. The other important pottery met with is the famous Northern Black Polished Ware, which is found lying in abundance on the site. Most of these sherds having thin section, are made of well-levigated clay. The types include dishes, convex-sided bowls, lids, carinated *handis*, etc. The painted designs consist of bands, dots, wavy lines and semicircles. The other ceramics are red wares of the Kushana and Gupta Periods. A few sherds of glazed ware were also noticed.

Bricks and Architectural Remains

It is difficult to assess the extent of architectural activities on the basis of limited surface exploration. The bricks, thickly scattered all over indicate a vigorous architectural activity at the site in ancient period. The size of bricks — varying in dimensions from 43 x 25 x 6 cm to 25 x 20 x 4 cm, indicate that they have been used in constructions in different periods. The bricks of 43 x 25 x 6 cm and 35 x 20 x 6 cm have been reported from Basarh,[13] Kausambi[14], Sarnath,[15] etc. from the early N.B.P. levels. It would not be unreasonable to postulate that the present site was an urban centre during the N.B.P. period, i.e. from *circa* 6th *c*. B.C. to 1st *c*. B.C. The other type of bricks, moulded ones, bearing anthropomorphic figurines and floral designs are also met with. Archaeological evidence shows that this type of brick was widely used in the Gupta and post-Gupta period.[15] After the 9th century A.D., the use of such bricks is not documented by archaeological finds.[17] A wall running from north to south measuring about 90 cm. in width has been exposed by a *nullah*.

Sculptures

The site is strewn with fragments of stone sculptures. Most of them are mutilated extensively and badly defaced, hence their identification is not possible. However, two images from the site are almost intact. A stone slab measuring 45 cm x 40 cm portrays the figures of Umā-maheśvara. The figures are similar to those found at many places in north India.

The other interesting image from the site now being worshipped under a peepul tree at the western outskirts of the site near Tiwaripura village and measuring 65 cm x 63 cm is made of reddish sandstone. The central deity is two armed and is shown in a standing posture surrounded by the ten incarnations of Vishṇu. On the right side of the central deity is a figure of Vamana, beautifully carved. The garland of roundish beads (*rudraksha*) worn by Vāmana is skilfully depicted. Above this figure, Vāraha is shown uplifting the earth by his left hand. According to mythology, Vishnu in the form of Varaha saved the earth from the clutches of the demon, Hiranayākṣha. On the top, a fish has been portrayed showing Matsyavatara aspect of Vishnu. Brahmā has also been depicted at the top of the slab. On either side of Brahma two flying Vidyadharas, holding garlands in their hands, are shown. On the left of the central deity a tortoise with two riders on its back, a male and female, is also visible. It is to be noted here that in the *dasavatara* panel, the tortoise has been shown in its natural form. The depiction of male and female figurines on the back of a tortoise is not common. It has not been possible to identify these figurines. The central deity has been carved beautifully. An oval halo decorated with eight petalled lotus has been shown behind the head. The two-armed image does not possess any attributes, viz. weapons, etc. in the hands of Vishnu. Below the right hand of the deity, a fierce-looking figure with a long moustache is sculptured.[18] Without specific attributes the identification of the figure is hazardous.

There are two other fragments of stone portraying a chariot driven by seven horses. The upper parts of these slabs are missing. At the northern outskirts. of the mound a temple known as Anandi Maa temple is situated. Though the temple is modern, the deity installed in it seems to be an ancient one. A two-armed female goddess is shown seated on an elephant holding a thunderbolt in her right hand. According to Markandeya Puraṇa,[19] Aindri, the consort of Indra, should be depicted as seated on elephant.

These finds are indicative of the potentiality of the site. Only an extensive exploration and selective excavations would bring out the ancient past of the region.

NOTES AND REFERENCES

1. Ranki is situated at a distance of about 60 km on the west from the district headquarters of Pratapgarh in U.P. The author visited this site twice, once in January 1980 and again in March 1982. For the archaeological findings of the site—See *Bulletin of Museum & Archaeology*, No. 27-28, pp. 9-16. The author is of the view that the present site Ranki could be identified with Alvi, an ancient town of Kosala *Janapada*. However, Cunningham and Hornele have identified Alvi with modern Neval in Unnao district. N.L. Dey has tried to locate this town about 45 km north-east of Etawah district of Uttar Pradesh. See B.C. Law, *Historical Geography of Ancient India* (Hindi tr.), 117.

2. Bihar is situated in Kunda sub-division of Pratapgarh district. For its archaeological material see, Cunningham, *Report of the Archaeological Survey of India*, Vol. IX.

3. About 3 km west of Phulpur town of Allahabad, there is a mound known as Kasarawaldih yielding N.B.P. and other ceramics.

4. For the location of this site see 3 above.

5. Mahnaidih is situated 7 km north of Saidabad station of N.E. railway in the Allahabad District. For the remains of the site see author's paper, An unnoticed Uma-mahesvara Image from Mahnaidih, *Drishtikona*, Vol. II, pp. 41-43.

6. The earliest pottery on the site is the N.B.P.

7. Purani Kashi situated at a distance of 3 km south of Aurai town in Varanasi district of U.P. is an important archaeological site. The site abounds in early pottery and stone sculptures.

8. Semaradhinath is situated about 40 km east of Allahabad city on the bank of the River Ganga. Probably this was named after Semaradhinath which is an epithet of Lord Siva. The site has yielded N.B.P. sherds, Ekamukha Siva Linga and several other fragments of stone sculptures belonging to Gupta and post-Gupta periods.

9. Sitamarhi is located about 2 km away on the west from Semaradhinath, on the bank of the Ganga. Local people call it as a place to which Valmiki belonged.

10. Lachhagiri—situated about 10 km west from Sitamarhi is a site of immense archaeological importance. The sporadic exploration of the site has revealed the presence of N.B.P. sherds, ring-wells and several fragments of stone-images and architectural pieces.

11. Chhatanaga situated adjacent to the mound of Jhunsi, ancient Pratisthana, seems to be an abode of Chhatranaga. Naga worship was prevalent in the area of Prayaga Mandala in the ancient period. The Puranas mention many Nagas of this mandala in ancient times. For example, Kambala, Asvatara, Bahumulaka, Vasuki, etc. See *Matsya Purana* More & ed., Calcutta; 56.34 *Kurma Purana* Varanasi, 1980, 33.28.

12. *Annual Report of the Archaeological Survey of India*, 1910-11.

13. Rahul, Sankrityayan—*Puratattvika Bibandhawali*, Allahabad 1958, p. 8-9.

14. *Ibid.*, p. 8-9.

15. *Annual Progress Report of Archaeological Survey of India* (Northern Circle) 1907-8, pp. 32-33.

16. *Ibid.* p. 33.

17. In the Vishnu Purana a terrible form of Lord Vishnu is described.

18. *Markandeya Purana*, (More & ed. Calcutta).

8

A Mahaparinirvana Panel in the National Museum Collection

Shashi Asthana

The National Museum, New Delhi has acquired a sculptured panel, which though fragmentary, is still extremely significant from the point of view of art history. The sculpture has been carved on Mathura blotchy red sandstone. With low relief carvings of animated human figures against the background of a vast plain surface, the panel represents a beautiful composition. The human forms are standardized and generalized as also the trees, and both are made to match each other and pipal leaf engravings are seen in both and was the prototype for them. This is, in fact, the hallmark of the Mathura-Kushana style. There are many other diagnostic features, viz. turbans, crests, garlands, etc. which would assign the sculpture to the Kushana period of the 1st-2nd century A.D.

The panel is in narrative style and depicts an episode of Buddhist origin. However, when complete the sculpture, a long tablet, must have depicted a chain of episodes from one or more stories, since in one corner of the extant remains there are some indications to that effect. The central panel is, however, vivid and extremely suggestive of a theme which is common in the Gandhara School but rare in the Mathura School.

The scene is located in a garden. In between two trees is placed a long rectangular solid object, mostly damaged, bearing criss-cross design making a mesh of diamond-shaped pattern. Since the design is bordered with a thin vertical ribbon, it appears to be the portrayal of a piece of cloth with patterned design. In other words, the long rectangular object has been shown covered with a beautiful linen. Nearer the right end, the barrel-shaped object carries two strings of a heavy garland. Behind it is a human head with a boat-shaped cap; the decorations being completely worn out. This is flanked by a pair of human heads, seen on either side. These four heads look alike—delicate and princely. They are seen with typical Kushana turbans with broad frontal band and leaf-shaped crests, decorated with jewels. The ears are adorned with heavy rings. From behind the dense foliage of the trees two celestial nymphs are seen emerging. The one on the right carries on the shoulder a basket full of flowers supported by left hand; the raised right hand is shown showering a handful of flowers. The one on the left, whose left hand is missing, is shown lowering a heavy garland over a long box-like object. Thus the artist has successfully shown the act of veneration of the long object by the celestial beings: in the former part of the scene the nymph had already garlanded and is in the act of throwing flowers while in the latter the garland is being lowered; since the other hand is missing, it is difficult to ascertain whether this figure also was performing a similar act as that of the nymph on the right.

What does this scene represent? The correct identification depends on the identification of the long object. In order to ascertain it let us consider the following points:

First, that the object is rectangular in shape since there is a marked foreshortening in the upper rows of diamonds of the covering cloth.

Secondly, that since only the five heads of the attending human beings are shown, it indicates that the object was placed on some high pedestal, or else it was nearly five feet deep.

Thirdly, that it was a long object, nearly six feet in length, since even though five men were standing (or sitting) in a row, shoulder to shoulder, there was still space for two more men for one on either end.

However, it is difficult to ascertain whether the object was in two parts—one a lid and the othera container, or else it was one solid object. In order to ascertain this we will have to take into account similar objects shown elsewhere. The Mathura sculptures do not help us here since it was not a popular theme with them. But the Gandhara sculptures can help us. One may cite at least three examples in which a long barrel-shaped object occurs in a similar context.

There are three reliefs, one housed in the Lahore Museum[1], one in the Indian Museum, Calcutta[2] and the third belongs to the Gai Collection, Peshawar.[3] The first two reliefs present a long barrel-shaped box placed on a couch along with three monks at the back and a sala tree, and the second relief depicts disciple Subhadra with three sticks on his shoulders. The third one presents a barrel-shaped box placed on a couch surrounded by seven monks. The lid of the box is decorated with a number of rosettes.

The 'long box like object' in these examples and in many others has been identified by all scholars as the Buddha's coffin. In all likelihood, therefore, the long rectangular object in this example also is a coffin in which the dead body of the Buddha was preserved till the time of cremation. For this we have textual references also.

The *Mahapariniravana Sutta*[4] informs that first the dead body of Buddha was wrapped in as many as five hundred layers of cotton, and then it was covered with wool. Finally, it was lowered in a double iron box full of oil for several days before cremation. The *Sutta* gives a graphic description of several other events which occurred just before and during the period of mourning. For example, it mentions that before the Buddha breathed his last Saint Subhadra came to become the last disciple of Buddha.[5] Subhadra, a moving mendicant, had only a tripod of three sticks and a pouch like water bowl. In the Gandhara and Mathura sculptures both the tripod with the bowl hanging from the top-knot of the sticks as well as Subhadra squatting on the floor appear repeatedly in the scene of *Mahaparinirvana*. The tripod with pouch like water bowl is invariably present there, almost like the symbol of Subhadra's arrival or presence.

The *Sutta*[6] also mentions that on hearing the news of Buddha's death, the most venerable Mahakashyapa also left for Kushinagara where Buddha's body was lying in state in a couch kept between two sala trees.[7] According to this text[8] a host of celestial beings, including tree spirits, visited Buddha to pay homage.

The *Sutta*[9] further informs us that on hearing the news of *Mahaparinirvana* of the Buddha, Sakra or Indra came from the celestial world to pay special homage. Similarly, four Malla Chieftains also assembled to pay homage at the time of cremation, dressed in new clothes to light the funeral pyre.[10] They had, of course, to wait the arrival of Mahakashyapa who was half way to Kushinagara.

In the light of this literary evidence when we look at the sculpture again we start wondering whether the scene represents the *Mahaparinirvana* of the Buddha. The lower portion of the panel is missing, hence Saint Subhadra is not seen but the tripod with the pouch like bowl is present beside the right hand tree. In other words, the *Sutta's* description tallies with the sculptural representation. Similarly, even though a large part of the tree on the left is missing, the tree spirits may be seen emerging out of the foliage. The five human heads, four in identical head-gears and the fifth in a different head-dress, also tallies with the Sutta's description: the central one represents Sakra's while the others represent the Malla chieftains. The iron box filled with oil and containing the body of the Buddha is represented by the long rectangular object covered by a patterned cloth.

However, by the side of the tripod one can see a narrow ladder. It is common knowledge that it represents the descent of Buddha at Sankissa (identified with Sankisa in District Fatehgarh, U.P.) from Tushita-heaven where he had gone to preach to his mother. This must have formed part of the next panel where a more graphic scene might have been depicted. Thus, the ladder does not form part of the scene of our immediate concern.

To this suggested identification of the scene, that it represents the *Mahaparinirvana* scene both in terms of the *Mahaparinirvana Sutta* and on the analogy of the Gandhara practice, calls for a few further observations

To begin with, it may be argued that the four princely figures may represent the personified versions of the guardians of the four cardinal directions and not the Malla chieftains since, according to one version, the 'Dead body of the Buddha' was taken into the city centre from four different directions.[11] However, this suggestion does not appear to be sound since the four heads are absolutely identical wearing princely headgear. In other words, had they been different from each other, they may have represented four different directions.

It brings us to the question whether there is any other similar representation of the *Mahapariniravana* in the Mathura art or not?

In the Govt. Museum, Mathura there is a Kushana railing pillar (J. 17) with a panel which represents a somewhat squarish box bedecked with garlands. The box is placed on a throne and a parasol is held over it. Recently, Rani Srivastava[12] has suggested that this box may represent the Buddha's coffin. However, Vogel[13] and Agrawal[14] had earlier identified this box as only a relic casket. In this context it may be observed that the near squarish form and comparatively small size of the object would favour its identification as a relic casket and not a coffin, which must in all circumstances be long, whether it is barrel-shaped or rectangular or tubular. Near squarish stone box containing relic caskets were found a long time back in the core of the brick stupa at Piprahwa, District Basti. Hence, to our mind, the views of Vogel and Agrawal appear to be nearer the truth.

Thus, this panel turns out to be unique in the gamut of Mathura School of art. Significantly enough, such *Mahaparinirvana* scenes with coffins never appeared before and after the Kushana period.

REFERENCES

1. Ingholt, H. *Gandharan Art in Pakistan*, New York, 1957. pp. 94-95, Catalogue No. 143.
2. Majumdar, N.G. *A Guide to the Sculptures in the Indian Museum*, Pt. II, p. 73, Pl. XIa.
3. Ingholt, H. *op. cit.*, p. 95, Cat. No. 144.
4. *Mahaparinirvana-Sutta*, V, 26; VI, 35.
5. *Ibid.*, 52-64, VI, 40.
6. *Ibid.*, VI, 36-39.
7. *Ibid.*, 3-4.
8. *Ibid.*, V, 10-14.
9. *Ibid.*, VI, 16.
10. *Ibid.*, VI, 42.
11. *Ibid.*, VI, 31.
12. Sharma, R.C. *Buddhist Art of Mathura*, New Delhi, 1984, p. 247.
13. Vogel, J. P. *Archaeological Museum at Mathura*, Varanasi, 1971, (Reprint), p. 146.
14. Agrawal, V.S. Catalogue of Architectural Pieces, *Journal of U.P. Historical Society*, 1951, p. 14.

9

Location of Pava

K.D. Bajpai

THE historical geography of the trans-Sarayu region is of an absorbing interest. The rich archaeological and literary evidence bearing on the history and culture of that area, has been utilized by several scholars. In the past this region included the *janapadas* of Kosala, the autonomous states and the main land of Magadha. The Vedic-Puranic religions, Buddhism, Jainism and the Yaksha and Naga folk-cults flourished side by side for a long period. This is confirmed by the literature of different pantheons as also by archaeological evidence.

Almost since the beginning of the 19th century, attention of scholars has been directed to the study of this region, endowed with political and cultural potentiality. Locations of a good number of the major sites of the trans-Sarayu region have been decided. Even then, doubts are sometimes raised about the established identifications. Recently in a section of the press the site of the Buddha's *nirvāṇa* has been reported to be the village Kusi in the Muzaffarpur district of Bihar.[1] It is a well-known fact that the site of *Kusinārā* has been identified, on sound evidence, with Kasia in the Deoria district of U.P.

Identification of another important site, Pāvā of the Mallas, still bristles with controversy. Ancient Buddhist and Jaina literature give ample references to this town. The *Mahābhārata* mentions Pāvā several times.[2] All this indicates the unusual significance of Pāvā even in the pre-Buddha period.

When we study the literary evidence referred to above, it is known that the Mallas belonged to the Ikshvāku branch of the solar race.[3] They first formed a monarchical state and then became a republic. This kind of change can be noticed in several other such republican states of ancient India. Like the kingdom of Panchāla, the *Mallaraṭṭhha* (Malla-rāshtra was divided into two branches. The first was the proper branch, with its capital at Pāvā; the other was the southern one with its capital Kuśāvatī, later called Kusīnara. Both the branches were having congenial relations between them and also with their neighbouring republics.[4]

It may be mentioned here that the overall behaviour of the large Kosala kingdom was friendly towards the republics, particularly with the Vajjis, the Lichchhavis and the Mallas. As compared to it, the imperial Magadha power, on the other hand, entertained a spirit of jealousy towards the republics and aimed at swallowing them at appropriate moment, believing in *Mātsya-nyāya* (the big fish devouring the smaller ones). This tendency is clearly seen during the time of Ajatashatru of Magadha.

Credit should go to several republics, particularly the Lichchhavis, the Vajjis and the Mallas, for respecting and maintaining a spirit of tolerance among the chief religious thoughts of the times. It is enlightening to notice that the Vedic-Puranic faiths, Jainism, Buddhism and the cults of the Yakshas and Nagas found a congenial atmosphere for their growth in these republics. This had its obvious impact on the neighbouring monarchical states of Kosala, Kasi and even Magadha. The Mallas took an exemplary role in this direction. This is proved by the literary and archaeological evidence.

Before the time of the Nandas, the rulers of the Haryanka and the Sisunaga dynasties of Magadha did not attack the Mallas. At the demise of Sakyamuni at Kusīnārā, the Magadha ruler Ajātaśatru sent his request to the Mallas for the portion of the relics. When the unscrupulous Magadha monarch Mahapadmananda caused destruction of most of the republics,[5] the Mallas also fell a prey to it although they could not be wiped out totally. They continued even after the great havoc caused by that despised destroyer of democracy.

It was in the year 1952 that I made a detailed survey of the trans-Saryu region in my capacity as Archaeological Officer, Uttar Pradesh. The major sites covered by me were Sahet-Mahet, Piprahwa, Khukhundu, Padrauna, Kasi, Kahun, Fazilnagar-Sathiaon and Basārh. Pāvāpuri near Nalanda and Rajgir were also visited. As regards the sites located in the present Deoria district, I could notice a large number of old mounds, monuments and art-relics. It was refreshing to find antiquities related to the Vedic-Purāṇic faiths, Buddhism,

Jainism and the folk-cults at one and the same site in that district.

My on-the-spot study at Padrauna and the surrounding region convinced me that Cunningham's identification of Pāvā, capital of the Mallas, with Padrauna,[6] was correct. My esteemed learned friend, Prof. N. Dutt of the Calcutta University, and myself wrote a detailed work *Development of Budhnism in U.P.*[7] wherein we have identified Pāvā of the Mallas with Padrauna.[8]

In October, 1985 I again visited Kasia and Padrauna in the company of Sri B.P. Khetan of Padrauna, who has written a few articles on Pāvā.[9] I surveyed the entire area of mounds and also saw the material obtained from the site. The finds are stone sculptures, bricks and pottery. The sculptures represent Jaina, Buddhist and Brahmanical remains, generally of the early medieval period. I was informed that several important relics from the site had been removed. One stone sculpture from Padrauna, assignable to the Sunga Period, is now preserved in the State Museum, Lucknow.

The source-material, so far available, confirms that the celebrated town of Pava, closely associated with Gautama Buddha and the Jaina Tirthankara Mahavira, can be identified with the present site of Padrauna (ancient *Padaravana*), capital of the northern Malla-rashtra.

Here it would be worthwhile to trace briefly the history of the Mallas.[10] The word *malla* derives its name from Chandraketu Malla, son of Lakshmana, younger brother of Rama. This is mentioned in the *Ramayana* as follows:

चन्द्रकेतोश्च मल्लस्य मललभूम्यां निवेशिता ।
चन्द्रकान्तेति विख्याता दिव्या स्वर्गपुरयिथा ॥

Uttarakāṇḍa, Bombay edn. 102.9

(i.e. Malla Chandraketu established his capital in the Malla region. The town was called Chandrakanta, which was beautiful like Amarāvatī.).

The description in the *Rāmāyaṇa* indicates that the region and the dynasty ruling over it were both called *Malla* after the name of Chandraketu. This prince was the younger son of Lakshmana, as known from the previous context. This confirms the association of the Mallas with the Ikshvakus of Ayodhya. Angada, the elder son of Lakshmana, was made ruler of Kārupatha (parts of Basti and Gorakhpur districts) with its capital at Angadīya.[11]

Chapters 101 and 102 of the Uttarakānda of the *Rāmāyaṇa* have retained the tradition as to how Rama, in consultation with his brothers, made necessary arrangements to extend the old limits of the Kosala kingdom and to administer it properly as a *Chakravarti.* He was particular about the region extending in the east upto the Gandakī River.

It is possible to locate ancient town of Chandrakāntā near present Padrauna. In course of time, the new township of Pāvā grew up as the capital of Malarāshṭra.

The conventional town-names Aṇgadiyā and Chandrākantā, after the names of the two sons of Lakshman, do not seem to have continued for long. During the time of the great sixteen kingdoms (*mahājanapadas*), the name Pāvā became well known as the capital of the northern Malla kingdom. By then the monarchical nature of the kingdom had changed into a republican state.

Due to geographical and political considerations, the Malla kingdom was divided into two parts: the north and the south Malla-rashtra. This can be compared with the division of Panchāla or that of the republican state of the Yaudheyas. The capital of the southern Malla is mentioned in some works as Kusāvatī, later known as Kusinagara. Prof. Raj Bali Pandey and several other scholars have confused the two ancient towns, both bearing the name of Kuśavatī.[12]

It may be pointed out here that the town of Kuśāvatī mentioned in the *Raghuvamsa* of Kalidasa (XV, 97 and XVI, 1-25) was not Kuśīnagara. It was located in the south Kosala (present Chhattisgarh). I have identified it with Kosala (near Malhar, in the Bilaspur district of Madhya Pradesh).[13] In the *Rāmāyaṇa*, it is said that the town Kuśāvatī of Kusa was founded by Rama across the Vindhya mountain.[14] The description given in the *Raghuvamsa* (XVI, 25-35) of Kusa's journey from the southern town Kuśāvatī to Ayodhya is definite on this point. The great poet Kālidāsa had a clear conception of geography from south Kosala to Ayodhya. In his account of Kusa's north-ward journey from Kusavati to Ayodhya the poet has mentioned the Vindhyas, the River Revā (Narmada), the Pulindas (tribals of the Vindhyas) and finally the River Ganga before reaching Ayodhya.

It is not possible to say as to when and how the name Kuśāvatī was given to the town which became famous as Kusinagara (Pali Kusīnārā) at a later time. It seems that the presumed association of King Kusa's name with Kusinagara is unwarrented. Had it been founded by Kusa the name should have been Kusanagara. During the Buddha's time Kusīnārā was not counted among the prime towns like Śrāvastī, Vaiśālī and Rajagriha. This is evident from the dialogue of Ananda with Buddha.

The actual location of Śrāvastī, said to be the capital of the kingdom of Lava (younger son of Rāma) is no definitely known. The name Śarāvatī[15] was quite popular and was used both for a town and a river in ancient literature. It appears that this river flowed through Haryana and Rajasthan.[16] From the literary references to the River Śarāvatī. I am tempted to identify it with the celebrated River Śarasvatī, which flowed in the southwestern direction and drained into the Arabian Sea.

According to the Pāli sources, the rivulet Kakutthā (modern Barahī, a tributary of River Hiranā or Chhoti Gandak)[17] formed the dividing line between the north and south Malla kingdoms. The River Sadānīrā(Gandaki) separated the Malla kingdom from the Vajji *janapada*.

From the Buddhist and Jaina evidences we can infer that the town of Pāvā was liked both by the Buddha and Mahāvira. This was obviously due to its location near the River Sadhānīrā, its bracing climate and its religious catholicity.

Like the towns of Mathura, Kāsī, Kuśāvatī, etc., the name Pāvā became popular and was adopted at several other places. At a distance of 10 km north-west of Pāvā, there is a village called Papaur.[18] In the present Nalanda district is the *Pāvāpuri* Jaina tirtha. In the Panchamahal district of Gujarat there is a Pavagiri. In Gujarat, again, is located Pāvāgarh near Champaner.[19] There is a reference to Majjhima-Pāvā, which was also called Apāpāpurī (later called Pāvāpurī).[20]

In the Jaina tradition, giving details of twenty-five and a half territories forming part of the Mauryan empire, the 22nd name in the list is given as Bhangi with its capital at Pāvā.[21]

Apart from being a political and religious centre, the chief town of Pāvā near the Gandakī River was a commercial centre. The main route from Śrāvasti to Vaiśālī passed through Pāvā. The Buddhist and Jaina literature gives an indication of the prosperity of Pava, where several rich businessmen resided. A reference to the *sulka-sala* (custom office) of Hastipala of Pava is found in some Jaina texts.[22] *Kammara-putta* (blacksmith's son) Chunda of Pava was a rich man. Buddha had reached Pava along with a huge congregation of monks, who were all entertained by Chunda.

When Buddha was on his way from Pava to Kusinara, he noticed a carvan of 500 carts, following Alar Kalama, marching from Kusinara towards Pava.[23] The road was utilized for religious and commercial purposes.

In the old Gazetteer of Gorakhpur it is recorded that in the year 1878, while salvaging a pond near Padrauna the remains of a wooden boat were found. It may indicate that the old course of the River Gandaki was not far off the present town of Padrauna.[24]

In the *Dighanikaya* (II, p. 198 ff) we find the details of Buddha's last journey to Kusinara via Pava. According to it, Buddha left Vaisali casting his last look at it. He then crossed Bhandagama, Hatthigama and Jambugama and reached Bhoganagara where he directed his disciples to give special attention to observance of moral precepts (*sila*), meditation (*samadhi*), acquisition of knowledge (*panna*) and attainment of emancipation (*vimutti*). He then gave them instructions for checking up the authenticity of *Buddhavachana*.

From Bhoganagara he moved on to Pava and stayed at the mango garden of Chunda, the blacksmith's son, who invited him for the forenoon meal. Chunda prepared *sukaramaddava* (a kind of mushroom)[25] and offered it to the monks. Buddha asked Chunda to serve *sukaramaddava* to him alone and not to the monks as they would not be able to digest it. He took it and became seriously ill with excruciating pain.[26] He then left for Kusinagara, which was at a distance of about 18 km. to the south-west of Pava. He then accepted an excellent robe offered by Pukkusa Mallaputta, who became his lay-devotee. He then took his bath at *Kakuttha nadi* and went to the Salavana of the Mallas at Kusinagara.

At Pāvā Buddha had consecrated the Mote-hall (*ubbhaṭaka*) of the Mallas, wherein the Mallas used to hold their meetings. They held Buddha and Mahāvīra both in high esteem, as is borne out from ancient literature. During the life-time of the two great personalities, they continued to honour them. After their demise they perpetuated their memory in the most appropriate manner by the construction of stupas.

The republican constitution of the Mallas was of a high order. They gained recognition among their contemporary ruling powers on account of their well-organised administration.

After his supper at Pāvā, the Buddha expressed his desire to proceed towards Kuśīnagara. He was quite confident that he would be able to cover the distance (about 18 km) between the two places in time. It is not correct to presume that Buddha's ailment had reached its pitch and that he was on his death bed at Pāvā. Had this been the case, he would not have stirred from Pāvā. From his discourses on some important matters with Ananda and others, at Pāvā and on his way to and also at the *Śāla-vana upa-paṭṭana* of Kuśīnagara, it is evident that although feeling pain, Buddha was quite alert mentally and hoped to improve. He controlled the agony as is borne out from the *Mahāparinivvana sutta* (section 140). He drank water and took bath in the River Kakuttha on his way to Kusīnārā.

After reaching the sala-vana, the condition of the Great Master deteriorated. But there also he maintained his balance and expressed his significant views about the true religious path, about behaviour towards women, about his impeding funeral rites (like those of a *chakravarti*) and about the four categories of *stupas* with their full details.

It is enlightening to note here that after consoling Ananda, the Tathāgata gave exhortation to the congregation of monks telling them about the great mental and spiritual qualities of Ananda.[27]

The special liking of Buddha for the land of the Mallas is clearly indicated in his conversation with Ananda. Ananda made a request to the Lord to choose, as the site for his *parinirvāṇa*, from any one of the six large cities, viz. Champā, Rajagaha, Satvāthī, Sāketa, Kosambī and Banarasī. Buddha emphatically declined this and made his clear decision in favour of Kusīnārā of the Mallas. He told Ananda about the glorious past of Kusinara, which was once famous as great Kusavati, having been the capital of the *chakravartī Mahāsudarśana*. Buddha told Ananda to inform the Mallas of Kusīnārā to prepare for his last rites. The wishes of the Lord were duly implemented. He ordained one Subhadra and finally gave his last sermon.[28]

The Jaina tradition also has preserved significant references to the kingdom of the Mallas and their town Pāvā. Malla-raṭṭha has been included among the sixteen *mahājanapadas* in Jaina literature.

Bhagavān Mahāvīra had a great fascination for Pāvā, capital of the Paveyyaka Mallas. He gave his sermons at Pāvā. The works like *Pariṣhiṣhṭa parava* clearly mention that Mahāvīra obtained *nirvāṅa* at Pāvā, where along with Lichchavis and others, nine Malla chiefs attended the last rites of the prophet, which were celebrated with eclat. The Buddhist works, *Majjhima Nikāya*, *Aṭṭhakathā*, etc. refer to the demise of Nigāṇtha Mahavira at Pāvā.[29]

The testimony of Jinaprabha Suri is of considerable importance in this regard. He visited most of the *tirthas* mentioned in his work, before compiling the same. In a section of his work, the writer says that Bhagavan Varddhamana stayed in the *śulkasālā* of Hastipala of Pāvā and gave his last sermon before laying his mortal remains on the *Amavasya* night in the celebrated town of Pāvā.[30] It is significant to note that the writer has observed the geographical sequence in his work *vividha-Tīrthakalpa*. He mentions *Apapa* (*Pāvā*) *puri* after giving the details of Kausambi and Ayodhya in the previous two sections (12 and 13) of the work. Again, it is of particular interest to note the name of the town *Aāapā* given by the auther in sections 14 and 21 of the work. He has explained as to how later on the town's name became current as *Pāvā*.[31]

Bhagavan Mahavira chose Pāvā to lay down his mortal remains. Gautama Buddha came to know about this when the end of the Buddha was approaching, he also preferred the *śālavana* near Kuśīnārā in the same Mallarashtra. Both the prophets did this due to obvious reasons. They had considerable liking for the Malla territory and its residents. The last rites cf Mahāvira were attended by the Mallas, the Lichchhavis and others including the ruling classes of Kosala and Kasi. On the demise of Buddha, the Mallas played the chief role. Other autonomous states also joined them and built stupas over the relics of Buddha in their respective territories.

It may be noted here that the then ruler of Magadha did not take interest worth mentioning on the demise of the two great personalities of that time, Mahavira and Buddha. The name of the Magadha chief is conspicuous by its absence in the case of Mahavira. It was only to get a portion of the relics of the Buddha, along with others, that the Magadha monarch Ajastasatru presented the case of Magadha. For this purpose he did not care to personally visit Kusinara, but he sent his messenger. This action seems to have been taken by the ruler at the request of the people of Magadha. Ajatasatru was jealous of the fame of the Mallas.

On the reliable evidence, it is certain that the place of the *nirvana* of Mahavira cannot be the present Pavapuri in the Nalanda district of Bihar, which area was located in the main Magadha territory. No ancient archaeological relics are known from that site. On the other hand, Padrauna and the region around is known for such relics.[32]

Efforts have been made to identify Pava with Sathiaon, about 16 km to the south-east of Kusinara. There are several ancient mounds in the twin villages of Sathiaon and Fazilnagar. The identification was first proposed by A.C.L. Carlleyle.[33] He gives a detailed account of the ancient mounds of 'Chetiyaon' and Fazilnagar, including the "ruins of a large stupa" on the top of the *dih* of Fajila. Carlleyle concludes: "I think we may now, with considerable certainty, identify this ruined stupa with the famous stupa of Pava, which contained one of the eight portions of the relics of Buddha."[34]

Carlleyle raises two objections to the identification of Pava with Padrauna suggested by Cunningham. The first is that even the direct distance from Kusinagara to Padrauna is considerable for the Buddha to cover it by foot. His second point is that Padrauna is "totally out of the way of the route from Vaisali to Kusinagara". These objections are unwarranted. Firstly, the distance between the two places is not very considerable. That commercial road passed through the two places has already been mentioned. As regards the second point, clear evidence is available to show that there was a route between Vaisali and Kusinagara via Pava (Padrauna). This route was followed by the two great prophets, by the disciples of Bavari and by Mahakasyapa and others.

After Carlleyle, several other scholars have tried to prove the identification of Pava with Sathiaon.[35] The reasons given by these scholars in support of their identification do not stand the test. It is wrong to suppose that the ancient name of Sathiaon was *chaitya grama*.[36] The field work conducted by the University of Gorakhpur in the year 1979 at the site brought to light an important clay sealing. The Gupta Brahmi legend on the sealing reads *Sreshthigramaagraharasya*. This indicates that the ancient name of Sathiaon was *Sreshthigrama* and not *Chetiya-grama*.[37]

No ancient Jaina relics, worth mentioning, are reported from Sathiaon-Fazilnagar. The few stone sculptures discovered there represent medieval Brahmanical images.

Besides the Buddhist and Jaina works, references to the Mallas are found in the Brahmanical literature also. In the *Manusmriti* (X, 22), the Mallas are mentioned along with the Lichchhavis. In the *Mahabharata* (II, 27, 11 and IV, 1, 9) they are referred to with their town Bhogavat (same as Bhoganagara).[38] Varahamihira in his work refers to the Mallas.[39]

Carlleyle and others, who are against the identification of Pava with Padrauna, have not paid necessary need to the famous ancient route passing from Pratishthana, through Sravasti to Vaisali. This route is described in several texts, one of which is the *Parayaya-vagga* of the *Suttanipata*. In this section the story of a Brahamana called Bavari is narrated. Born at Sravasti, he had emigrated to the Asmaka (Assaka) country and was residing on the bank of the Godavari.

Bavari sent his mission of disciples to pay respects to the Tathagata, who was at that time residing near Vaisali. The text gives the main halting places on this long route. They are mentioned in the following order: Patitthana (Paithan), Mahissati (Maheshwar), Ujjeni (Ujjain), Gonaddha (near Vidisha), Vedisa (Vidisha), Vanasahvaya (Tumain in Guna distt.),Kosambi, Saketa (Ayodhya), Savatthi (Sravasti), Setayya, Kapilavatthu (Piprahwa, Basti dist.), Kusinara, Pava and Bhoganagara (all the three in the Malla kingdom), the Magadhan city of Vesali and the Pasanakachetia.[40] The route from Sravasti to Rajagriha (beyond Vaisali) was well known to the Buddha and Mahavira and to several of their followers. This is confirmed by the literary accounts. Almost all the accounts include the names of Pava and Kusinara as the chief halting places due to their importance.

If we study the locations of the Asokan pillars, erected in the area between Lumbini and Vaisali, we notice the striking fact that the Maurya emperor took particular care to select suitable spots falling on the main routes. Unfortunately, some of his pillars fixed on the trans-Sarayu area seem to have been lost.[41]

The archaeological field work conducted at Padrauna since the time of Buchanan and R.M. Martin till the recent times has brought out some valuable facts bearing on the antiquity of Padrauna.[42] A headless standing stone image, described by Martin (his plate IA) seems to represent a Buddhist image with seated miniature Buddha images and attendants. The other stone image in *Padmasana* shows a *Jina* with triple umbrella over the head and seated on a beautifully carved pedestal. These two images can be assigned to 10th-11th centuries A.D.

During my recent visit to Padrauna I saw several stone sculptures said to have been recovered from the mounds of Padrauna. Mention may be made of a *Tirthankara* image seated in *Padmasana* finaked by *maladhara ganas* and of Yakshi Ambika, on a decorative pedestal holding a child and lotus stalks. Remains of the images of Siva, Kubera and some other Brahmanical deities were also seen. The period of these can be bracketted between c.A.D. 650 and 1100.

The archaeological materials which survived the Muslim destruction, is not preserved there at present. Some of the antiquities from here have been removed to other places. A study of all the materials is necessary. I may mention here one important stone sculpture found at Padrauna, and now preserved in the State Museum, Lucknow (Museum no. 55-283). According to the details in the Museum register, the sculpture is made of red sandstone. It is a fragment of a colossal Yaksha image, with a tenon and can be assigned to 2nd century B.C.[43]

General Cunningham in the first volume of his Reports of the survey conducted during 1862-65, has given a brief but valuable account of the large mound at Padrauna. He did some digging also on the highest part of the mound and found some large size bricks with rounded edges similar to those discovered at Buddha-Gaya and Giryek. He inferred the existence of two stupas at the site, one big and the other small, and of a big courtyard about 100 feet square.[44]

There has since long been pilferage of bricks and other materials from the ancient mounds at Padrauna. This has caused a good deal of loss of evidence in regard to the antiquity of the site.

Early in 1985 the Archaeological Survey of India conducted partial excavation at Padrauna. It is very necessary that a thorough exploration of the area in and around Padrauna is made and the big mound at the site is duly excavated.

REFERENCES

1. Eg. *Janasatta* (Delhi), dated 22.7.86.

2. For literary references see Raychaudhury, H.C. *Political History of Ancient India*, 7th edition (Calcutta, 1972), pp. 113-15.

3. Other contemporary ruling dynasties belonging to the solar race were the Kosalas, the Śākyas and the Moriyas. The Magadha rulers belonged to the Naga race.

4. This can be compared with the good relations among the Mitra kingdoms of northern India during the post-Asokan period. In the *Kalpasūtra* and some other Jaina texts, there is a reference to nine Lichchhavi and nine Malla *ganas*.

5. This is alluded to in the *Kaliyugarāja-Vrittānta* (III,2), wherein it is stated that the greedy and mighty Magadha king was the destroyer of all rulers. He first conquered his neighbours, belonging to the Ikshavaku race, and thereafter other independent powers of Panchalas, the Kurus, etc.

6. Location of Padrauna in Deoria district of U.P. is at 26° 54'N, and 83° 59'E. See Cunningham, *Archl. Survey of India Report* (*A.S.R.*) 1862 to 65 Vol. I (1871) pp. 74-76; *The Ancient Geography of India* (reprint Varanasi, 1963), pp. 366-67 with map showing Travels of Hiuen Tsang.

7. Publication Bureau, Govt. of U.P., Lucknow, 1956.

8. *Ibid.*, pages 14, 17, 124, 350-55.

9. Sometime back Sri Khetan presented a paper on Pava in a seminar organised at the Banaras Hindu University on the History of Kashi. The paper evoked a good deal of interest among the scholars present.

10. The Mallas belonged to the Vashishtha *gotra*. They were exhorted as the *Vasishthas* by the Buddha. See the *Mahāparinirāvna sutta, sutras* 257-76.

11. *Rāmāyaṇa*, VII, 102, 5-8.

12. Pandey. R.B. *Gorakhpur Janapada aur uski Ksatriya Jatiyon ka Itihasa* (Hindi), Gorakhpur, 1946, pp. 76-8.

13. K.D. Bajpai, *History and Culture of Madhya Pradesh* (Ahmedabad, 1984), pp. 34-5, 41; Bajpai, *Cultural History of India*, Vol. I (Kanpur, 1985), p. 23.

14. *Rāmāyaṇa* VII 198, 4.

15. According to N.L. Dey, Śarāvatī appears to be the corruption of Śrāvasti. See the *Geographical Dictionary* 3rd edition (Delhi, 1971), p. 181. The basis for Dey's assumption is the description in the Ramayana (VII, 1084): *Śrāvastīti Purī ramya śrāvita cha Lavasya ha.* From the evidence of the *Rāmāyaṇa* and other literary sources it is definite that the kingdom ruled over by Lava was to the north of the kingdom of Kusa cf. *Kosaleshu Kusam vīram Uttareshu tathā Lavam. Rāmāyaṇa* (VII, 107, 7.).

16. For a detailed discussion on Śārāvatī See Sircar, D.C. *Studies in the Geography of Ancient and Medieval India* (Delhi, 1960), pp. 209-13.

17. Cunningham, *Ancient Geography.*, pp. 366-67, and map.

18. Some scholars have identified Papaur with ancient Pava. See Motichandra, *Sarthavaha* (Hindi), Patna 1966, pp. 17-18; See also Sankrityayana, Rahul *Buddhacharya* (Sarnath, 1952), p. 352.

19. Joharapurkar, V. *Tīrthavandana-Sangraha*, (Sholapur 1965), pp. 155-56.

20. *Vividha-tīrtha-kalpa of Jinaprabha Suri* (Singhi series, 1934), *Kalpas* 14 and 21. Hindi translation by Agarchand and Bhanwarlal Nahta (Mevanagar, 1978), pp. 56-57, 76-101. This Majjhima-Pāvā is the same as the main town of Pāvā (modern Padrauna).

21. *Brihat Kalpa-Bhāshya*, pp. 3263 ff. Dr. Motichandra has located Bhangi in the Hazaribag and Manbhum districts. cf. *Sārthavāha*, pp. 76-77.

22. *Vividha-tirthakalpa*, p. 34.

23. Cf. *Mahāparinirbaṇa* sutta, sectionsl 33-34, 149-54.

24. The word *Kārupatha* used for the road indicates that it was used by craftsmen of different categories.

24. *Gazetteer of Gorakhpur* (1909), p. 279.

25. Several European scholars wrongly translated the term *Sūkara-maddava* as 'boar's flesh.' This inaccurate meaning has been followed by others also. As the Chinese texts have rightly explained, the word represents 'a kind of edible fungus or mushroom.' See Dutt N. and K.D. Bajpai, *Development of Buddhism in U.P.*, (1956), pp. 124, 324.

26. *Mahpāarinirbaṇa Sutta*, sections 175-195.

27. *Ibid.*, 201-204.

28. *Ibid.*, 205-235.

29. For details see *Kalpasūtra* (Sacred Books of the East series Vol. XXII, p. 266; *Tiloya-Paṇṇatti* (IV): Prachina Tirthamala Sangraha (Hindi), Bhavanagar, (1921), pt. I, p. 16; *Tīrthavandana-Samgraha*, (Sholapur, 1965), p. 157; Jain Balabhadra *Bhārat ke Digambara Jaina Tīrtha*, Vol. I (Bombay, 1974), pp. 175-77; Muni Nagaraja, *Mahavira evam Buddha ki sam--samayikata*, (Delhi, 1968) pp. 121 ff.

30. *Vividha-tīrthakalpa*, p. 34.

31. The dropping of the initial letter a, as a grammatical norm, can be noticed in several ancient names eg. *Ayodhana, Ayodhyā, Avimukta, Achirāvati*, etc. The name Apapapuri has been used by some other writers also. See *Jain Balabhadra op. cit.*, p. 175 and Joharapurkar, *op. cit.*, p. 157.

32. The sculptural relics found at Padrauna can be assigned to a period between 2nd century B.C. and 11th Cent. A.D. The early Jaina sites of Khukhundu, Kahaun, etc. are located nearer to Padrauna than to Nalanda. For details about the new Pāvāpurī, near Bihar Sharif, see A Cunningham, *A.S.R.*, Vol XI, pp. 170-71; Joharapurkar, *op. cit.*, p. 157, Also see Pandey R.B. *op. cit.*, p. 110.

33. *A.S.R.* XVIII, pp. 101-14- plates *II* and *VIII*.

34. *Ibid.*, p. 113.

35. Mention may be made of Dr. Raj Bali Pandey (*op. cit.*, p. 78); Bhikshu Dharmarakshit, a *Kusinagara Kā Itihāsa* (Hindi), pp. 24-6, Jain Balabhadra *op. cit.*, pp. 176-78 and map of Kosala janapada facing p. 153.

36. Pandey, *op. cit.*, p. 78.

37. For the arguments against the identification of Sathiaon with Pāvā see Upadhyay Bharat S., *op. cit.*, pp. 322-24. Dr. Upadhyay points out the difficulty in regard to the equating Pāvā with Padrauna on the lone evidence of the *Sumangala-villāshinī*, wherein the distance between Pāvā and Kuśīnārā is given as 3 *gavyūtis.* The distance given in that work seems to be observed that the measurement of a *gavyūti* differ from time to time, cf. *Amarākośa*, II 2, 18.

38. Chatterjee, A.K. *Political History of Pre-Buddhist India* (Calcutta, 1980), pp. 190-91.

39. *Brihatsamhitā*, V 38. In V 41 of the work the Mallas are mentioned along with the Videhas. Kern while commenting on the word *Malla*, alludes to the proficiency in wrestling (*bahū-yuddhajña*).

40. Sircar, D.C. *op. cit.*, pp. 206-7; Upadhyay, Bharat, S. *op. cit.*, p. 32-33, 540.

41. B.P. Khetan's cyclostyled paper on *Pāvā* (read at the Varanasi Seminar), pp. 15-19.

42. For details see Martin, M. *History Antiquities.*

43. *Topography and Statistics of Eastern India*, Vol. II, reprint 1976): pp. 354-57; Cunningham, *ASR*, I, pp. 74-6 and *Ancient Geography of India*, pp. 366-67.

43. Association of the Yakshas, both with Buddhism and Jainism, is well known. In the *Udāna* (Hindi translation, p. 8) there is a reference to the *chetiya* called *Aja-Kalapaka* at Pāvā, where the Buddha is said to have stayed. The name of the Yaksha of Pāvā is given as *Ajakalāpa* in the *Udāna.*

44. Cunningham, *ASR*, I, pp. 74-76.

10

'Copper Hoard' Implements in the National Museum Collection: 1986

S.P. Gupta

TILL 1964, the National Museum, New Delhi had not a single example of Copper Hoard artefacts. However, during the last two decades it has built up a sizeable collection of 93 artefacts and some fragments there of. Here a brief history of the acquisitions of copper implements in the Museum is recorded.

In 1965, Prof. Jagdish Gupta of the Hindi Department of the Allahabad University, who is an eminent scholar of not only literature and art but also archaeology, was pursuaded by the present author to donate to the National Museum his personal collection of antiquities—terracottas, seals and sealings, copper implements, etc. He met Dr. Grace Morley, the then Director of the Museum, and agreed to part with his collection, but strictly on commercial basis. He also told her that he would not sell all the antiquities in one lot since he felt he had developed emotional attachment with the objects which he had collected over long years. Thus, in 1965, he sold us only four copper implements, 2 flat celts, 1 bar celt and 1 harpoon, through the Art Purchase Committee of the Museum.

In the following year one Sri Surendra Mohan Misra from Chandausi, Distt. Moradabad, U.P. suddenly turned up in the Museum and showed us a copper anthropomorphic figure whose two legs were broken apart. He desired to know its importance and wished to sell it to the Museum. We practically jumped at the offer and acquired it for obvious reasons. He informed us that he had located it by the side of a tank near his village while returning from there after a wash. In 1966 itself, Prof. Gupta sold us 2 more flat celts, 1 antennae sword and 1 harpoon. As earlier, he informed us again that he goes to his native town Shahabad, Distt. Hardoi in Uttar Pradesh once or twice a year and collects the implements from the local shopkeepers who deal in metallic vessels since these persons while selling new pots and pans also purchase old metallic objects, complete or broken, even scraps. Prof. Gupta had initiated them in the basic knowledge of the Copper Hoard implements so that they did not refuse to acquire them when someone brought these artefacts to them.

In 1967, Prof. Gupta further gave us 2 harpoons and 1 antennae sword. Then for a couple of years we did not get any example from any source.

In 1970, suddently a gentleman, named Sri A.K. Thakkar, from Mehsana, Distt. Mehsana in Gujarat came to the Museum with 4 antennae swords which he claimed he had located at a place near Modhera, Distt. Mehsana, otherwise famous for its sun temple. We again jumped at it since some of these implements were somewhat unusual in form.

In 1971, after a lapse of four years, once again Prof. Gupta brought to us 5 celts, and one copper lamp, the latter, however, need not necessarily have belonged to the Copper Hoards. We requested him to enrich the museum collection through his greater efforts since we did not get these objects through regular art dealers.

During one of the following meetings of the Art Purchase Committee, an art dealer from Hyderabad, Sri Tandon, brought to us a harpoon with the tang shaped like the bust of woman with blurred features. He fixed the price at Rs, 75,000/-. The Committee, however, did not buy it since it was practically twenty times the price we paid for a harpoon, and secondly, the experts felt that the object may not even be genuine since such an example was never reported earlier.

In 1975, after a lapse of four years, we again acquired from Prof. Gupta 10 flat celts, 1 shouldered celt, 1 double axe or *parasu* and 1 antennae sword. Then once again for about eight years we did not receive any object of this category from any source although we have been telling art dealers to look for these objects.

Finally, in 1984, one Sri Bal Mukund Agrawal, an antique dealer from Delhi, brought to the Museum 2 harpoons which we acquired. By now more art dealers also came to know of our interest in acquiring Copper Hoard objects. In the following year, we acquired more of these artefacts.

In 1985, one Sri Pramod Puri, another regular art dealer from Delhi, came forward with some objects. We, however, purchased only 1 shouldered celt and 1 flat celt from him which he claimed he got from another dealer. In the same year, Prof. Gupta sold us 4 at celts, including two fragments of perhaps one splayed celt,

2 shouldered axes, 2 spearheads, 4 antennae swords, and 3 tanged weed-chisels or *khurpis*.

In 1986 from one Śri Tariq Ahmad Chishti, a Book-seller from Amroha, Distt. Moradabad, U.P. we acquired 2 flat celts and a harpoon. We, however, could not buy a number of copper rings since the price he demanded for them appeared to be on a higher side. By now Prof. Gupta's son, Sri Abhinava Gupta, also got interested in the Copper Hoards. Being a young man, he toured a number of local markets in Districts Kanpur, Unnao, Sitapur, etc. in U.P. collected objects and sold them to us. These objects include a lugged axe with elliptical head, 3 shouldered celts, 23 flat celts, some fragmentary (in one case two fragments may as well belong to one single example), 3 chisels, 2 harpoons, 5 spearheads (three of which are fragmentary and 1 weed chisel or *khurpi*).

Prof. Gupta also gave us some molten pieces, some rough ingots and some very small fragments of tools which, it is hoped, will be soon scientifically analysed.

Observations

Of the 93 Copper Hoard implements in our collection till 1986, only a dozen or so examples require our special attention. *Antennae Swords :* A group of four 'antennae swords' came from Modhera in Mehsana Distt. of Gujarat. This is the first discovery of such weapons in Gujarat. As a matter of fact, except for a broken ecliptical artefact, identified as anthropomorphic figure, coming from the late levels of Lothal, we had so far no knowledge of the presence of Copper Hoards in Gujarat. Antennae hilted double edged 'knives' and 'swords' were, however, known from Maharashtra and Andhra Pradesh, the former coming from Chandoli, in Chalcolithic levels of the second half of the second millennium B.C. and the latter from undated levels of a rock-shelter at Kallur. It may be noted that the Modhera-Mehsana hoard is also undated.

The antennae hilt, it may be observed, has a large variety. The Modhera-Mehsana hoard itself has at least three varieties:-

(i) low angle antennae (the prongs are thus nearly horizontal), making about 10% to 20% angle in relation to the vertical axis of the blade).

(ii) high angle antennae (the prongs are thus highly splayed, making about 30° to 45° or more angle in relation to the vertical axis of the blade), and

(iii) middle angle antennae (the prongs are thus moderately splayed, a making about 20° to 30° angle in relation to the vertical axis of the blade).

In one example, interestingly, the antennae ends have been beaten flat in the form of a fan, with sharp edges; it is indeed unique. It may also be observed that the central ridge on the blade in this example is also different from the other three examples: it has a broad rounded spine, starting from the base of the blade and running upto the tip as against the sharp raise line running from the tip of the blade till the point from where the antennae ends emerge in other three examples. It may be noted that, except for this unique example, where the two antennae or wings are of equal size, of the two antennae one is always shorter than the other.

Prof. Jagdish Gupta's examples from the Gangetic basin are slightly different than all the examples found in peninsular India. Often the antennae is small, and some what horizontal—in example the ends are incurved, in another, where only one antennae is preserved the end has been pressed a little flat; in yet another example the antennae ends are outcurved. Varieties can be worked out in still larger numbers, depending upon various factors one may consider, still only broad categories may be valid in terms of funtionality and typology. In any case, typological considerations show strong regional differences. If it is true, then we may not be justified in clubbing all the antennae hilted 'knives', 'swords' and 'rapiers' in terms of single culture-complex, even though technologically they may all be put in a single basket.

Spearhead with a central hole : There is an example of a medium sized spearhead with central hole, meant possibly for fastening the tool with its wooden handle with the help of long. In the Neolithic period, China had such a device on stone axes.

Tanged Weed-chisels : There are some short tanged blades with sharp edge. We have called them weed-chisels or *khurpis*. If our functional identification is correct, the presence of such tools woud indicate that some kind of agriculture was also practised by the Copper Hoard people in the upper Ganga basin.

Lugged Axe : This year we purchased a lugged axe with elliptical working-end and straight base. It was found at Mohamadabad, near Sitapur. The elliptical end, it is significant to note, resembles, to a great extent, the elliptical end of an anthropomorphic figure. However, instead of 'hands' of the usual anthropomorphic figure, it has two rectangular lugs. Similarly, instead of 'legs', of the usual anthropomorphic figure, it has straight base. But, significantly enough, it has exactly the same kind of innumerable short vertical chisel-marks as any 'anthropomorphic figure' bears on its body, including the one from Lothal. But such marks are present in other examples as well.

Typologically and functionally the tool was thus meant to be an axe and not an anthropomorphic figure.

11

Natesa Scultpures in the Early Art of Central India

Sudha Malaiya

The rhythmic movements of dance, at once capturing the minds of the onlooker is personified in Nataraja Siva; Siva the beautiful (*Sundaram*), representing the ultimate truth (*Satyam*) which is immanent, eternal, ominpotent, ominiscient and the formless one. He assumes Sadasiva form, to enjoy the ecstasies of his own cosmic dance, as fancied by the Kakatiya commander-poet and Natyavisarada Jayasenapati.[1]

Most of the gods and goddesses of the Hindu pantheon have been depicted in dancing poses. However, dance is most closely associated with the tutelary deity of *Natya*, i.e. Nataraja, the 'king among dancers', who is usually credited with the creation of dance as an art form. The mythology of Siva is full of references to the different forms of dance favoured by him. This explains why the dancing images of Siva have always remained favourite theme with the ancient sculptors, as compared to his other forms.

This also accounts for the *nrittamurtis* being deaւc with as a special category, separate from the *ugra* and *saumya* forms, occupying much greater place in *Silpasastras*. There are innumerable references to his dance in literature, viz. such as '*nrityapriyo, nityanritya, nartanas, sarvasadhakah* in *Linga Mahapurana* (1.65, 74) and *Vadyanrityapriya Nrityasila* and *sugiti* in *Vayupurana* (240,142, 43). The praises sung by poets and devotees in epigraphic records reflect *Nrityadhipati's* fondness for dance. He is called '*Nartesvara*' in Bharella (Decca) inscription: *Nrittesvara* in Isanvarman Sambor Preil Kuk inscription, Cambodia; *Advallan* in Chola inscriptions; *Natyesvara* in Norod inscription of Vyomadiva and *Charisancharanapravina* in Chandreh stone inscription.[2]

These epithets make it quite clear that Nataraja is also one of Siva's several names, which shows his association with and his mastery over dance. Thus, in general, all the dancing images of Siva can be described as Nataraja[3] or Natesa or Nateswara. The bronze Nataraja or the *Nadanta* mode of dance which became standardised in Tamil country by the 10th century A.D. is not the only form of Nataraja as generally understood. But uptill then, the concept of Siva as Natesa, the dancing god, lacked stylisation.

The *panchakrtyas*[4] and the aesthetic value and spiritual significance of the cosmic dance of *Mahasailusha* (greatest actor) of this universal stage, whose fourfold *abhinaya* represents cosmos in dance, might have been discussed in much detail. Yet it becomes meaningful only when its exact nature and formal aspects are comprehended.[5] For this we have to depend upon *Natyasastra* where the *tandava* of Siva is described meticulously, not in terms of myth or occasion, but in terms of the precisely articulated movements, definite poses and disposition of limbs, because when the symbols used in iconography are translated into the gestures of dance, then only the spectators or the scholars can refer briefly to the different aspects of Siva without going into the details.

Silpasastras borrowed their norms almost totally from *Natyasastra* for the sculpting of the *nrittamurtis*. The iconographic texts like *Vishnudharmottara Purana*[6] (*c*-5th-7th, Cent. A.D.) and *Samaranganasutradhara*- (A.D. 998-1026) discuss the *hastamudras, sthanakas* and *rasadrishtis*, as delineated in *Natyasastra* and Sutrapatamandana in his *Devatamurtiprakarana*[8] (*c*. 15th Cent.-A.D.) directs all the *nrittamurtis* to be sculptured on the basis of *Natyasastra*.[9]

In this way the kinetic vocabulary of dance is a key to understand the meaning of the various iconographic details of a Natesa which is a veritable encyclopaedia of mythological references. On the other hand, *nrittamurtis* in the form of more intelligible visual modes, also shed great light on the obscure and not too well understood textual definitions provided by Bharata. It is, therefore, appropriate to analyse the *nrittamurtis* or *Nrityapriya*, in terms of the 108 units of dance called *karanas* or the *Sivatandavas*[10] and their constituents known as *chari, sthanaka, nrittahasta, hasta, pada* and others.[11]

Saivagamas also enumerate 108 modes of Siva's dance but only nine *nrittamurtis* or seven *tandavas*[12] are discussed.[13] Orissan iconographic text *Silaprakasa* (2.196-20 B) describes three types of dancing images of Siva called *Natambaras*. A careful study of these reveals that there is not much difference between the iconographic treatment of *nrittamurtis*, *tandavas* and *Natamaras;* but as far as their dancing pose is concerned, they do not exactly correspond to the *Natyasastriya-karanas* and represent only a few of them such as *bhujangatrasita*, *urdhvajanu*, *parasvajanu*, *lalatatilaka*, *Lalita*, *svastika* and others, which will be discussed later. The feet position of the *Ananda*,[14] *Gauri*, *Sandhya* and *Uma tandavas* correspond to the first, second, third and fourth *nrittamurtis* which have left or right *bhujangatrasita pada* (like Bronze Natarajas) and four hands (except six-handed *sandhyathandava*). Tripura[15] and *Kalika tandava* are near to fifth and sixth sixteen-armed *nrittamurtis* having right foot touching the head. *Samharatandava* is close to the eight-armed seventh and eighth *nrittamurtis* and first *Natambara* having one *urdhvajanu* or *parsvajanu*. Ninth four-armed *nrittamurti* having one *samapada* and the other *kunchitapada* corresponds to the second *Natambara*. The third *Natambara* has *svastika* feet position, not mentioned in any of the texts, but profusely illustrated in the sculptures. The differences that occur in all of them are minor, relating to the number of arms, use of left or right foot and hands, and the dress and attributes. The basic idea behind all of these dances is more or less one and the same—the manifestation of primeval rhythmic energy.

Attempts to study *nrittamurtis* on the basis of the *Natyasastra* have been made by Gopinath Rao, (Sivaramamurti, Kapila Vatsyayan,[16] Annie Marie Gaston and others. First two of these scholars, recognised the primacy of the *Natyasastra* and could have been aware of the fact that *karana* is a cadence of movement. However, they identified the *nrittamurtis* in terms of *natyasastriya karanas* in a manner as if *karana* is a static pose, without examining the difference between the two media—plastic and kinetic. They did not realise that only a frozen movement after or before the movement can be depicted in the sculpture; thus only a degree of probability of identifying certain movement can be suggested. Exact identification is not always possible. Nor was there any attempt to correlate *natya* and *silpa* texts, neither to compare the movement of *karana* arrested by the sculpted *karana* panels in the south at Thanjavur, Chidambaram, Kumbhakonam, Vriddhachalam, etc. This naturally led to grave errors in the study of dance sculptures, Kapila Vatysyan for the first time studied the *nrittamurtis* in their proper perspective, i.e. in terms of the grammar of dance. Gaston analysed only hand and feet positions of Natarajas without identifying the primary, intermediary or final stage of the *karana*.

The concept of the dance of Siva is as old as the text of the *Mahabharata* (7.80, 39, 40; 13.14, 15, 17, 154, 156) where we find a clear picture of Siva as a great dancer, along with the iconographic concept of multi-armed Siva carrying attributes dancing in the company of Devi and the *ganas*.[17] However, the sculptural representation of Siva's dance start appearing only in the Gupta period which proliferated in medieval period. The paucity of early iconographic material probably accounts for the absence of Natesa sculptures earlier than the Gupta period.

Many, if not all of the dance *karanas*, of which Siva is the very embodiment, according to Jayana, have been picturesquely protrayed as they were, in the early sculptural art of Central India. By the time of the Guptas, dance had become an accepted part of worship in the Hindu temples of Central India. This practice has been referred to by Kalidasa. This resulted in the increase in the variety of Siva's representations. The temples of Nachna, Bhumra, Tumain, Adhbhar, Sirpur, Malhar and Rajim preserve many Natarajas of this period. These can conveniently be studied under three broad categories, according to the position of lower limbs and the manner of the contact of one or both the feet with the ground. The rationale for this lies in the fact that once the feet take a definite position the body assumes a stance accordingly. These are as follows:

1. *Sama-kunchita/Agratalasanchara/suchi* (one foot in complete contact with the ground, while, only the forepart or toes or the big toe respectively of the other).

2. *Svastika* (both the feet crossing each other, either in *sama-tryasara* or in *sama-kunchita*);

   and

3. *Bhujangatrasita* (one leg lifted up and extended across the body, as in bronze Natarajas).

Within these basic formats emerge many sub-categories depending upon the variations in the use of *hastas* and their *hastakshetras*, position of head and movement of torso, etc.

One of the finest and most important examples of the early Natarajas of the first category comes from Sirpur. Dancing on the rocky heights of Kailasa for

Himalayaputri, the eight armed and *tribhangi* Kailasa pati (Pl. 11.I) exhibits all the grace and beauty characteristic of the Gupta art. Its main right arm, extended across the body, is in *karihasta* or *gajahasta* with *katakamukhashasta* (according to *Hastamuktavali* and *Balaramabharatam*). Sivaramamurti and Annie Marie Gaston have identified it with *samdamsa* and *hamsasya hasta* respectively, which is incorrect. Main left hand, though broken now, must have been near the ear or shoulder after the *vivartita* action either in *abhaypataka* or in *abhayasamdamsa-hasta*. Head and neck are slightly tilted towards left in *anchita-sira anchita-griva*. *Parsva* (sides) is slightly *prasarita* (extended) towards the right and the *kati* (hip) is *udvahita* (deflected) towards the left. Therefore, there is a slight shift of weight on the left *samapada*.

Both the knees are bent and out-turned in *parasvajanunatajanu* according to the *Balaramabharatam*. This is the first stylization which distinguishes a simple standing position from a dance movement. As rightly observed by Vatsyayan[18], dance sculptures of the period from the 7th century to the twelfth and thirteenth century A.D. have been largely identified as 'dance' on account of this basic stance termed *ardhamandali* and also known as *ukkaramandali* in the South. Right *suchipada* clearly resting on big toe is placed at a distance of one or more *talas* from the *sampada*. The stance of the lower limbs, thus, can be identified as the variation of *asvakranta* or *mandalasthanaka*[19] and the initial position of *suchi* or *saktasya* or *janitachari*[20] etc. The pose of the body on the whole corresponds to the textual description of *lalitakaran–'karihasta bhavevdmo dakshinascha vivartitah, bahusah kuttitah pado gneyam tallalitam budhaih'—Natyasastra* (4.93).

Though, the left hand is required to be in *kanihasta* pose, the same movement is generally repeated through opposite hand and foot, according to the dance tradition. *Kuttita* is a toe-heel movement which has been depicted in sculpture through *suchi kunchita* or *agratalasanchira pada*. Chidambaram *lalita karana* panel (Fig. 1) depicts the same hand and feet position, while the Thanjavur one (Fig. 2) portrays left *dolahasta* and right *kunchitapada*. Probably it represents the intial position of the *karana*.

Chandrasekhara's perfectly arranged *jatamukuta* adorned with *ardhachandra*, *ekavali*, *kankana* and *yagnopavita* add to his glamour. Two of Siva's hands carry his characteristic attributes *damaru* and *trisula*—symbolic of creation and destruction. The upper two hands hold the snake as canopy, signifying the serpent of eternity as the embodiment (*tirobhava*). One left hand in *adhomukha-samdamsa-hasta*, shows him demonstrating the technique of dance to his pupils. His first disciple, Tandu is seen between his leg while his son, the eternal child Kumara is shown riding his peacock. They appear to be proving their competence as learners by imitating him accurately. The other left hand of *Urdhavameghra* is shown fondling Devi's chin, who is sitting in *kurmasana*. It shows that *Paramayogi* is *Paramasringari* too. Ganesa mounted on his rat completes the domestic setting. Below right a *mardangika* playing on threefold *mridanga* (consisting of *urdhavaka*, *alingyaka* and *ankika*), provides the necessary beat while a *panivadaka* claps his hands to keep time.

A great masterpiece as it is, it has been a trend-setter for the iconography of the Natarajas of North and Central India. The presence of overhead snake, Devi on left fondled by her husband, *urdhavalinga*, the *aharaya*, the number of arms and the *lalita* pose became stylised by the 8th century. They almost answer to the description of the second *Natambara* of *Silpaprakasa*. The feet position also corresponds to the ninth *nrittamurti* of *Sritattvanidhi*. However, in essence it is closer to the *sandhyatandav* which Siva dances in gay abandon for his consort on the heights of Kailasa, surrounded by his family. *Lalita* pose caught the fancy of the ancient sculptors the most, who enthusiastically carved most of the dancing Siva images in this particular pose until the medieval period in Central India and adjacent regions. Another Gupta wonder, the eight-armed *samabhangi* and *trinetri Nrityasila* comes from Adhabhar (Pl. 11. II) depicting similar pose through opposite limbs. This can be taken as an accurate depiction of the second variety of *lalita karana*. Though less dynamic and lesser known this particular piece is hard to surpass for its rare combination of the spiritual contemplation with the restrained movement and perfect poise. Siva has almost stationary right half *dakshinardha* and whole body from head to toe is in *sama* but for the dynamic *Vamardha* displayed by left *parsvajanunata-janu* and *suchipada*. The latter along with the presence of a percussionist confirm that Siva's main activity is dance here. He is probably teaching soft-dance *lasya* to Sivakamasundari, through his *Vamardha* which stands for the feminine half of his Ardhanarsivara aspect. The main right hand *abhaya-pataka* conveying benevolent assurance to the restless souls, the *bhala* adorned with the third eye like a *tilaka*, the neck garlanded by serpent of eternity in two or three folds, well arranged *jatamukuta* studded with *chintamani* jewel, well defined features and serene countenance, introvert gaze of the half closed eyes and one left hand carrying *khappara* are enough to enhance the beauty of the yogi and Nartesvara, combined in one. The lack of dynamism

FIG. 1

FIG. 2

FIG. 3

FIG. 4

in the above example, however, is compensated in its, a little later representative from Malhar Museum, (c. 6th-7th century A.D.), 'portrayed in the same pose (Pl. 11. III). Mahakala's sixteen arms, the rapid swirl of which raises blasts, beautifully represent the *bhujataruvana* of Kalidasa. It is a typical northern feature that travelled from Ujjain to all over India. The performance of Mahesa, the greatest practitioner of *Naty--sastra*, is witnessed here by his colleagues Vishnu and Brahma assembled above on their respective vehicles and Nandi. They were conspicuously absent in previous examples and make up here for the absence of Siva's sons. Bhavani standing in svastika pose with *abhagna vaksha*, hanging but crossed *dolahastas* fulfill the requirements of *sanna-takarana* according to Bhattatandu's explanation.[21] *Nurajavadaka* with his *pushkaratraya* is the only accompanist.

Yet another eight-armed *Nrittesvara* from Malhar Museum protrays the same pose with right *karihasta* and left *Kuttita* foot and comprise the third variety of *lalita* pose. The presence of right *dola hasta* instead of *karihasta* has imparted a specific character to the eight-armed Girisa (Pl.11.IV) from Rajivalochana temple, Rajim. The pose, thus can now be identified as the primary state of the *lalitakarana*, according to the Thanjavur *lalita karana* panel as well as the *janita karana*. The latter requires, a *mushtihasta* placed on chest, a *dolhhasta* and an *agratala pada*. It is used as a starting point for many *karaas* (N.S., 4.154). Chidambaram *janita karana* panel (Fig. 3) exhibits the same hand position but *suchipada* is inexplicably absent there. The main left *samamsahasta* shows that the Sarvasadhaka is teaching *lasya* to Girija here, whom he is caressing with the other left *ardhachandra hasta*. A *mardangika* on the left and a cymbal player on the right seated in *utkatikasthanaka* complete the orchestra. Siva's arrested crown and similar necklace represent the typical features of the art of south Kosala.

The ealiest examples of our *svastika* category come from Tumain, Sakor and Nachna. The eight-armed Mahesvara dancing without any accompaniment, is from Tumain (Pl.11.V) having *samakunchita* feet crossing each other. It is a beautiful representation of *ardhasvastika-karana, savastikasthana* and *svastika desi chari* derived from *savstika pada*. Its hand position—right *samdamsahasta* znd left *mushti* or *katakamukha hasta* placed on the hip above the navel—answers to the commentary that provides for the provisional use of *katihasta* (hand placed on hip) instead of a *karihasta*. It also resembles the Thanjavur and Chidambaram *ardhasvastika karana* panels (Fig. 5 and 4). Except for the hands holding the snake and *damaru*, rests are mutilated. The pose corresponds to the third *Natambara*. It is significant for its remarkable simplicity.

The hand position according to *Natyasastra* is represented by the ten-armed Bhutesa which occupy the *lalatabimba* of the door lintel that is the only extant part of the now ruined Saiva temple at Sakor.[22] It has right *karihasta* and left hand placed on the chest. The music is provided by the *bhutas* whose musical instruments are invisible. So are the attributes of the *bhujataruvana*. Sravani is the only spectator. Its close parallel posewise is a four-armed *Nartanasila* from Nachna (Pl. 11.VI). However, its architectonic treatment and the occasion of dance—when the *Paramavadaka* is providing the music for the dance of the *Paramanartaka* himself, have given it a special significance. This is a rare example of unique aesthetic sense. The sculptor has handled his subject with admirable skill by arranging both seated and standing figures in the same panel occupying, the same width of space. This could be done only through a dance sculpture. Its permanent value, however, lies in the fact that formless Sadasiva has simultaneously assumed two forms here—*Vinagana* and Nrittesvara to provide music for his own cosmic dance. The whole treatment is distinguished by a balance and well-defined features.

Another Gupta example in the earliest representation of *bhujangatrasita* mode, known to most people as the Nataraja pose, is represented by an eight-armed Sankara from Bhumra (Fig. 6). Carved skillfully is a circular medallion of now ruined temple of Bhumra[23], this image is enough to prove the origin of this pose in the North. It predates the first southern representation of this pose in the seventh century A.D.—the Nataraja image in a Pallava cave temple at Sivamangalam (Tamil Nadu). Its right *samapadatryasra pada* is planted on the ground, an abode for the tired souls struggling in the toils of *karma*. Left foot or the *padmapada* is lifted up and extended with the help of *chinnakati* and *udvarittauru*, across the body to grant eternal bliss to his devotees. Both the main hands are placed in the chest region either in *abhyayapctaka* or in *katakamukha hasta*. Rest of the hands are either mutilated or carry conventional attributes. The pose can be identified as *saiva desi sthanaka* of *Bharataranava* (336) and the final position of *bhujangatrasita chari* and *bhujangatrasita-karana*.[24] The expression on the face clearly bespeaks of a man frightened by the sight of a serpent. Hands are optional according to the text, though the commentary requires one *katakamukha* and other *dolahasta*-"*kramaineko dolahastahaparah katakasya iti*" (*Abhinavabharati*).[25] Despite the difference in the position of hands, the pose of the body anticipates Nataraja pose and is closer to Thanjavur *bhujangatrasita-karana* panel

Fig. 5

Fig. 6

Fig. 7

(Fig. 7). It a'so corresponds to the first and second *nrittamurtis* and *Ananda* and *Gauritandavas*.

The enigmatically smiling four-armed Pramathadhipati from Nachna (Pl. 11.VII) is nearer to *bhujanganchitakarana* panel from Chidambaram (Fig. 8) which has right *dolahasta* and left *urdhavarechita hasta*. However, the identification of this imageis controversial. According to Sivaramamurti[26] it is the of first Siva's five forms—*Vamadeva Sadyojata*, *Tatpurusha*, *Aghora* and *Isana*—showing his democratic attitude, as he has chosen to be a dwarf when present amidst his *ganas*. But we know for certain of the references about the *bahubhuji pramathas* in *Vuya* and *Matsya Purana*. Many scholars, thus, do not agree with Sivaramamurti and the matter is still open for discussion.

Another example comes from Nachna in the form of four-armed Nataraja (Pl. 11.VIII) only the bust of which is fortunately preserved. The twist of the bust and the hand-position is similar to that of the dance performance shown in Fig. 3 though the pose cannot be ascertained.

This analytical study and representative samples is more or less comprehensive account of almost all the known Natarajas from the early art of Madhya Pradesh. Even so, this is sufficient to prove the popularity of dance form in this area. An idea about the prevalent dance styles and common poses can also be formed. Varieties of *svastika bhujangatrasita* and *lalita karanas* were the favourite modes of dancing *Karihasta*, *pataka*, *samdamsa*, *katamukha*, *mushti* and *allapallava hastas* seem to have been very popular. But we do not come across any Nataraja in the *urdhvajanu* and *vrschika* poses, so eloquently portrayed through the then contemporary *ganas*. Nor does the extreme position of the *vrschika-pada*, the *laltatilaka* or the *urdhvatandava* which became a popular pose in south Indian art, figure here. Surprisingly enough the Bhumra-Nataraja is the only *bhujangatrasita* representative of its own kind. It disappeared totally from the later Natarajas of this region.

No posterior views or profiles of Natarajas are seen. As far as iconographic details are concerned overhead snake, *damaru* and *trishula* are the most common attributes. Vertical third eye, *jatas* either tied up in a knot or partly tied up and partially flowing down on the shoulders were the features that re-emerged later. Natarajas also are not shown with mustaches which is a typical Gupta feature. No Ganga flows from out of Siva's *jata*. Nor any *apasmara* writhes under his feet, though the concept was not new at this time and could be traced back to as early as the bronze seal of Mauses. Though, not much deviation from *Natyasastra* took place uptil this time, yet sculptors had enough freedom to portray the cosmic dancer in a variety of poses.

NOTES AND REFERENCES

1. Raghavan, V. (ed.) *Nritta Ratnavali of Jayasenapati*, Madras Government Oriental Series Madras, 1965, 1.1.

2. Also see Sivaramamurti, C. *Nataraja in Art, Thought and Literature*, National Museum, Delhi, 1974, p. 4-5.

3. *Ibid.*, Gaston, Anne-Marie, *Siva in Dance, Myth and Iconography*, Oxford University Press, Delhi, 1982, have all over used Nataraja for all the dancing images of Siva.

4. *Srishti* (Creation), *sthiti* (preservation), *samhara* (destruction), *triobhava* (embodiment) and *anugrha* (His grace).

5. Vatsyayan, Kapila, Siva Natesa: Cadence and form in Meister W. Michael ed. *Discourses on Siva*, Bombay, 1984, p. 191-92.

6. Shah, Priyabala, ed. *Visnudharmottara Purana*, Vol. III, part 1, Gaekwad Oriental Series, Baroda, 1958.

7. Bhattacharya, B. ed., *Samarangana Sutradhara of Bhojadeva*, Gaekward Oriental Series, Baroda, Vol. I.

8. Sankhyatirtha, V.M. (ed). *Devatamurtiprakarana of Sutrapatamandana*, Calcutta, 1936.

9. Sastri, Madhusudan (ed.) *Natyasastra* of Bharata (NS) (1971 and 1975) (edited and translated) part 1 and part 2, Hindi ed. Kashi Hindu Vishavidyalaya, Varanasi, 1971 and 1975.

10. The fourth chapter of *Natyasastra*, where the karanas are described is called *Tandavalakshanam*.

11. For details see *Natyasastra*, *op. cit.*, Ch. IV, VIII, IX, X, XI and XII.

12. *Silparatna*, *Kasyapasilpa*, *Asmumadhedagama*, *Uttarakamikagama*, *suprabhedagama* and *Purvakaranagama* discuss *nrittamurtis;* while in *Sritattvanidhi*, *Mayamata*, *Silpasamgrha* and *Karanagamas tàndavas* are described.

13. For details see Rao, Gopinath, (1968), *Elements of Hindu Iconography*, 2nd ed. Vol. II, part 1, Motilal Banarasidas, Delhi, 1968, p. 224-57; Sivaramamurti, 1974, *op. cit.*, p. 150.

14. Also known as *Nadanta* or *Sabhapatinritya*, it is the mode of dance that attracted maximum attention of scholars.

15. It is also known as *Urdhvatandava* or *Kalitandava*. Whether the *tripuratandava* and *Samharatandava* are related to *tripuravijaya* and *gajasurasamhara* we are not sure of.

16. Vatsyayan, K. *Classical Indian Dance in Literature and the Arts*, Sangeet Natak Academy, Delhi 1968.

17. Sivaramamurti, 1974, *op. cit.*, p. 78 ff.

18. Vatsyayan, K., *Dance Sculptures in Śarangapani Temple*, Society for Historical and Epigraphical Research, Madras, 1982, preface.

19. *Natyasastra*, 10.34, 16 and 25 respectively.

20. *Ibid*, 12. 172-173; 10.65 respectively.

21. *Swastikau charanau kritya karihastam, cha dakshinam' vakshah sthane tatha vamardhasvastikamadiset*— *Natyasastra*(4.82)

22. *Sangitasamayasara*, 7.160.

23. See Banerjee, R.D. (1924) *The temple of siva at Bhurma* Memoirs of the Archaeological Survey of India, No. 16, Calcutta 1924.

24. *Natyasastra*, 10.42.

25. *Kunchitam padamukshipya trayasramurum vivartyet, katij-ananuvivartachcha bhujangatrasitam bhavet*—*Natyasastra* (4.84).

26. *Ibid.*, & p. 170 and 114.

12

Kamesvara Temple at Galiavalli

M. Krishna Kumari

Galiavalli is a small village situated about 15 kilometres away from Rajam in Bobbili Taluk of Vizianagaram district, Andhra Pradesh. At Galiavalli, the temple is dedicated to Siva under the name Kamesvara, now locally known as Kamalingesvara. The temple is similar to the Orissan style of temples in plan and construction. So far, no attempt has been made by the art historians and art critics to bring out the importance of the art and architecture of this temple, though it is located close to the temples of Narayanapuram, Jayati, and Sarapalli in the Vizianagaram district,[1] which show the Eastern Ganga patronage of temple art and architecture in northern Andhra. In the present paper, it is proposed to study in detail the architectural and iconographical features of the Siva temple at Galiavalli which reflects the popular local styles and the royal patronage and to ascertain the date of its construction.

The Kamesvara temple facing east, rises to a height of about 10 metres from the ground and is without any *antarala* and *jagamohana*. The *mandapa* in front of the sanctum appears to be a later construction. But the image of seated *nandi* about 51 cm high in the present *mandapa* appears to be an ancient one. The temple is built of soft-textured Khondalite, which can be obtained from the neighbouring places. Just like the temples of Mukhalingam and Bhubanesvar, it is observed that no cementing material was used in the construction of the temple. Large blocks of stones, neatly cut and dressed, were placed one above another in their pre-determined positions and held in place by their weight and balance.

The ground plan of the temple shows that the sanctum is square internally and stands on a *triratha* plan externally with a wide projection in the centre of its external faces. The elevation of the temple can be divided into three sections, the base (*bada*) including the wall-portion, the tower (*gandi*) and the apex (*mastaka*). The *bada* consists of three mouldings resembling those of Parasuramesvar and Vaital-Sisiresvar group of temples at Bhubanesvar and that of Madhukesvara temple at Mukhalingam. The base mouldings (fig. 1) consists of three levels in which the topmost is square in section and decorated with rectangular panels of sculptures; the second level is not decorated but rounded in section and finally, the lowest level also plain, is called, *khura* or hoof after which it is shaped. According to *Silpa Prakashsa*, this type of temple is known as *rathayukta*, with its base being widely projected in the centre.[2] The *jangha* is decorated with three *devakoshtas*, of which the central one is wider than the other two and are decorated with the figures of Ganesa, Karttikeya, Mahishasuramardini and the images of the *dikpalas*. The niches have overhanging eaves at its top with images.

The doorway of the sanctum is of the *trisakha* variety, like those found in the temple of Somesvara and Madhukesvara at Mukhalingam with the floral motifs on it. The *dvarapalas* are found at the bottom of the doorjambs and are carved inside square niches. The two niches on the east wall contain the images of Parvati. The lintel of the doorway can be observed by climbing the *mandapa* which carries the figures of nine planets in a long row and Gajalakshmi beneath it.

The *sikhara* of the temple (Pl. 12. I) rises up straight for more than half of its height and then begins to curve inwards. Like the early Orissan temples, the tower of Kamesvara temple, has in the centre on each of its faces a wall-projecting vertical band which is continued up to the top from the base below. It is decorated with several *chaitya* arches diminishing in sizes as they go up. The wide *chaityas* at the bottom contain cult images. Vertically, the *gandi*, is divided into seven *bhumi-barandis*, each of which is covered by a *bhumi-amla* moulding with fluted *amlas* in the angles in the *kanika-paga*. The *gandi* is divided into five *pagas*, i.e. a central *raha-paga* two-side *anuratha-pagas* and two outer most *kanika-pagas*. On top of the *bisama*, above the *gandi* are carved four *mandis* facing different directions. The *beki* is capped by a heavy fluted *amalaka* and *khapuri*. Inside the temple, the sanctum has no ceiling but shows the corbelled roof. The *pranala* is seen at the *kumbha* level of the base mouldings on the northern side of the temple.

As regards the sculptural art and iconography of the temple, it shows all the characteristics of the medieval art. In the centre of the sanctum is found a *linga* on a rectangular *panuvattam*. Parsva-devatas represented are Ganesa, Karttikeya and Mahishasuramardini. The niches on either side of the central niches contain the images of *dikpalas*. The *koshtas* contain narrative scenes from mythology. The floral designs and narrative panels are enclosed within dotted outlines and appear to be a local practice which is not found in any of the Orissan temples. Similar treatment of the niches can be seen in the Dibbhesvara temple at Saripalli.

According to the *Silpa Prakasa*[3] the architect should place the image of Ganesa in the central niche on the south wall of the temple. The image of Ganesa here (Pl. 12. II) conforms to this description as well as to the iconographical features described in the *Brhatsamhita* and *Saiva Agama* texts.[4] He is four-armed, seated on an *asana* with his left leg folded and the right leg hanging down. The right hands carry a rosary and elephant goad and the left hands sweet-meat and *parasu*. He wears *Kiritamukuta* and the trunk of the god is shown as touching the sweet-meat held by his left hand. The sacred thread and armlets are of snakes. Two flying vidyadharas carrying garlands in their hands can be seen on either side at the two top corners. The mount of the god, the mouse, is carved as moving to the left with a long tail. Strings of bells are found as ornaments on the neck and anklets of Ganesa.

The central niche on the west wall of the temple contains the image of the two-armed youthful Karttikeya (Pl. 12. III) carved almost in round which conforms to the description given in the iconographic texts.[5] He is seated in *ardhaparayanka* pose on a stool, with his right foot resting on a peacock, his mount. He holds a *sakti* in his right hand and a *kukkuta* (a fowl) in his left, the head of which is broken. He wears pearl stringed *yajnopavita* and a beautiful *hara*. The hair is arranged in such a way that the side strands fall over his shoulders. His body is covered with a garment extending up to his knees and the folds of the drapery fall down from over the *asana*. The peacock with its tail is carved below the seat of the image and is looking on its lord. The image under study with two arms appears to be the *satvika* form of the god and represents him as *yoga bera*. Generally in the north Indian images, Karttikeya is shown either seated on his mount, standing in front of the mount or riding and has either two or more hands and faces.[5]

The image of Mahishasuramardini on the north wall of the temple (Pl. 12. IV) conforms to the descriptions given in the *Silparatna* with slight variations.[7] The image is ten armed and is shown in an aggressive pose, where the three prongs of the *sula* pierce the demon. Her right hands carry a sword, wheel, trident and a *vajra*, while her left carry a bow, *naga*, a sword, battle-axe and her natural left hand presses down the upturned head of the demon. The sword in the upper right hand is held horizontally over the head of the goddess. She is carved as standing firmly on her left leg and her right leg is placed on the back of the demon. The demon holds a sword tightly in his hands. Here the demon is shown as emerging from out of the decapitated head of the Mahisha. This feature is in contrast to the earlier examples of the depiction of the goddess wherein the demon below the feet of the deity is shown with a human body and a buffalo head. The goddess wears *kundalas*, jewelled armlets and *katisutra*.

The images of the *dikpalas* carved in the niches on the three outer walls partially conform to the description in the *Brihatsamhita*, *Silparatna*, *Amsumadbhedagama Suprabhedagama* and *Purvakaranagama*. Agni, Nirriti, Varuna, Vayu, Isana and Kubera are carved as standing with two hands along with their respective *vahanas*.

Though the figure of Agni (Pl. 12. V) carved in the south-eastern niche corresponds to the description in *Vishnudharmottara*,[8] it shows two-armed god standing in *samabhanga* holding a rosary in his right hand and a water-vessel in his left. He has a beard, an angry stare, long waving tongues of flames emanating from his body, sacred thread and few ornaments. The lower garment extends up to his ankles. His mount, goat, is carved to his right side. To his left, is carved a dwarfish attendant holding flames in his right hand.

The image of Nirriti, the god of evil, carved in the south-western niche (Pl. 12. VI) shows the *dikpala* standing on the back of a man, who is shown lying flat on the ground holding a sword and shield tightly in his left hand. He wears a long *yajnopavita*, *katisutra*, armlets and bracelets. He is adequately decorated with *ratnakundalas*, *hara* and *jatamukuta*. To his right side is carved a male attendant holding a sword in one of his hands.

The image of Varuna, found in a niche on the western wall, (Pl. 12. VII) is carved as standing in a very graceful pose. It shows him holding a looped noose by its end in his left hand which rests on his hip with a water-vessel in his right hand. He is decorated with jewelled head-gear, *ratna-kundalas*, necklaces, pearl *yajnopavita* and waist girdle. An oval halo is carved around his head. Below the feet the wavy horizontal lines and a *makara* with its mouth open behind his feet indicate water. To his right side is carved the miniature figure of his consort Gauri standing in abhanga pose carrying the stalk of a lotus flower in her left hand. The image described above is similar to the figure of Varuna of the Raja Rani temple of Bhubanesvar[9] and does not correspond to the description in *Vishnudharmottara*.

Vayu, the lord of the north-west direction is described in the *Vishnudharmottara* as two-armed, his two hands holding the two ends of the scarf worn by him, his garment being inflated by wind. *Silparatna* lays down that he has a flag in the left and the right hand is in *varada mudra* and his mount[10] is a stag. The image of Vayu carved in the niche to the north-west side partially corresponds to the description given in *Silparatna*. Here Vayu is shown as two-armed, standing in the *abhanga* pose holding an *ankusa* in the right hand and a flag in his left hand. He is decorated with *patra-kundalas, kantha-mala*, long *yajnopavita* and bracelets. His lower garment is inflated by wind emphasising his swift motion. To his right is carved a standing attendant with stag head.

Curiously, Isana, the lord of the north-eastern quarter does not occupy his allotted position in the outer side of the sanctum, instead the image of Kubera is seen in its place. The image of Isana on the northern wall of the temple corresponds well with the description given in *Vishnudharmottara*.[11] Here he is called Gaurisvara which is another name of *ardhanarisvara* Siva. This conjoint aspect of Siva and Uma can be seen in the image of Isana. He is carved as standing with two hands, the right hand holding water-vessel and the left hand resting on an indistinct long object. From head to feet, the two halves are clearly demarcated. A prominent breast is shown on the left half. The right half wears *jatamukuta;* the hair on the left is arranged in a big knot at the top and is decorated with ornaments. He wears a single stranded *yajnopavita* and *katisutra*. He is shown with an oval halo round his head and a male attendant to his right side. In each of the two top corners a lotus is carved.

The image of Kubera carved in the north-eastern niche conforms to the features described in *Amsumadbhedagama*.[12] It describes the god as two-armed, the hands being in *varada* and the left hand holding a club, having a sheep for his mount, attended by his consort and the two *nidhis, sankha* and *padma* in the form of two powerful spirits. The image of Kubera here (Pl. 12. IV) is carved as standing in (*abhanga* on a *padmapitha* with two hands, the right hand in *varada mudra* and the left hand holding a *sakti*. He wears a long *yajnopavita* and *katisutra*. The lower garment is shown up to his thighs. The hair is arranged as in a *kiritamukuta* and the side strands fall over his shoulders. His mount, sheep, is carved as standing facing right, to his right side. To his left is carved the powerful spirit, *sankha nidhi*. Lotus flowers are carved in the two top corners.

In addition to the images described above, loose sculptures of Lakulisa and Ganesa are to be seen within the precincts of the temple. It appears that the cult images are carved on loose slabs and then fitted into the shallow niches in the walls.

The decorative motifs and scroll-work patterns on the doorjamb and around the niches are drawn from Orissan tradition. The temple walls are decorated in relief of religious and secular subjects or themes. Women performing dance, playing music (Pl. 12. IV) and men engaged in hunting and battles (Pl. 12.VII) are proportionately and beautifully carved. The sculptors made a bold departure from convention and introduced many popular folk-themes in their art. The graphic portrayal of men and women returning from a hunt and the warriors sculpted with a variety of dresses, men riding horses (Pl. 12. V) are meant to display the might and power of the Eastern Ganga empire. Further, the portrayal of the monkeys in action in a narrative manner around the *koshta* containing the image of Vayu leads one to suggest that delightful fables are drawn from the famous epics. Thus the icons as well as sculptures of the temple not only created to meet the needs of religious minded people but also served to attract the common folk and the masses.

There is no foundation inscription referring to the construction of the Kamesvara temple. But two inscriptions of Anatavarama Choda Ganga[13] (A.D. 1077-1147), are found on the walls on either side of the entrance to the temple. Of them, one is dated in his 47th victorious regnal year and registers the gift of lamp by Vittapa Nayaka, a *kannada mangali* to Lord Kamesvaradeva of Galiavalli. Recently two sets of copper plates grants were recovered near the temple complex. Of them, the plates with larger dimensions, edited and published by me, belongs to 11th century A.D. while the other set is roughly three centuries earlier. The recovery of these two sets of plates near the temple strengthens the belief that the area in which the temple was located was under the authority of the Ganga rulers of Kalinga. Probably it was under their patronage that the Siva temple at Galiavalli was constructed and maintained.

The architecture of the temple is the typical example of the *rekha deul* of Orissa. The elevation of the wall-portion and its tower bear close resemblance to the Somesvara temple at Mukhalingam[14] and Muktesvara temple at Bhubanesvar. The carving of the nine planets in a row on the lintel of the doorway of the sanctum and the figure of Gajalakshmi are similar to those of the Somesvara temple of Mukhalingam. It has been observed by K.C. Panigrahi and J.N. Banerjea, that in the Siva temples of Bhubaneswar only eight planets are shown in the earlier one Ketu being a later addition. Further, *Vishnudharmottara* which belongs to 5th century A.D. suggests the depiction of only eight planets omitting Ketu.[15] The image of Karttikeya with a cock in his left hand is carved on the west wall and the image of Ganesa with his mount on the south wall suggests that it belongs to a later period. In carving the Mahishasuramardini image, the demon below her feet is shown in human form emerging from the animal. K.C. Panigrahi suggests that this type of depiction is to be seen only in the later images.[16]

Thus on the basis of the study of the architecture, iconographic progression in the above said images, as well as the epigraphs of the temple, it can be concluded that the Kamesvara temple was built in the middle of 11th century A.D. It may also be observed that the art and architectural traditions which were current in Orissa and Mukhalingam found their way into Galiavalli. The Gangas of Kalinga seems to have been responsible for the construction of the temples of Orissan style in northern Andhra, as his area was included in the Kalinga region in ancient times.

NOTES AND REFERENCES

1. Dehejia, Vidya *Early Stone Temples of Orissa*, Delhi, 1979, p. 133-134; *Telugu Samskriti*, (ed.) Vol. I (revised edition) 1983, p. 810.

2. Boner, Alice and Rath, Sadasiva *Silpa Prakasa of Ramachandra Kaulachara*, Leiden, 1966, II, 68-69, 66-69.

3. *Ibid.*, II, Appendix C, pp. 92 ff.

4. Rao, T.A. Gopinatha *Elements of Hindu Iconography*, Vol. I, Pt. II Appendix C, pp. 1-13.

5. According to the texts, he holds in one of his hands a spear or a trident and in the other a fruit or a cock. His mount, peacock, accompanies him. Rao; *op.cit.*, Appendix C, pp. 205-228.

6. Thakur, U., *Karttikeya in Literature and Art: Some Aspects of Ancient Indian History and Culture*, New Delhi, 1974, pp. 244 ff.

7. In the *Silparatna*, it is described that the goddess should have ten hands and should hold trident, sword, spear, wheel and bow in the right and in the left, the noose, goad, *khetaka*, battle-axe and a bell.

8. He is described as bearded, four-armed, four-tusked, three-eyed, riding a chariot with smoke standard drawn by four parrots and driven by wind, having his consort, Svaha, on his lap, holding flames, trident, and rosary in his hands. cf. Banerjee, J.N. *Development of Hindu Iconography*, p. 524

9. *Ibid.*, p. 527, Pl. XLVI, Fig. 1

10. *Ibid.*, p. 528.

11. *Ibid.*, p. 529.

12. *Ibid.*, p. 528.

13. A.R. No. 369 and 370 of 1934-35; p. 42.

14. Masthanaiah, B., *Temples of Mukhalingam*, p. 107-108.

15. *Ashtauva tatra kartavya grahah ketu vivarjitah/Suryassukrah kujo rahu sauris-chandro budho guruh/kramenanena kartavyam tatra rajan grahasitakam.*

16. Panigrahi, K.C., *Archaeological Remains at Bhubaneswar*, pp. 125-134. He points out that the earlier images of Ganesa are without his mouse while in later examples the mouse is present. In the case of Karttikeya, earlier images depict the god with just his peacock, while later examples include the cock. In the earlier examples of the Mahishasuramardini images, the demon is shown in animal from only and in later ones demon in human form from the decapitated head of the *mahisha*.

13

Bronze Age Culture of Thailand

Mahesh Prasad Madhukar

At the end of the Pleistocene period China, south of the Yangtze, shared a common prehistoric tradition with Indo-China, Thailand, Burma and West Malaysia, where the stone industries were dominated by pebble choppers, often with unifacial and unidirectional working. Stone mortars and pounders, bone spatulas and in the later stages, cord-marked pottery and edge-ground stone tools were also common. Collectively, this tradition is known as the Hoabinhian culture, from the province in Northern Viet Nam where it was first recognized.

Perhaps the best-known Hoabinhian site excavated in recent years is the Spirit Cave, near Mae Hong-Son in north-western Thailand. The sequence spans the period 10500-7500 years ago and there was a cultural change about 8800 years ago, when the Hoabinhian pebble industry was enriched with ceramics, quadrangular adzes and polished slate knives—a change interpreted as the arrival of an alien farming culture. The wide range of animal species in Hoabinhian sites suggests a broad-based foraging economy, and although some plant remains from the Hoabinhian levels at Spirit Cave have been tentatively identified as beans and peas, most of the plant specimens are from wild forest trees and perennials and need demonstrate no more than the harvesting of species that have remained useful and are often cultivated today.

By the middle of the fourth millennium B.C. there were certainly village settlements on the easily worked soils of the seasonally dry Sakon-Nakhon basin in north-eastern Thailand, and over the next two millennia they expanded south into the Mun River basin and on the margins of the wetter central plain of Thailand. Two thousand years, from about 5500 B.C. to 3500 B.C., of which little is known beyond the continuing Hoabinhian forest culture, separate the end of the Spirit Cave sequence from the basal levels of sites such as Ban Chieng and Non Nok Tha. As in Northern China, it is still not possible to recognize in any detail the processes that transformed the small mobile collecting societies into sendentary farmers. The early graves at Ban Chieng, for instance, have a striking black-burnished pottery with incised designs above cord-impressed bases that (though generally South-east Asian in style) has no obvious local antecedents. It has been called 'Neolithic' but the most recent excavations at Ban Chieng make it clear that tin-bronze ornaments and weapons were present in the earliest phase of Ban Chieng, as at Non Nok Tha.

It is claimed, on the evidence of an increasing number of radiocarbon tests, that bronze was first cast in the north of Thailand at a hitherto unsuspected early date: possibly before 2000 B.C., with greater probability before 1000 B.C. This conclusion rests chiefly on the intensive study of a single site (that of Non Nok Tha) and is involved in complex problems of stratigraphy. Many will look to the similar study of comparable sites, the establishment of evidence *in extenso* before, giving their quest to this revolutionary conclusion on the course of technological progress in an area once regarded as remote from the main highways of progress in Asia. But whatever conclusion the controversy may reach, and whatever precise dates may be established, the old view that the introduction of advanced bronze-working was in any sense an aspect of the Hinduisation of south-east Asia, or took place only shortly before that process began, is now shown to be wholly mistaken. It is very likely that there were prehistoric contacts between India and the western parts of south-east Asia and between China and the eastern parts of the area, before the influence of Indian 'Colonization' and religion began to be felt. Even iron would appear to have been first used in the region, perhaps having spread there from India, several hundred years before we find the first evidence of Hinduism or Buddhism.

In the development of research into south-east Asian prehistory as in other parts of the world, it is possible to distinguish between two different approaches or tendencies each producing its own kind of contribution to the overall picture. The approach is centred upon the collection and analysis of individual finds, their types and distribution, whilst the other concentrates upon the sequences of cultures suggested by the excavation of specific sites. Both approaches are necessary, but either of them on its own must suffer from severe limitations. It is important to recognize that during the first half of the twentieth century, the picture of south-east Asia which was presented by prehistorians was to a very large extent based upon only the first approach. It is true that there were a number of excavations during the 1920's and 1930's but the majority of them were unskilled, undertaken by archaeologists more interested in recording finds than in establishing stratigraphy. Moreover, a great many of the finds which entered into the work of comparative analysis were studied in museums, and their original provenance was often only very approximately known. With the development of more scientific excavation in south-east Asia since the mid-1950's, some of the theories that were based only on the study of finds have come to be challenged.

The transformation of subject began with the arrival on the scene of a new generation of archaeologists in the 1950's, and complete revision of the old theories became necessary as a result of subsequent work during the 1960's. The application of increasingly strict principles of stratigraphy, combined with the growing use of scientific dating methods, made it possible to establish cultural sequences for certain sites.

In the countries of mainland south-east Asia, important work has been undertaken in Viet Nam and Thailand and to a lesser extent in Kampuchea. But it is in Thailand that excavation has produced the most startling challenges to old images of south-east Asian prehistory.

In Central Thailand, the Thai-Danish Archaeological expedition of 1960-62, led by P. Sorensen, was responsible for important excavations at two sites in Kanchanaburi province: Bankao and the Ongbah Cave. A few years later, a Thai-British team led by W. Watson and H.H.E. Loofs was responsible for excavating the sites of Kok Charden (Lopburi province) and Tha Muang (U Thong), the latter an important site in relation to the protohistoric period. A number of other important sites were found in north-east Thailand, where in 1964, W.G. Solheim II took the initiative in organising a field survey of localities about to be flooded by the reservoirs of Mekong Development Project. It was this survey which led to the identification of the now famous site at Non Nok Tha, where in 1966 and 1968 Solheim and D.T. Bayard found a cultural sequence which seemed to indicate that bronze was being worked at a remarkably early date. Other evidence pointing towards a similar conclusion, that the south-east Asian Bronze Age began long before anyone had supposed, came from a nearby site at Non Nong Chik, excavated by R.H. Parker and C.F. Higham in 1970 and from another famous site at Ban Chieng, near Udorn.

Much of our knowledge of the economy and technology of the early Bronze-using peoples of the area comes from only two sites: Non Nok Tha and Ban Chieng, both located on the rolling lowlands of north-eastern Thailand.

Non Nok Tha was the first site to give a clear indication of a distinct bronze period in south-east Asia. The mound of Non Nok Tha (Phu Wiang district, Khon Kaen province), like most other open sites in Thailand, is characterised by an exceedingly complex and hard-to-interpret stratigraphy, which is further complicated by the dense concentration of burials (205 recovered in the 1966 and 1968 excavations) and other cultural disturbance. As a result of this and other factors such as possible contamination, the absolute dates from the site do not form a single tidy sequence, but rather may be interpreted in terms of several sequences.

We have some thirty-two radiocarbon dates and four thermoluminescence dates from the site. So, we can construct at least four quite distinct sequences: (1) a 'latest' sequence, with the earliest pre-metal habitation at the site beginning about 500 B.C. and the entry of bronze at the beginning of the present era; (2) a 'traditional' sequence with first occupation at *c*. 900 B.C. and bronze at 700 B.C.; (3) an 'intermediate' or compromise sequence with pre-metal and bronze periods beginning at 1800 B.C. and 1200 B.C. respectively; and (4) the 'early' sequence, with first occupation of the site occurring prior to 3500 B.C. and bronze appearing about 2700 B.C.

The economy of the Non Nok Tha culture was apparently based on rice from the outset, as suggested by the use of rice chaff as a tempering material in pottery from the beginning of the early period. Domestic cattles, dogs and, very probably, pigs are also present from the earliest level; however the presence of deer and other wild species indicates a significant reliance on hunting and gathering as well. A variety of pottery was recovered in burials of the early period, most of them round-bottomed and cord-marked; some of the vessels had elaborate incised designs. A few fragments of bronze from the bottom level and a socketed axe from the top level indicate that bronze was in use, but rare, throughout the early period. It became relatively abundant at the onset of the latest period or sequence, which is marked by an elaboration of pottery types and finds of sandstone moulds, coarse ceramic crucibles and bronze artifacts, indicating casting of bronze at the site. Greater variations in wealth and burial style tentatively suggest increasing social stratification, perhaps the results of a growing trade in bronze, but the economic pattern of the early period continued. Some evidence for intermittent occupation may indicate that rice was being grown by swidden (slash-and-burn) method rather than in wet fields.

After a gap in the sequence the site was reoccupied in A.D. 1000 (the Late period) and abandoned some 150 years ago. The Late period inhabitants of the site used iron tools and cremated their dead, and appear to have been similar to the present day wet-rice farmers of the area.

Ban Chieng, near Udorn, is a small village in north-east Thailand, an area considered as "depressed" by the Thai government because of its generally sparse and certainly underdeveloped resources. In 1960 or '61, a Fine Arts Department Officer stopped in the village during a north-east inspection tour and picked up a handful of small sherds which he found unusual. These fragments of pottery were unique in terms of what was then known of the Thai prehistoric sequence, yet their significance was not to be fully realised until many years later.

Ban Chieng remained archaeologically undisturbed until July 1966 when Stephen Young, an American student, visited Ban Chieng during the construction of a village road. From the fresh road cuts he retrieved for scientific interest several large fragments and a few nearly complete pots painted with handsome and intricate red-on-buff spiral designs. Elizabeth Lyongs, then working as a consultant to the Fine Arsts Department, photographed and studied them and could find no parallel with other south-east Asian pottery or that of China and India.

The initial settlers of Ban Chieng were already adapted to a lowland, rice agricultural technology; they were skilled hunters, craftsmen, potters and, before the end of this initial phase, had either developed or somehow gained access to the technology of bronze metallurgy. The wealth of bronze, the astounding number of pots, the scarcity of weapons of war, and the ritual slaughtering of animal during funerary rites, all of which occur throughout the site, attest to a long period of economic prosperity, security and stability.

The five cultural layers present at Ban Chieng are described by the excavator as (1) Humus, (2) Late Metal Age, (3) Early Metal Age, (4) Late Neolithic, and (5) Neolithic; the presence of a metal bracelet in the fourth layer may indicate that small quantities of metal were present during this Late Neolithic period, or perhaps the artifact lay in a later disturbance. The Early Metal Age layer contained only bronze tools, while metal finds in the Late Metal Age layer we.e exclusively iron. Although the distinctive painted pottery begins in the fourth layer, it is concentrated mainly in the second and third layers. The pottery is stylistically different in the two layers; mainly large and round bottomed with crowded triangular and curvilinear designs in the bronze-period layer; and smaller and ring-footed with more open spiral designs in the iron-age layer above. Oddly enough the related vessels at Non Nok Tha are of the latter type.

Relationship is less clear but still quite apparent between Non Nok Tha and the site of Ban Chieng in eastern Udorn province. It is sufficient to say that ties with Non Nok Tha are evident between the distinctive (and beautiful) red-on-white pottery found in abundance at Ban Chieng and similar but cruder vessels which occur sporadically in burials at Non Nok Tha. Ties are equally apparent in a number of stone, metal and clay artifacts; the bronze and even the iron tools recovered from Ban Chieng resemble the bronze tools from Non Nok Tha in their use of socketed rather than tanged hafting.

Ban Phak Top, about 26 km south west of Ban Chieng, resembled Ban Chieng but on a smaller scale. The vast majority of pots were black and incised; there were virtually no examples of the classic Ban Chieng red-on-buff painted ware. The stratigraphy of Ban Phak Top contrasted with that of Ban Cheing in several ways. The soil in the lower layers was quite hard and very difficult to remove. Several of the layers were very thin, in contrast to the rather thick layers at Ban Chieng. In addition, several layers contained large quantities of shells which were almost certainly refuse of the prehistoric inhabitants.

Unfortunately, no burials were unearthed but it is likely that the density of burials at Ban Phak Top is considerably less than at Ban Chieng. Bronze objects are often found in burials containing the black incised pottery. We have no reason to doubt this assertion which tends to corroborate the association of black incised pottery and bronze at basal Ban Chieng.

There have also been recovered polished stone adzes, worked bone objects and many small pieces of bronze. The analysis and chronometric dating of this material, now underway, will establish the extent to which the occupation of Ban Phak Top was contemporaneous with that of Ban Chieng and will enable us to evaluate hypotheses about the interrelationships between the two sites.

Don Klang site is located approximately midway between Ban Chieng and Non Nok Tha. The location of Don Klang is remarkably similar to that of Non

Nok Tha, 25 km to the south-west, and 2.5 km from the foot of Phu Wiang, a larger sandstone monad rock (a residual mountain standing above an eroded plain).

One of the important problems in understanding the evolution of the Ban Chieng cultural tradition is the role played by metallurgical technology. No evidence of smelting had been found at Ban Chieng although there was ample evidence for melting and casting. At Don Klang, on the other hand, metal, probably iron, was reduced from ores by smelting.

In contrast to the Ban Phak Top excavation, 16 burials were unearthed at Don Klang. Many bronze and iron objects from layers in the upper half of the site, including iron axes and knives in direct association with several burials were recovered. Small finds recocovered at Don Klang as well as Ban Phak Top and Ban Chieng include worked bone, polished stone adzes and clay pellets. Spindle whorls and beads (variously made of glass, stone and bone or shell) are common to Don Klang and Ban Chieng.

Despite the apparent dissimilarity of the upper level Ban Chieng and Don Klang pottery, one has the definite impression that further analyses will reveal a certain degree of cultural affinity between the two sites. In the lower levels, the relationship between them seems more definite. In the lowest Don Klang burial, the sherds with incised curvilinear designs which should cross date both basal Non Nok Tha and phase III at Ban Chieng (2000 B.C., among its significant finds are jar burials of children, sophisticated hunting activity, and some bronze artifacts). Moreover, a fixed burial was found in a lower layer at Don Klang. This and the flexed burials in the lowest layers at Ban Chieng constitute the first flexed burials discovered in sites belonging to the Ban Chieng cultural tradition.

Ban Tong is located 5 km south-east of Ban Chieng. The most interesting feature of the site was the absence of a clearly defined mound. Nine layers were recorded, the deepest being over 3 metres below the surface. Two burials were found. The upper contained a very large pot with an incised and painted spiral design around the neck. On typological grounds, this burial should be related to phase IV (1600 B.C.—1200 B.C., among its significant finds are numerous bronze objects, bimetallic artifacts showing the initial appearance of iron smelting and foraging) at Ban Chieng. The lower burial was cut into the sterile soil and contained only a cordmarked pot.

The major site of Bankao, in western central Thailand, provides considerable evidence for the traditionally late date of appearance of bronze and iron in the region. The site is interpreted as a Neolithic occupation area with later Neolithic burials, save for two burials with iron tools which supposedly derive from a later iron period.

Further evidence for the antiquity of bronze in this area comes in the form of two radiocarbon dates of charcoal from the cave site of Tham Ongbah to the north-west of Bankao.

Sometime before 1000 B.C. the development of wetrice cultivation, in conjunction with the water buffalo for ploughing and the use of iron tools, made possible one of the major population shifts in the region's prehistory: the movement from the rolling lowlands to the hitherto unsettled alluvial plains that now support the vast majority of South-east Asia's people. Perhaps stimulated by population pressure, groups began to move on to the deltas of the Red and Chao Phraya (and probably Mekong) rivers early in the first millennium B.C. This is seen in Phase I of the Chansen site on the Chao Phraya plain, where there was a sizeable village of wet-rice agriculturists using both bronze and iron. The investigation of one of a large number of moated and walled sites on the Chi alluvium in north-eastern Thailand indicates that these were probably occupied by iron-using rice farmers shortly before 500 B.C. Finally, sites of the Go Mun culture on the Red River delta dating from before 1000 B.C. indicate that a similar phenomenon was taking place there. The overall picture is one of movement to, and agricultural intensification on, the alluvial plains, and the growth of large villages and, later, towns. The growth of population, incipient urbanization, the control of water resources and the spread of water-borne trade all combined to produce a situation ripe for the introduction of Indian religio-political concepts at the beginning of the Christian era. The evidence suggests that the south-east Asians themselves took an active part in acquiring a number of cultural traits from India that enabled them to produce their own civilizations in the first few centuries A.D.

Thus, according to the archaeological evidence, the flowering of civilization in Thailand was neither early nor rapid. By 1000 B.C. the region was already well-populated and technologically advanced; as late as A.D. 500 there had been little change. Although small towns, minor kings and degree of literacy (in foreign languages) existed here and there, the average Thailand people of the 6th century still lived much as had their ancestors lived a thousand years before.

14

Ethnoarchaeological Survey on Ceramic Production

Valentine Roux

One of the objectives of ethnoarchaeology is to test the validity of some of our archaeological interpretations with the help of ethnographic surveys.

In this case, we focused on the quantitative evaluations of protohistoric ceramic productions and on the relevance of observation data upon which the evaluations are founded. With this as our framework, at the time the Indo-French Archaeological Mission was surveying in Haryana, we considered the possibility of calculating a rate of ceramic productin based on those observation data usually accepted in archaeology.

In archaeology, the following four criteria are used to evaluate ceramic production:

(1) The number of kilns; this being generally associated with a fixed number of yearly firings;

(2) the volume of ceramic residues, directly correlated with the rate of production;

(3) density of sherds per square metre which is supposed to vary with respect to the production rate; and

(4) the surface area of the craft activity area. This area is defined as that surface occupied by ceramic residues (pottery wastes and ceramic slags), kilns (firing ditches, constructed kilns), tools (turn-wheel, polishers, etc...) and all associated fittings. The surface area of the craft activity area is supposed to vary in relation to production intensity.

Criterion no. 1 is not relevant to our study considering the numerous ethnographic counter examples. Particular mention is made of the case of the Haryana potters for whom the yearly number of firings ranges from 2 to 12 and for whom the number of firing ditches does not necessarily corresponded to the number of working craftsmen.

CHAPRT 1: NUMBER OF DITCHES, POTTERS AND YEARLY FIRINGS IN 7 VILLAGES IN HARYANA

Village	No. of ditches	No. of potters	No. of firings per year and per potter
Devan	2	2	2-5
Kaimri	7	15	6-12
Bhagana	5	3	4-5
Umra	5	4	4-6
Tosham	5	4	10
Jamalpur	3	2	2-6
Mudhal Khurd	6	12	2-8

Criteria no. 2 and no. 3 are just as difficult to accept. After having studied the relationship between the volume of ceramic residues and the rate of production in some fifteen firing diches, it was found that the volume and the density of the ceramic residues do not vary only with respect to the rate of production but also according to the following factors:

(1) The rate of breakage during firing this ranges from 5% to 25% from one village to the next (depending on dexterity of potters, location of kiln, grade of earth, etc...).

(2) Different ways of covering the kiln. The covering is made of constantly renewed earth or else from the burnt ditch earth which is thus regularly recycled. According to this volume and density of residues vary significantly.

(3) The reuse of ceramic residues as back-fill (to fill up roads, ditches, courtyards, foundation support, etc....). In this case the volume of residues observed is not related to the amount actually accrued over any number of years.

(4) Localization of refuse area. When the area is located in a depression and thus under water during the monsoon, the residues are so scattered about that the heaps are no longer visible and that the density of sherds becomes very slight.

(5) Whether refuse area is isolated or not: if it merges with the domestic refuse area, the volume and the density of ceramic residues is no longer indicative of the production rate.

These variations are shown in the chart no. 2.

when the kilns are located on the periophery of the village; in this case, we must draw up a large surface area so as to include within the same area not only the kilns which may be scattered over several dozen metres, but as well the refuse areas visible in this case. Bhagana and Tosham are cases in point. The periphery of Bhagana has three firing ditches each located a few dozen metres from another. The refuse areas are found in the immediate vicinity. According to archaeological criteria the craft activity area has an area of 1248 m^2. On the other hand, at Tosham, the firing ditches are inside the living quarter courtyards and the residues were used as back-fill in various places in the villages. If we add together

CHART 2: COMPARISON OF VOLUME RESIDUES FROM 7 FIRING DITCHES AND THE CORRESPONDING RATE OF PRODUCTION

Village		Residues Area (m^2)	Residues Vol. (m^3)	Production Pots (1-201)	Breakage %	Breakage nb	Age of Ditch (year)	Firings per year	No. of Pots per ditch (151)
Umra	1	12.60	13.86	12.000	20%	2400	3	6	400-600
	2	72	72	9.000	13%	1287	6	4	300-400
	3	42	50.40	19.000	23%	4370	10	4-5	200-350
	4	36.50	40.15	67.250	25%	16812	10	5	500-1000
Bhagana	5	37.68	5	148.500	20%	29700	45	3-4	400-500
	6	74.58	34.80	45.000	15%	6750	15	5	400-500
	7	45.30	19.63	40.000	25%	10000	15	4	500-600

And now to the last criterion, surface area of the craft activity area. This has no cognitive value for reasons given earlier in this discussion, namely that the surface area and volume of residues are not exclusively dependent upon the rate of production. Moreover, study of numerous potters' areas clearly shows that the surface area of the craft activity areas as previously defined varies basically according to the actual location of the kilns and their layout.

When the craft activity areas are inside the village, the area is restricted, limited to living quarter courtyards with no possible extension beyond. In these courtyards kilns and residues are found reused as a covering at firing time. The craft activity area does not include the residues areas spread about in and outside the village and which cannot be localized especially where sherds were used as back-fill. Conversely, the surface area of the craft activity area is much greater

the areas of the 3 courtyards with a ditch, the craft activity area has an area of only 327 m^2. Now, the Tosham potters, with an annual average of 10 firings, produce exactly twice as much as their counterparts in Bhagana.

Conclusion

In conclusion, it emerges from our ethnoarchaeological study that the material data relevant on archaeological sites judged for evaluating ceramic production have no cognitive value due to their multifarious nature. It is only by comparing production from site to site in the same region or production from one period to another on the same site that evaluation becomes possible. Using such an approach, the evaluation would be rough but logically sound and thus more acceptable than evaluation based on the four criteria given at the beginning of this paper.

15

The Pre-industrial Mines of India

Dilip K. Chakrabarti

I. Introduction

The purpose of this paper is to argue that India offers a tremendous scope for investigations in the history and methods of pre-industrial mining and that whatever has been understood about this deserves proper attention. Three facts clearly stand out. First, India has had a long history of metallurgy. By the time of the Indus civilization whose mature phase possibly began around 2800 B.C. (Chakrabarti 1978, 1982) the knowledge of copper, tin, gold, silver and lead was securely established, and the tradition continued right through the subsequent phases of the Indian protohistoric and historic sequence. Iron appeared sometime in the second half of the second millennium B.C. The antiquity of the use of zinc goes back to the late centuries B.C. or the early centuries A.D. (Neogi 1979: 41). The point to note is that these metals occurred adequately in the subcontinent itself. Secondly, there are extensive belts carrying remains of preindustrial mining of different metals in various parts of India. Their dates are meagre, and if the nineteenth century reports are any indication, the preindustrial mining operations continued in several parts of the country till the middle of that century. The long history of the use of metals in India suggests that a good number of these mines have possibly a history going back to the protohistoric and early historic periods. Thirdly, as far as the history of Indian mining is concerned, there is hardly any detailed literary source. The only worthwhile ancient literary reference is found in the *Arthasastra* of Kautilya (c. third century B.C.) but even this does not provide much information beyond the fact that mining during this period was conducted by the state which attached great significance to it as a "source of treasury" (Chakrabarti n.d.). It is not possible to attempt in the Indian context what Healy (1978) has done for mining in the Graeco-Roman context on the basis of textual data. The reconstruction of the history of Indian mining, a thoroughly neglected field among the Indian archaeologists and historians till now, can be done only through an intensive documentation and study of the surviving mining remains and the determination of their dates both by radiocarbon method and the associated archaeological samples. The traces of pre-industrial mining operations, in fact, constitute the only clue to the history of Indian mining. The nature and distribution of these traces associated with various metals, some direct references to them in the nineteenth century records and the limited number of dates available for them will have to be, in the present state of research, the core theme of this paper.

II. The remains of preindustrial mines

1. *Copper*

In the context of archaeology the following copper-mining areas deserve more attention than the rest : Rajasthan, Bihar, Andhra, Madhya Pradesh and the Garhwal-Kumayun belt of Uttar Pradesh.

In Rajasthan the copper-mining areas are mostly along the eastern flank of the Aravallis, extending from Bharatpur, Alwar and Khetri regions in the northeast to the south of Udaipur in the southwest reaching as far as Amba Mata on the border of Rajasthan and Gujarat. The old working localities which have been reported from Bharatpur are Nithahar (26°58' : 77°06'), Basawar (27°02' : 70°07'), Hathori (27° : 77°10'), Khankhera (26°58' : 77°06'), and Khareri (26°11' : 77°56'). A more than 3m deep pit has been reported at Khankhera and old slag heaps are said to occur at Khareri. The possible significance of the preindustrial working of copper ore in the Bharatpur region (Roy 1958 : 124-125) has been highlighted by the recent discovery of 16 harpoons, 7 celts, 2 chisels, 7 swords and 1 hooked rod, all typical Gangetic valley "copper hoard" specimens (c. first quarter of the second millennium B.C.) at Mallah in the Ghana sanctuary near Bharatpur.

In the Alwar zone the most impressive occurrence of old mines may be seen at Khoh Dariba (27°10' : 76°27') in the form of vertical shafts which definitely go up to 60m in depth. At one point the circular mouths of these shafts extend intermittently for about 1 km. Fragments of timber have been found embedded in the rock debris of old shafts (information from N.K. Kherada, mining engineer, Hindusthan Copper Corporation, Khoh Dariba). Another important locality in this zone is Pratapgarh (27°15' : 76°13'). The strike-length is about 10-12 km and falls into two blocks—Madhupura block (northern) and Nagel block (southern). There are 200-300 close-spaced vertical shafts, some going up to 90 m in depth, in this locality (information from Utpal Bose, Geological Survey of India, Jaipur). There are also other comparatively minor old working localities in the Alwar zone (Roy 1958 : 121-124) but perhaps nowhere is the scale of old mining operations in this area more clear than at the modern town of Bairat which is located on the top of an old and huge copper slag heap. Bairat was an early historic city going back to the third century B.C. and later well-known for its Mughal mint. That the Alwar zone was an important copper-mining area in the third century B.C. need not be doubted. Its potential as a prehistoric source of copper will need further study.

The Khetri belt is the most well-known copper-bearing belt in Rajasthan and equally well-known for its old workings. The detailed mapping of the distribution of old workings in this singularly important area still remains to be done, and all that one can do here is to emphasize the scale of preindustrial operations. In Khetri (28° : 75°51') "old workings are found near the top of a ridge, some 500 feet above the surrounding plain country. There is an underground gallery known to be more than two miles long, following the strike of the formations. Some deep shafts connect with the underground gallery" (Roy 1958 : 126). At Babai (27°53' : 75°49') in the same area "the workings are quite irregular, commencing as narrow inclines, widening out into large chambers, contracting to narrow burrows, and ramifying as the ore led the miners, but their general direction is with the dip of the slates at an angle of 30° to 60°" (Heron 1917, cited in Roy 1958 : 128). Perhaps the most impressive remains can be seen at what is called the Madhan mine in Khetri. The entrance to the upper part of the mine is on the top of a hill where the subsidence of 100 feet in depth over an area of 200 feet by 300 feet has exposed an old stope which can be reached by a 50 feet by 20 feet opening. The opening was rendered safe by the preindustrial miners by means of stone pillars. The depth of this mine was more than 100 m and ventilation shafts can be observed at various points on the hill slope. The scale of mining operations in this area is also exemplified by the huge slag deposits looking like hillocks at Singhana (28°06' : 75°54') and also by the innumerable smaller slag heaps on the bank of a local river, Kharkera. Singhana was the most important smelting place of the area. It has been estimated from the Singhana heaps that 5-6 million tonnes of ore were exploited by the pre-industrial smelters of Khetri (information from A.L. Soni, geologist, Hindusthan Copper Corporation, Khetri).

A little away from Khetri but still within the general belt is the old mining area of Baleshwar near Nim-ka-Thana. In the hills overlooking the valley there must be more than 100 old workings both in the form of vertical shafts and open trenches dug into the hillside. The whole area is littered with slag.

The importance of the Khetri copper belt as a probable source of Harappan copper is generally accepted and has recently been given an added support by the discovery of the evidence of copper-smelting at the contemporary sites in the Cholistan area of Bahwalpur (Mughal 1980). Besides, one notes the wide occurrence of mature Harappan and early Harappan sites in northeast Rajasthan itself and the neighbouring Haryana and east Panjab. Another dimension has been added to the significance of this copper belt by the discovery of a large number of copper artificats (more than 1000 in number, including arrowheads, rings, bangles, spearheads, chisels, balls, celts, etc.) at the site of Ganeshwar which is located very close to the Baleshwar valley. This site falls squarely in the middle of the third millennium B.C. (Agrawala and Kumar 1982). Another point of interest in this context is the wide occurrence of old workings in the Mahendragarh-Narnul area of Haryana, which is not far from Khetri and must be visualized as a part of the Khetri belt. That this area is rich in copper artifacts is understood from the mere fact of frequent appearance of "copper hoards" in the local market for their metallic value (information from R.C. Agrawala, formerly Director of Archaeology and Museums, Rajasthan). In the same context the apparently minor old workings reported in Bikaner (Roy 1958 : 125) assume great significance because they are closer to the Harappan area. The localities are : Bhadasar (28°18': 74°22'), Dariba (27°39': 74°22') and Biramsar (28°02' : 74°47').

Although old copper workings have been reported from the Ajmer area of central Rajasthan, the next important focus of their occurrence is in southeast Rajasthan. Archaeologically the earliest occurrence of copper in this region is at Bagor, phase II, dated in the early part of the third millennium B.C. and that the copper metallurgy was well-developed in the second half of the third millennium B.C. is evidenced at the site of Ahar near Udaipur. There are many minor workings near Udaipur itself, which the Ahar smelters could have exploited. As far as Bagor is concerned, there is an important copper source at Kotri Dariba, 22 km east of Bagor. Besides, in the same region there is the Rajpur-Dariba mining complex which is now known primarily for its lead-zinc ores but was used earlier for copper as well. The hillsides of Rajpur-Dariba are extensively pock-marked by old shafts, scoops, etc.

In the Chhotanagpur plateau section of Bihar and adjacent West Bengal and Orissa copper ores have a wide dissemination but the most significant occurrence lies in the Singhbhum-Hazaribagh belt. Old workings abound, but the following localities deserve special mention—Baragunda (24°4′ : 86°7′) in Hazaribagh and Rakha (22°38′ : 86°27′)—Mushabani (22°31′ : 86°28′) localities in Singhbhum. Baragunda (Ball 1880 : 254) is the site of 48 ancient copper mines which extend all along the outcrop and average 25-30 yards in width along the main line. The major smelting area seems to have been Giridih, about 3 km away, where large mounds of slag covering several acres of ground may be observed. The richness of the old workings in and around the Rakha mines will be apparent from the fact that between the Rakha mines and Roam, an area of several acres was found to contain slag to a depth of 6 feet and that slag from this place was used in the concrete for King George's Dock in Calcutta port in 1926-28. The surface of both the main lodes at Mushabani (the Main Lode and the Western Lode) is marked by old workings and "these old workings at Mushabani are among the largest within the copper belt, and are continuous throughout the length of the lodes" (Dunn 1937 : 101). The following observation of Dunn on the old copper miners of Singhbhum is worth quoting:

> "The skill of these ancients is indicated in the manner of their mining. Down to the depth at which they ceased working, usually water level, they have left no workable copper except in the pillars for holding up the walls; they have picked the country as clean as the desert vulture picks a carcass. Looking over some of these old workings it is often remarked that "they must have worked over it with tooth picks". Even their spoil heaps provide no abundant specimens of copper" (Dunn 1937 : 54).

Copper-using cultures in the adjacent areas of Bihar and Bengal go back at least to the middle of the second millennium B.C. and there is no doubt that the Chhotanagpur plateau was through the ages the source of copper in eastern India. Early historic coins have been found in the copper-working belt, and more significantly, there is a report of the second millennium B.C. pottery of eastern India near the Rakha mines (personal information from F.R. Allchin, based on his study of D.H. Gordon collection). In this contest it must also be noted that old copper workings occur in the Chhotanagpur plateau even outside the Singhbhum-Hazaribagh belt and some of them are found well outside the known copper-bearing. For instance, in the West Bengal district of Bankura there are remains of at least two old copper mines—one at Chhedapathar where one notes old shafts for about 1 km and the other at Tamkun where the remains of an open shaft into the side of a hill are clearly visible.

In Andhra attention should be paid to at least four districts : Kurnul, Bellary, Nellore and Guntur, all of which have been found to contain many old workings. Copper mines, hundred feet deep and several hundred feet long, have been reported from Nellore (Ball 1980 : 242). In Guntur, for instance, the ancient copper mining activity

> "is revealed mostly by old workings of the nature of long, open trenches following the lodes in the direction of the strike. Some of these workings, which are accessible today, have reached a depth of 100 feet or more from the surface in the direction of the dip of the lode" (Ziauddin 1961 : 119).

There are second millennium B.C. copper-using cultures in Andhra and the possible significance of these old workings is easy to see.

Archaeologically we would like to put some emphasis on the occurrence of copper and related old workings in the Balaghat area of Madhya Pradesh and the Kumayun-Garhwal belt of Uttar Pradesh. The significance of the Balaghat source will be obvious from the fact that Gungeria in this region as many as 424 copper implements weighing about 826 pounds came to be reported in 1870 (Neogi 1979 : 12). The traces of old copper mines are apparently abundant in the Kumayun-Garhwal belt (Ball 1880 : 267), and considering that this belt is located just to the north of the Gangetic plain, their possible significance to the protohistoric copper-using cultures of the upper Gangetic valley cannot be overlooked. Moreover, the recent discovery of protohistoric and early historic sites in this region is a pointer in this direction.

2. *Tin*

Contrary to the general impression, tin suitable for preindustrial smelting and use does occur in India, notably in the Chhotanagpur plateau section in Bihar and the Bastar area of Madhya Pradesh. The Bastar deposit is extensive enough to be exploited commercially at present and an earlier report suggests its preindustrial use as well. The Chhotanagpur deposits are not commercially viable now but a nineteenth century report on Hazaribagh describes preindustrial tin smelting leading to the preparation of ingots in moulds and another report from the same area refers to preindustrial tin mining. Trenches and pits have also been observed along the length of a cassiterite occurrence in Ranchi district (for the details, Chakrabarti 1979). That the Chhotanagpur tin resource was being opened up at least in the beginning of the first millennium B.C. has recently been demonstrated by the find of 10% tin in a copper ring found in the protohistoric level of Bahiri in Birbhum district, West Bengal (information from P.K. Chattopadhyay, Durgapur Alloy Steels). The possible archaeological significance of the Bastar tin deposit has not been worked out yet.

3. *Lead*

Lead in India occurs primarily in the Chhotanagpur plateau, Andhra, Rajasthan, Madhya Pradesh and the Himalayan belt of Panjab and Uttar Pradesh. Archaeologically its antiquity is well-attested right from before the Indus civilization. It was used widely in the early historic period for coinage and ornaments (for the details, Nanda 1981). Here attention will be drawn to only two lead-mining areas, one in Andhra and another in Rajasthan. In Andhra the most significant evidence comes from the Varikunta (15°03′ : 78°52′)—Zangamrajupalle (16°46′ : 78°53′) belt which lies along the eastern flank of the south-central part of the Nallamalai range. Ancient workings have been reported at Gadageribodu, Varikunta and Zangamrajupalle. The main ancient workings at Gadageribodu are mainly quarries of 10-20m width and a few metres deep extending for about 150-250m strike length. At Varikunta the most important group of ancient workings is found in the Gavulabhavi area. These workings extend for a strike length of 1200 m.

"The ancient workings consist of linear pits and trenches, shafts and inclines developed laterally underground in the form of drifts and slopes dipping at steep angles to the east in the eastern part and to the west in the western part. One of the surface diggings extends for about 280m along the strike. The main underground mine had been developed for a length of over 100m, the initial 30 m being a partly stopped drive, followed by two parallel drives interspersed with stops and connected by cross-cuts at regular intervals. The deepest accessible stop in this mine is approximately 90m below the surface" (Rao and Rao 1977 : 88).

In view of the significance of lead in the coinage of the early historic period of this region, lead old workings such as this assume considerable significance.

What gives the Rampura-Agucha deposit in Bhilwara district, Rajasthan, is not merely its extensive mining activity going back to c. third century B.C. at least but also the location of a large archaeological site in its immediate vicinity. The lead-zinc mineralisation in Agucha (25°50′ : 74°14') village extends for about 1500 m, being 115m wide at its maximum. At several places along this belt heaps of old mine debris up to 8m in height are noted. Ancient mine workings figure on the surface as old trenches and pits, underground drifts rises, inclines and stopes in exploratory mine development and as irrigation wells which were ancient shafts. In addition, there are indications of extensive old workings obtained during drilling carried out for modern exploration of the deposit. According to Tiwari and Kavida (1984 : 85) "most of the ancient mining was continued up to 80m in depth below surface. However, in some parts the old workings extend up to 125 m depth". About 70,000 sq. m area was found covered by slag dumps and in these dumps it was possible to pick up sherds of *c.* 200 B.C. The Agucha mound which is about 1 km long goes back to the pre-Maurya (pre-300 B.C.) period, and there is no reason to doubt that the site which shows extensive occurrence of slag on the surface came in response to the mining of the local ores.

Finally, it is worthwhile to draw attention to the following observation of Ball in the context of lead : "there is probably no metal of which the ores have been formerly worked to so large an extent, excepting of course those of iron" (Ball 1880 : 281).

4. *Silver*

In its native form silver occurs rarely in India but as argentiferous galena it is known significantly from Andhra and Rajasthan where this occurs in lead or lead-zinc deposits. In Rajasthan, for instance, silver was collected in this fashion from the lead-zinc ores of Zawar, Rajpur-Dariba and Agucha. At Agucha, according to Tiwari and Kavida (1984) "silver, mostly associated with galena, assays 50 gms per tonne of ore" and the main target of the preindustrial miners was galena-rich ore-body. Among the ore minerals at Rajpur-Dariba the galena component is 2% (information from Sohanlal Sharma, Geologist, Hindusthan Zinc Limited, Rajpur-Dariba). At Zawar a sample assayed showed more than 10 ozs of silver per tonne of lead (Ball 1880 : 236). Silver occurs prominently in the Indian archaeological contexts right from the Indus civilization and was used extensively for coinage in the historic periods (for the details, Nanda 1981).

5. *Gold*

The alluvial gold has been washed and collected in various parts of India but the old mining activities for reef gold are apparently known principally in the Kolar, Hatti and Gadag regions of Karnataka in the south and partly in the Chhotanagpur plateau in the east. In the Champion Reef mine of the Kolar field the average depth of the old workings is 150 feet but the maximum depth goes up to 275 feet. In the Ooregum Mine of the same field the average depth of the old workings is 100 feet and the maximum depth noted here is 250 feet (Hatch 1901 : 18). The most important locality in the Gadag region seems to be Kabulayatkatti where the old workings reached a depth of at least 300 feet. At Hatti old workings were recorded up to the maximum depth of 640 feet (Allchin 1962: 201).

In the Chhotanagpur plateau the evidence of old workings seems to be comparatively limited. As Maclaren (1904 : 69) puts it : "In no case in Chhotanagpur. . . were deep ancient workings discovered comparable in the slightest degree with those of Mysore or even with those of the Wynaad. The deepest uncovered reached a depth of no more than 15 feet. . . "

Allchin (1962, n.d.) has pointed out that the antiquity of the southern goldfields goes back to the neolithic settlers of the region in the third millennium B.C. and that the location of a number of Mauryan epigraphs (third century B.C.) in this region underlines its importance during that period.

6. *Zinc*

Zinc appears to have been worked formerly in the Agucha lead-zinc deposit, the Rajpura-Dariba lead-zinc-copper deposit and the Zawar lead-zinc deposit of Rajasthan. Of these the Zawar deposit is the most famous, not merely for its rich mineral deposit but also for its impressively abundant traces of old workings extended all over the 25 km mining belt and apparently going down to a depth of 90m below surface (information from L.K. Gurjar, Hindusthan Zinc Limited, Zawar). We also draw attention here to the observation of Kerr-cross (1950 : 9) that the Zawar miners went to depths exceeding 500 feet. More than 1 km valley leading to the mining area at Zawar is covered by smelting debris and clay retorts for zinc smelting. The comparatively late antiquity of these remains at Zawar may be deduced from the occurrence of about 8, 13th-14th century Jaina temples in the area and also from the fact that the distillation of zinc in tubulated covered retorts occurs in some alchemical texts of the 12th and 13th centuries A.D. (Neogi 1979 : 78-79).

7. *Iron*

Iron suitable for preindustrial smelting occurs virtually all over India outside the alluvial zones and thus the issue of mining is not significant in this case (for the details, Chakrabarti 1976). However, in certain areas, notably in Madhya Pradesh, open cast mining for iron has been recorded in the nineteenth century (Ball 1880) but there is no reason to assume that the tradition has a high antiquity.

III. The issue of dates

Attention has been paid in the preceding section to the possible archaeological association of different preindustrial mining areas. The total number of C-14 dates available for the old mines is about 15 (Agrawal and Kusumgar 1975, Agrawal and Margabandhu 1975-76, Agrawal, Margabandhu and Sekhar 1976, Agrawal, Krishnamurthy, Kusumgar and Pant 1978). The earliest available date for the south Indian gold working is 760± 150 B.C. (PRL-253) whereas the earliest date from presumably copper working at Rajpura Dariba in Rajasthan is 1260 ± 160 B.C. (PRL-208b). The Amba Mata copper working in Gujarat yields a date of 160 ± 200 B.C. (PRL-53). Most of the other dates, almost exclusively from Rajasthan and Karnataka, are mediaeval. The available dates are not at all representative of the different areas and the probable phases associated with them. All the samples came from random collections.

IV. The nineteenth century records

While the relevant geological literature refers to preindustrial mines in many cases it is not generally helpful for a specific insight into the modes of preindustrial mining. From this point of view Dixon's account of lead-mining near Ajmer in 1831 (Dixon 1831), an anonymous author's account of the Singhana copper mines near Khetri in the same year (Anonymous 1831) and Brooke's description of the Khetri mines in 1864 are invaluable. Brief records of this kind exist in other contexts as well (cf. Ball 1880) but none is as important as the three publications mentioned above.

Dixon's lead-mines were in the hills near Ajmer. Their openings were at the height of 100 to 350 feet from the level of the plain, spread along for about 300 yards. After the colouring of the rocks showed presence of, or proximity to, the ore, a performation was made in the rocks, sometimes unsuccessfully. The basic task was to follow a vein and when a number of veins showed up the major one was followed leaving the minor ones for the future. The opening was not expanded more than what was necessary for a man to move on his hands. There was no system to remove underground water and the miners generally removed themselves to the upper ground once water was encountered. Particularly hard stretches of rock were calcined by fire. This was usually done at the end of the working day so that the miners could begin work at the spot next morning. The mining implements consisted of two or three hammers of different weights, a few chisels or wedges edged with steel and some one-armed picks. The miners used to enter the mines about sunrise, divesting themselves of "every attire of clothing" and carrying a small lamp in their hands. The ore was crushed before being put in bamboo baskets which were then transported to the mouth of the mine in the following manner:

> "As the gallery is not sufficiently high to allow of the workmen standing upright, they sit on their haunches, arranged in a row, from 4 to 12, according to the capacity of the mine, and pass the baskets from one to another. When the whole has reached the foremost man, they move upwards, and again range themselves. This is continued until the mouth of the mine is attained." (Dixon 183$_1$)

The disputes regarding the ownership of a vein were settled by the miners' council by erecting a wall of loose stones at the points of contact. This meeting of channels also helped ventilation for which no special provision was made otherwise. According to Dixon the lead-miners of Ajmer did not spend more than 3 to 4 hours a day in the mines and looked "very healthy".

The anonymous recorder of the Singhana copper mines near Khetri saw numerous openings giving access to galleries, honeycombing the hills in every direction and extending, according to a local tradition for a length of 2 miles. The shafts, usually a rude oval of 5 by 4 feet or 4 by 3 feet with their sides notched in such a way as to obviate the necessity of ladder, descended to a sufficient depth before galleries were driven out in various directions. The resistant rocks were split by large wood-fires which were left to burn for about 3 days. As equipment every miner had a lamp placed upon his head, a small wicker basket, a hammer and a mining chisel. The mining season lasted from October to the setting in of the rains. The rain water was baled out at the commencement of the ensuing season. The day's proceeds were collected in a public place and put up on auction to the proprietors of furnaces. According to this report the miners died early, generally between the age of 35 and 40.

Brooke's report on Khetri (Brooke 1864) is more detailed. It is related to the Kolihan mine whose entrance was about 300 feet above the level of the plain and which descended at an angle of 60°. Sometimes for about 10 to 20 yards it was only just sufficient "to admit the recumbent body of a man", but occasionally it widened into "considerable chambers", according to the richness of the rock that had been removed. The way of baling out water was to arrange a chain of human beings passing pitchers to the mouth of the mine. The mines were owned by the miners themselves and managed by the miners' council. Each year, after the rains, various branches of the mine were auctioned by the general council with the miners acting as the bidders. Labour on daily wage was also employed by the individual owners of the mining right. The collected ore at the end of the day (180-250 pounds per mine, in wicker baskets weighing 6 pounds each) was put up on auction to the furnace-owners.

There is not a single old mine in India, which has been scientifically investigated in detail. In this situation the records such as the ones mentioned above constitute almost the sole evidence of the preindustrial mining procedures in the country, which possibly remained unchanged through the ages.

Acknowledgement

I am deeply indebted to Dr. J.C. Shaffer who made possible a joint study of some of the old mining areas of Rajasthan in December, 1982.

REFERENCES

Agrawal, D.P. and Kusumgar, S. 1975. Tata Institute Radiocarbon Date List-XI. *Radiocarbon* 17: 219-225.

Agrawal, D.P. and Margabandhu, C. 1975-76. Ancient gold workings: Some new C-14 dates. *Puratattva.* 7: 139-140.

Agrawal, D.P., Margabandhu, C. and Sekhar, N.V. 1976. Ancient copper workings: some new C-14 dates. *Indian Journal of History of Science.* 11: 133-136.

Agrawal, D.P., Krishnamurthy, R.V., Kusumgar, S. and Pant, R.K. 1978. Physical Research Laboratory radiocarbon dates. *Current Science* 47: 607-610.

Agrawal, R.C. and Kumar, V. 1982. Ganeshwar-Jodhpura culture: new traits in Indian archaeology. In *Harappan Civilization* (ed. G.L. Possehl). Delhi: Oxford & IBH Publishing Co., pp. 125-134.

Allchin, F.R. 1962. Upon the methods and antiquity of gold-mining in ancient India. *Journal of the Economic and Social History of the Orient.* 5: 195-211.

Allchin, F.R. n.d. Antiquity of gold mining in the Gadag region—Karnataka. In *Madhu: Recent Researches in Indian Archaeology and Art History* (ed. M.S.N. Rao). Delhi : Agam Kala Prakashan, pp. 81-83.

Anonymous. 1831. On the copper works at Singhana near Khetri in the Sekhawati country. *Gleanings in Science.* 3: 380-384.

Ball, V. 1880. *A Manual of the Geology of India, Part III. The Economic Geology.* Calcutta: Geological Survey of India.

Brooke, J.C. 1864. The mines of Khetri in Rajpootana. *Journal of the Asiatic Society of Bengal.* 33: 519-429.

Chakrabarti, Dilip K. 1976. The beginning of iron in India. *Antiquity.* 50: 114-124.

Chakrabarti, Dilip K. 1978. The Nippur Indus seal and Indus chronology. *Man & Environment.* 2: 90-91.

Chakrabarti, Dilip K. 1979. The problem of tin in early India—a preliminary survey. *Man & Environment.* 3: 61-74.

Chakrabarti, Dilip K. 1982. "Long barrel-cylinder" beads and the issue of pre-Sargonic contact between the Harappan civilization and Mesopotamia. In *Harappan Civilization* (ed. G.L. Possehl). Delhi : Oxford and IBH Publishing Co., pp. 265-270.

Chakrabarti, Dilip K. n.d. Mining in ancient and mediaeval India. In *The Cultural Heritage of India,* vol. 5. Calcutta: Ramakrishna Mission Institute of Culture (forthcoming).

Dixon, C.G. 1831. Some account of the lead mines of Ajmir. *Gleanings in Science.* 3: 111-115.

Dunn, J.A. 1937. The mineral deposits of eastern Singhbhum and surrounding areas. *Memoir of the Geological Survey of India,* 69 (part 1): Geological Survey of India.

Hatch, F.H. 1901. The Kolar gold-field, being a description of quartz-mining and gold-recovery as practised in India. *Memoir of the Geological Survey of India,* 33 (part 1): Geological Survey of India.

Healy, J.F. 1978. *Mining and Metallurgy in the Greek and Roman World.* London : Thames and Hudson.

Heron, A.M. 1917. The geology of northeastern Rajputana and adjacent district. *Memoir of the Geological Survey of India,* 45 (part 1): Geological Survey of India.

Ker-cross, D. 1950. Ancient mines and miners of India. *Indian Minerals.* 4: 5-10.

Maclaren, J.M. 1904. Auriferous occurrences in Chhota Nagpur, Bengal. *Records of the Geological Survey of India,* 31 (part 2): Geological Survey of India.

Mughal, M.R. 1980. New archaeological evidence from Bahawalpur. *Man & Environment* 4: 93-98.

Nanda, Rajni. 1981. *Lead and Silver in Early India: a Study of the Geological, Archaeological and Literary data.* M. Phil thesis: Delhi University.

Neogi, P. 1979 (reprint). *Copper in Ancient India.* Delhi : Janaki Prakashan.

Rao, B.B. and Rao, K.S. 1977. Lead deposits in Varikunta-Zangamrajupalle belt, Cuddapah district, Andhra Pradesh. In *Miscellaneous Publications, Geological Survey of India.* 27: 87-94.

Roy, B.C. 1958. Economic geology and mineral resources of Rajasthan. *Memoir of the Geological Survey of India,* 86 (part 1); Geological Survey of India.

Ziauddin, M. 1961. Ancient copper mining and metallurgy near Agnigundala. *Indian Minerals.* 15: 117-120.

16

Some Fresh Evidence from Sanghol Excavations, 1986

C. Margabandhu and G.S. Gaur

Excavations of a limited nature had been carried out at Sanghol for nearly a decade, albeit intermittently, revealing limited results.[1] However some new evidence of the Chalcolithic character of the settlement,[2] further highlighted the significance for carrying out large scale excavations here. The recent discoveries of the sculptures, pillars, cross-bars etc. from the stupa site also added knowledge of the religious edifices during the Kushana period[3]. All these required further excavations on a large scale to understand the settlement, its origins and growth. To achieve the above end excavations were resumed in this year to lay bare horizontally for understanding the planning of the township as also to add information pertaining to the material culture right from the early occupation of the site.

Sanghol (30°47′ N and 76°23′E), locally called Ucha Pinda, is situated 40 km west of Chandigarh on the Chandigarh-Ludhiana road in Tehsil Samrala, District Ludhiana, Punjab. The place is also approachable from Sirhind Railway Station, situated at a distance of 16 km from Sanghol.

The presence of dried up old channels at places would lead to believe that Sutlej, which at present flows about 10 kms away, was running nearby Sanghol and has shifted its course now.

Despite an early history of its discovery in the forties, an organised archaeological probing was undertaken only in 1968 by Shri R.S. Bisht, then in the Department of Archaeology and Museums, Govt. of Punjab. The work was continued further by Shri G.B. Sharma and his team of the same department. The Excavations Branch of the Archaeological Survey, New Delhi, joined this year with specific objectives detailed above. Although several Kushana sites have been excavated, yet the data pertaining to structures are limited to scattered evidences, particularly as those revealed from excavations at Mathura[4]. Apart from this, Kushana culture in totality including socio-economic aspects etc. is yet to emerge and here was an attempt to achieve this by horizontally exposing the Hathiwara mound which is the fortified citadel of the Kushanas. The information pertaining to the Kushana town planning, divergent building activities etc. was also to be gathered. Further problems of the overlap between the Bara and Painted Grey Ware (PGW) cultures and subsequently the Black Slipped ware strata prior to the Kushana remains, were also to be properly understood by digging systematically.

The site consists of an artificial mound with habitational deposit of about 18 m thick average with several separately demarcated, though adjacent, localities- which were inhabited at different periods of time. For example, during the Kushana rule, the ancient city of Sanghol was divisible into two part —fortified citadel and the open township—both closely situated. Even the surface indications suggested the separate entity of the Kushana citadel, locally called Hathiwara, which stood apart from the main town. Likewise, the area near the modern hospital on the south-eastern side of the mound was inhabited during the Gupta Period. This fact was testified during the earlier digging. So is the case about the extent of the ancient Bara village which appears to confine itself on the south-western side of the present village. This apart, the stupas which have also been referred to by Hiuen Tsang were built away from the main habitation in the peripheral zone during the Kushana times. Not only the two exposed stupas, but also the still buried religious edifices, which are identifiable from the surface indications, exist on the periphery of the township. The site extends over an area of 7,50,000 sq. m.

Protohistoric Sanghol takes it birth during the Bara Period which is characterized by six structural phases represented by piśe and mud brick walls and typical antiquities like terracotta bulls and balls, faience bangles

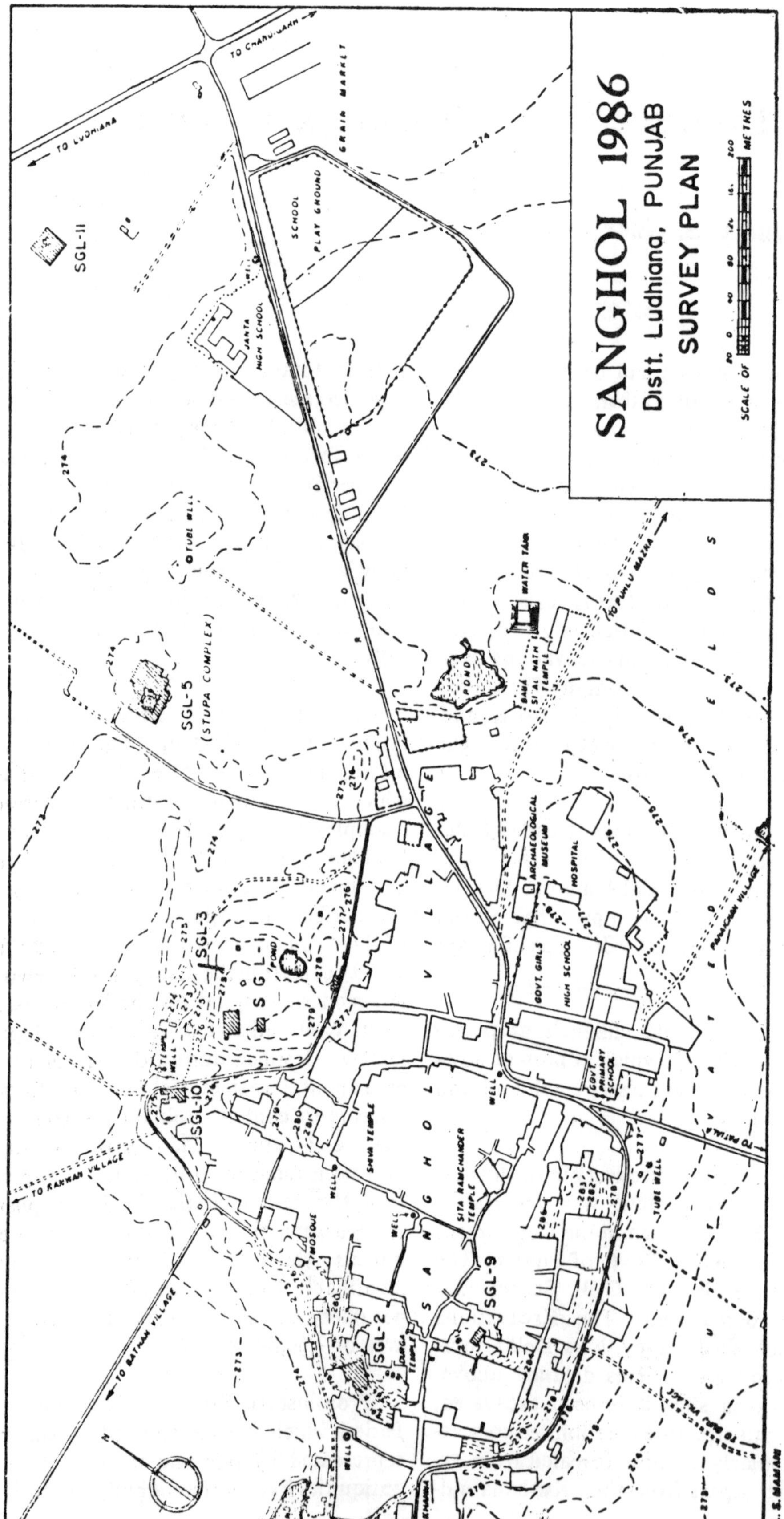
SANGHOL 1986
Distt. Ludhiana, PUNJAB
SURVEY PLAN
SGL-11
SGL-5
(STUPA COMPLEX)
SGL-3
SGL-1
SGL-10
SGL-2
SGL-9
SCHOOL
PLAY GROUND
GRAIN MARKET
JANTA HIGH SCHOOL
WATER TANK
POND
ARCHAEOLOGICAL MUSEUM
HOSPITAL
GOVT. GIRLS HIGH SCHOOL
GOVT. PRIMARY SCHOOL
SHIVA TEMPLE
SITA RAMCHANDER TEMPLE
MOSQUE
DURGA TEMPLE
SANGHOL VILLAGE
TO LUDHIANA
TO RAKHAN VILLAGE
TO BATHAN VILLAGE
TO KHANNA
TO PATIALA
TUBE WELL
WELL
N

FIG. 1

and beads, triangular and round terracotta cakes, the faience objects being found in profusion.[5] Curiously enough, only two structural phases were met with during the present excavation at SGL-10, an area contiguous to the Hathiwara mound, wherefrom the existence of Bara culture was not reported earlier.

The Bara culture at Sanghol is so rich and dominating that it had merged itself with both the succeeding cultures of the PGW and Black Slipped ware. The total thickness of the Bara deposits at Sanghol are more than 4 m Possibly this is the only settlement in this region of Punjab and Haryana characterized by the rich and thick cultural milieu of the Barans, thereby suggesting an early origin. Closer examination of the culture components of both the succeeding cultures relveals that the subuded Bara ethos was present in them. As the evidence goes, Sanghol was probably the nucleus of the Bara culture.

Generally speaking, the Bara pottery is distributed mainly in the Sutlej and Ghaggar basins. From this area it has possibly spread on to the Saraswati and Drishadvati in Haryana and subsequently to the Ganga-Yamuna Doab in the western Uttar Pradesh. This postulation is made considering the total cultural milieu with all its ramifications.

It has been stated earlier that undecorated pottery are found less in comparison to incised and painted ware at Sanghol.[6] This year's excavations has added more information regarding undecorated ware which is also found in good quantities.

On the present showing, the Bara culture is, to a certain extent, contemporaneous with the Indus civilization and continued to survive later. The likelihood that the Bara culture possibly owes its origin to the pre-Harappa culture as some of the painted motifs are exactly common to both. But the Bara culture had remained throughout a village culture with rural bias. The marginal contacts with the Bara and Harappa cultures are evident particularly in some common shapes like dish-on-stand, basin with flaring sides, large storage jars with bulging to bluntly carinated profile, etc. Further details are yet to be studied.

Sanghol was an important city and trade centre in the Kushana period at least from the first century A.D. to the third century A.D. The Chinese traveller Hieun Tsang's description of this place touches some aspects of the town, but the personality of Sanghol does not emerge from this.

Surface indications, topography, townscape and archaeological probings at various localities have enabled us to understand the settlement pattern of the town (Fig. 1.). The Kushana remains revealed by excavations consist of the following :

1. Citadel
2. The township
3. Fortifications
4. Adjacent peripheral area around the town with religious edifices.

The ancient mound of Sanghol measures 1000 m east-west and 750 m north-south representing a length-breadth ratio of 4:3 for regular habitation. The citadel and the township are situated respectively on the northern and southern sides. While the citadel area was inhabited mainly during the Kushana rule, the township was built on the habitational deposits of earlier times and is, therefore, on a higher level than the citadel. The citadel is rectangular in shape, and the lower town is elliptical. The palace-complex within the citadel area appears to be square on plan. So far as the fortifications are concerned, only the citadel area seems to have been fortified by raising a high mud wall, sometimes mixed with brick bats, etc. with an average width of 4 m. The fortified Kushana citadel measuring 340 m east-west and 210 m north-south encloses, on the western side, mainly a palace-complex measures 150 m square: excavations has already confrmed the existence of a palatial structure as the partially exposed two parallel walls indicate.

The non-habitational peripheral area roughly stretching 640 m from the main township was used mostly for religious estabishments, viz. stupas, residential monasteries and other buildings. On the present showing, a main stupa (wherefrom famous Sanghol Kushana sculptures have been found) and another stupa of smaller dimensions, though built on the same plan excavated this year, besides many votive stupas have already been exposed here. Needless to say, monastic complexes at both these places have also come to light. This apart, the peripheral area was subjected to extensive exploration, study of surface indications and plotting of various archaeological findings which collectively speak about the possible existence of some more stupas and monasteries, etc. This might also conform to the description of Hieun Tsang who had referred to the presence of twelve such stupas at Sanghol. This area was never regularly inhabited and that is the reason why pottery and antiquities from the stupa sites are much less.

A review of the above features of the settlement and distributional pattern in this Kushana town is perhaps suggestive of the well-differentiated social stratification caused by various levels of economic standard, Though this could be visualising too far, but still one could glean, at least superficially some sort of a society based on class distinctions. To quote an instance from Sanghol the nature of residential building in both citadel and the township are at variance. While in the citadel, where possibly the elite were living, the rooms are bigger and spacious, the walls are thicker and the neatly laid floors reveal variety; in the town, the houses are closely built with smaller rooms and thin walls; some of the walls of houses are built back-to-back while others leave no space in between. This seems to be the nature of the township, since similar feature of 'cluster' of houses was found in sections at many places exposed on surface. The increasing expansion of the township through building activity is also much in evidence during this period.

Despite the class distinctions in the Kushana society, the Kushana rule had benefitted the weaker sections of their subjects. This central authority over a large empire had probably encouraged free movement of people thereby bettering intercommunication which ultimately resulted in brisk trade of numerous objects from one region to the other.[7] Trade and increasd productivity gave birth to more capital followed by larger circulation of money. The Kushana rule is one of the periods in Indian history when such a vast number of coins were struck and circulated and this reached the common man, whose purchasing power was thus to a large extent improved. The Sanghol examples show that the copper coins from the houses of a common man are almost equal to that of a rich man. Such an even distribution of monetary power probably indicated some kind of pattern of like wherein, the main focus was the increase of trade and commerce supported by agricultural surplus to a certain extent. In other words this is apparently the result of substantial economic prosperity. Religious tolerance is also suggested by the fact that the figurines of gods and goddesses and other religious objects belonging to both Buddhist and Hindu pantheons have been found from the same level of occupation. The people living in the same space and time were practising the religion of their liking and leading a secular life. The Khushana society was thus secular.

As regards the town planning, the lanes and bylanes running parallel to the houses have been found. The data on this is still very limited as our area of operation was very small. Considering the thickness of the walls particularly in the citadel area, it may possibly be inferred that some of the Kushana houses were doublestoreyed in nature. We may now briefly discuss the results of the excavations undertaken.

Fourfold cultural sequence as reported earlier and given below was confirmed this year.

Period I Bara
Period II PGW
Period III Black slipped ware
Period IV Kushana and
Period V Recent times.

Period I

As already emphasized, this period was characterised by the typical Bara pottery with two exposed structural phases, represented by mud walls, both at SGL-2 and SGL-10 (I) at two different localities of the mound. Important pottery shapes included jars with collared, beaded or beaked rim or splayed mouth, large *lota*-shaped vase, squat dish-on-stand, jar with ring base, bowl-like lid with or without central knobs (Pl. 16.I). Several potsherds bearing exterior incision marking, various geometrical patterns have also been found (Pl. 16.II). The painted pottery, were however, limited in quantity. Important antiquities include terracotta bulls, and balls, faience pieces and beads.

Period II

As already elucidated above, the PGW culture does not appear to have a separate cultural horizon. The main pottery shapes included straight-sided bowls, cups and dishes with incurved sides and convex base; the associated red ware, though limited was present. Cooking was done on the simple single mouthed *chulah* with horse-shoe shape as evidenced by a *chulah* of similar description. The painted motif on the PGW included rows of dots, intersecting lines, groups of wavy lines, svastika, sigma, concentric semi-circles, spirals and vertical or oblique strokes below the rim band. Terracotta discs, balls, beads, bone points, etc. were also recovered.

Period III

This was characterised by black-slipped, burnished grey wave and associated red wares. Amongst antiquities mention may be made of bone points and beads made variously of terracotta.

Period IV

Having an average habitational thickness of about 2.6 m this period is divisible into two sub-periods. Period IVA is represented by bowls with incurved rim and dishes with flat base and vertical rim. In IVB bowls with vertically straight rim, sprinklers, vases with long vertical neck, ink-pot type lids, basins with prominently ribbed body and various kinds of jars are found. A new type of the sprinkler hitherto unknown from any excavated Kushana site is significant (Fig. 2) Thus this period was represented exclusively by a red ware industry. The use of stamped and incised decoration was remarkable. The motif included svastika, triratna leaves, flowers, tendrils, loops, circles and various other geometrical combinations.

The habitation strata showed five structural phases of which upper two were largely built of reused material and followed more or less the earlier plan. The houses were mostly made of burnt bricks of the size

33 x 21 x 7, 33 x 24 x 6, 30 x 20 x 5 and 23 x 15 x 6 cm. There is no standardization in the sizes of bricks. The two early phases were made of mud bricks. An inter-

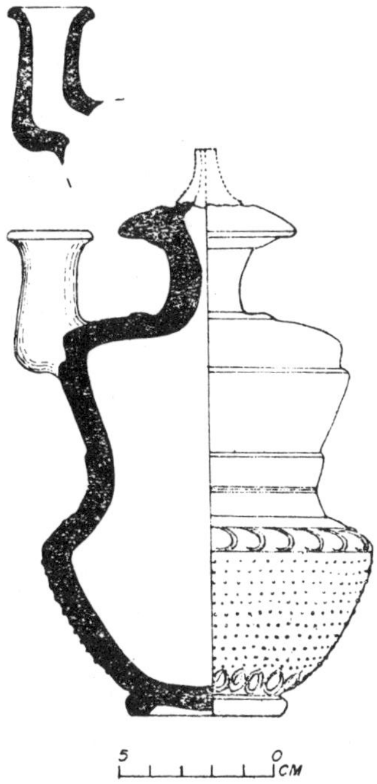

FIG. 2

mediary stage of mud and burnt bricks being used simultaneously was also noticed. As to the layout of this period, the houses were not oriented along the cardinal directions.

The largest wall, probably of a palace complex measures 14.10 m in length and 0.40 m in height with 13 courses exposed so far (Pl. 16.III). It has to be added here that a similar wall representing the outermost wall nearer to the fortification was also exposed. The latter is possibly the outer palace wall: between these massive walls are bigger halls connected by joining walls. Mention should also be made of a platform which roughly measured over 4.30 m in length, 3.25 m in width and 0.70 m in height which was completely traced. With a core of brickbats, it has a nice facing of complete bricks of which four courses are visible. The pronounced feature noticed here is the presence of robbed brick walls particularly in upper two phases; the top-most phase being completely destroyed. In front of one of the houses could be seen slopy brick-on-edge path probably for easy acccess to the house,

A noticeable feature with regard to the structures here is the closely-built houses (Pl. 16.IV) in the lower town are smaller in dimensions in comparison to those exposed at SGL-1 (citadel area).

An interesting feature noticed here is the different kinds of floors met with during the excavations in the Kushana houses. The floors are divisible into the following categories:

1. Burnt brick floor
2. Brickbat floors
3. Brick-jelly floor mixed with lime
4. Mud floor mixed with small kankars
5. Mud floors
6. Mud-clod floor
7. Cemented concrete floor made of lime, kankar and refuse, iron, etc.
8. Lime floor, and
9. Mud brick floor.

Several hearths of various sizes and shapes, namely circular, elongated, rectangular were found. These hearths seem to have been used for the purposes of cooking as well as for manufacturing beads, etc. Some workshops represented by rows of hearths have also been found (Pl. 16.V). One such iron-smith's workshop was noticed at SGL-10, a locality in the lower town. In front of the palace-complex was noticed in one of the excavated trenches, a clay ramp built in two successsive phases with the evidence initially of brickbats ramming. This was probably for the easy access to the palace inside.

By using floatation technique some grain samples have also been collected from various Kushana levels. The report of these palaeo-ethnobotanical investigations is still awaited. However, easily identifiable grains include rice, wheat, barley, pulses and *ber* (*Ziziphus jujuba*).

An isolated feature was noticed at SGL-10, a locality in the lower town, where the Bara culture of about 2.90 m thickness hereto unreported in this part of the mound was sealed by a thick sterile layer consisting of fine sand and clay over which sits the Kushana settlement. Other intervening cultures, namely PGW and black slipped are non-existent here. This probably denotes the later expansion during the Bara culture and was abandoned subsequently, only to be reoccupied during the Kushana period.

A structural complex comprising of a small stupa having two circles with inner diameters of 1.45 m and 3.70 m with eight spokes and a monastic complex on all the three sides of the former was also brought to light (Pl. 16.VI). This stupa, though smaller in dimensions in comparison to the main stupa exposed earlier (Pl. 16.VII). followed the same plan. Some pillar bases were also found, but their exact relationship with othe structures and nature remain indeterminate.

So far as the antiquities are concerned mention mary

be made of terracotta figurines (Pl. 16.VIII), beads and pendants of semi-precious stones, terracotta, bone and shell; balance, rattle, toy-cart frames, wheels; miscellaneous objects of bone, ivory, shell, copper and iron, coin moulds (Pl. 16.IX), of slate and terracotta and dice of bone and ivory. The antiquities of this period comprised numerous seals and sealings, some of them reading *Visnubhadrasya*, *sridhamma*, *Dhamasa*, *Haridatta*, *Nakshitasya*—in Brahmi characters of the 1st and 2nd century A.D. Seals and sealings bearing Kharoshti inscriptions are also not wanting. Some terracotta weights (?) of various sizes carrying on one of their surfaces incised straight lines on some and curved lines on the others. One of the specimens looks like a graduated scale as it carried smaller lines separated by one bigger line, in the middle instead of on the edges. Copper coins were also found in abundance belonging to the Indo-Parthian, Kushana and Huna rulers. Coins of Gondopharnes, an Indo-Parthian ruler, Vima Kadphises, and Vasudeva are noteworthy.

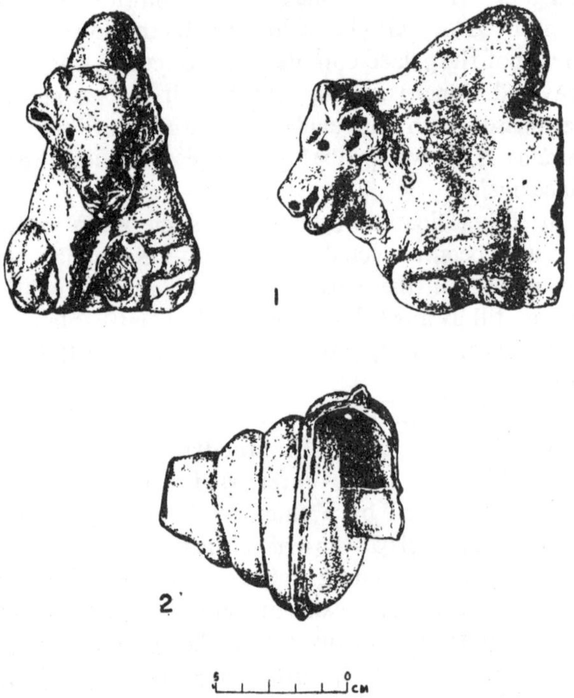

FIG. 3

The shell industry represented by finished and unfinished beads, bangles, pendants, etc. of this period at Sanghol is very rich. The evidences are suggestive of the fact that the objects were manufactured locally.

The most important find of the season is an inscription in ink written in concentric fashion on the interior of a late Kushana bowl. On palaeographical considerations this is datable to 2nd/3rd century A.D. Another importa1 t discovery of the year is a terracotta conch (Pl. 16.X) which was possibly attached with a life-size image of Vishnu. The conch which can still be blown and its sound being similar to that of the natural conch probably bespeaks of the high technique employed by a highly skilled and crafty potter. Ivory comb recalling the one from Taxila is also noteworthy (Pl.16. XI). A seated terracotta Nandi of the late Kushana times is also significant (Fig. 3).

Acknowledgement

We acknowledge with thanks Shri L.S. Mamani, Surveyor, Shri J.S. Bisht, Modeller and Shri B.B. Sharma, Photographer all of the Excavations Branch-II, Purana Qila, New Delhi for their valuable work in respect of the preparation of contour plan of Sanghol and antiquities drawings and photographs respectively. We are also thankful to Shri K.K. Sharma and S.K. Sharma of the Branch, Sarvashri G.B. Sharma, K.K. Rishi, Kuldeep Singh and Gurdev Singh of the Punjab State Archaeology to their active participation in the field work and for multifarious help and co-operation. We are grateful to the Director General, Archaeological Survey of India, New Delhi for making possible the above study and also permitting to publish it. The copyright of the photographs published rests with the Archaeological Survey of India.

REFERENCES

1. *Indian Archaeology—A Review* (*IAR*), 1968-69, pp. 25-26; 1969-70, pp. 31-32; 1970-71, pp. 30-31; 1971-2, pp.3 9-40; 1972-73, p.28;177-78, pp.43-44; Bisht, R.S. 'Transformation of the Harappan culture in Punjab with special reference to the excavations at Sanghol and Chandigarh; *Archaeological Congress and Seminar* 1972 (ed) Udai Vir Singh, Kurukshetra, 1976, pp. 16-22; Sharma, Y.D. and Sharma, G.B. 'Bara Culture and its Housing remains with special reference to Sanghol, *Indian Archaeology: New Perspectives* (ed) Sharma, R.K. Delhi, 1982, pp. 71-72; Sharma, Y.D. 'The Pre-Harappans in Punjab' *Puratattva;* 1979-80, pp. 32-8; Sharma, Y.D. 'Harappan complex on the Sutlej (India)', *Harappan Civilization* (ed) Gregory Possehl, 1983, N. Delhi, pp. 141-64.

2. Sharma and Sharma, *op. cit.*, 1982, pp. 73, 76; Sharma, *Puratattva*, 1979-80, pp. 32-33.

3. Gupta, S.P. (ed) *Kushana sculptures from Sanghol*, New Delhi, 1985.

4. *IAR*-1975-76, pp. 53 ff; 1976-77, pp. 54 ff.

5. Sharma and Sharma, *op. cit.*' pp. 72-3; Sharma, *op. cit.*, 1983, pp. 154-56.

6. Sharma and Sharma, *op. cit.*, p. 71.

7. Puri, B.N. *Indian Under the Kushanas*, 1965, Bombay, pp. 106 ff.

8. *IAR*—1968-69, pp. 25-26; 1969-70, pp. 31-32; Sharma, G.B. *Coins, Seals and Sealings from Sanghol*, 1986, Chandigarh, pp. 1-8.

17

Ayodhya of the Valmiki Ramayana: An Energizing Debate on its Identification

B.B. Lal

For the past nine years, the Indian Institute of Advanced Study, Shimla, in collaboration with the Archaeological Survey of India, has been working on a project called 'Archaeology of the Ramayana Sites.' While the overall direction and co-ordination of the project has all along been the responsibility of present writer, from the side of the Survey various officers, viz. Shri K.V. Soundara Rajan, Shri D.K. Sinha and Shri K.N. Dikshit, have participated from time to time. Under this project, Ayodhya, Nandigrama, Sringaverapura, Bharadvaja Asrama and Chitrakuta have been taken up for excavation, so as to ascertain their antiquity and archaeological contents.

At Ayodhya as many as fourteen different spots, including traditional ones like the Janam Bhumi, have been excavated by us. About a decade ago, the Banaras Hindu University had also dug trenches at three separate spots. None of these seventeen different trenches, however, has yielded anything which can be dated prior to the beginning of the Northern Black Polished (NBP) ware. Though in the lowest levels of the site there does occur the black-slipped ware, along with the NBP ware, there is no earlier and separate horizon for the former ware, such as, for example, we have in the case of Sringaverapura. On the basis of the 14C and thermoluminiescence dates, the earliest NBPW deposits at Sringaverapura are unlikely to go earlier than the turn of the eighth or seventh century B.C. On the transference of this evidence to Ayodhya, this site may go back to the beginning of the seventh century B.C. at the earliest. This indeed, is very uncomfortable evidence, for no one had expected the beginning of Ayodhya to be so late as that, particularly when one realises that the Painted Grey Ware associated Mahabharata sites, like Hastinapura, etc. antedated Ayodhya. This appears to be the main reason for some scholars to think that the ancient site on the bank of the Sarayu, known as Ayodhya, may not be the Ayodhya of the *Valmiki Ramayana* and they have advanced a number of arguments in this regard.

Spearheading this attack on the generally accepted identification of the site, even now known as Ayodhya in Faizabad District, U.P., with that of the *Valmiki Ramayana* M.C. Joshi, one of the Directors of the Archaeological Survey of India, published a paper in 1978 in the *Puratattva*[1] in which he sought to make out a case that Ayodhya was a mythical city, by referring to certain verses from *Taittariya Aranyaka*. After fully examining these verses as well as other references in the Vedic literature, the present writer[2] showed that these verses did not contain any allusion to a city called Ayodhya. On the other hand, the word *ayodhya* was found to have been used in that text in the sense of 'invincible' (*ayodhya*), and the reference in these verses was to the human body which, as the abode of the god, is invincible. This view was further substantiated by quoting Sayana's commentary on these very verses of the *Taittariya Aranyaka*. To recall Sayana says: *purti-sariramuchayate* whereby he emphasises that the word '*pur*' stands for the body. He then adds *ayodhya=karmagatimantarena kenapi prahartumasakya*, and thereby clinches the issue that the word 'ayodhya' stands for 'unassailable' or 'invincible' and *not* for a city, as Joshi had proposed.

In the long analysis of these verses the present writer had suggested that the word '*ashtachakra*' may denote the eight plexuses and the word '*navadvara*', the nine doors of the human body. On this Joshi has offered the following comment:[3]

> "Lal, after citing a number of textual references, concludes that the word 'Ayodhya' in the Vedic context has not been used as a proper noun but only in the sense of 'invincible'. At the same time, he feels that eight *chakras* and nine *dvaras* are respectively indicative of eight plexuses beginning with *muladhara* and nine gates (outlets) of human body like the eyes, nostrils, ears, etc. The major difficulty in accepting the interpretation of Lal is that the number of the *chakras* (plexuses) is believed

to be only six without *sahasrara*. With latter's inclusion their total number would be only seven and not eight as inferred by him."

While the book of Hinze may well refer to only seven plexuses, there do exist references to even nine plexuses in ancient Sanskrit literature.[4] Be that as it may, the main point at issue about these verses was whether the reference therein was to a city, with eightfold fortifications and nine gateways or not. And the answer, as already clarified above, is that in these Vedic verses the word *'ayodhya'* does not stand for a city. It is thus likely though not proved, that Ayodhya as a city may not have existed at the time of the composition of the *Taittariya Aryanyaka* which is generally thought to be composed around the eighth century B.C.

However, in his second paper,[5] the main point that Joshi wishes to make is that the place now known as Ayodhya is *not* Ayodhya of the *Valmiki-Ramayana.* He unfolds his arguments as follows :

> "Ayodhya mentioned by Valmiki in his *Ramayana* as the capital of Kosala is often identified with a small town of the same name in District Faizabad, U.P., on the right bank of the Sarayu or the Ghagra. But a critical examination of the geographical data available in Valmiki's narratives does not justify the commonly accepted identification of the ancient city with the modern one. The major points of disagreement are as under:
>
> According to Valmiki's description, Ayodhya was situated at a considerable distance from the River Sarayu flowing at that time in a westward direction and joining the Ganga at some distance.
>
> *Adhyardha yojanamgatva nadim paschanmukhasritam*
> *Sarayum punyasalilam dadarsa Raghunandanah*
> 118 CX *Uttarakanda*
> *Adhyardha yojanamagtva Sarayva dakshinetate*
> 11 XXII *Balakanda*
> *Tau prayatau mahavirayau divyam tripathagam nadim*
> *Daddrisate tatastatra Sarayvah sangame subhe*
> 5 XXIII *Balakanda*
>
> The location of modern Ayodhya, however, does not tally with the details given in the above cited verses; for instance, the present city stands in close proximity of the river and not one and a half *yojana* away from the town site. According to D.C. Sircar one *yojana* is equal to nine miles (14.4 km) and therefore one and a half *yojana* would be thirteen miles and a half. Even if this distance is taken to be somewhat less than what has been stated by Sircar, it would hardly justify the present location of Ayodhya in terms of the epic.
>
> Further, the Sarayu today flows eastward and not westward (*paschanmukhasritam*) and joins the Rapti (ancient Achiravati) and not the Ganga which is contrary to the Ramayanic references."
> 5 XXIII *Balakanda.*

Joshi has thus made three points which according to him, stand in the way of identifying the site on which there stands the present town of Ayodhya with Ayodhya of the *Valmiki Ramayana.* To recall, these are :

1. Valmiki's Ayodhya was 1.5 *yojanas* away from the Sarayu and not on its bank as the present Ayodhya is.
2. In the days of the *Ramayana*, the river was flowing in a westerly direction in which it does not flow at present.
3. The Sarayu now joins the Rapti and *not* the Ganga as mentioned by Valmiki.

We may now examine the three points serially. For this we shall have to go the context itself in which the verses concerned occur, for thus alone can their import be appreciated. The verse *adhyardhayojanam gatva sarayva daskhine tate* (I. XIII 11 of Gorakhpur Ed. or I 21.9 of Baroda Ed.) occurs in a context when Dasaratha agrees to the request of Visvamitra to loan him the services of Rama and Lakshmana to kill the demons who were troubling the sages in the area where his (Visvamitra's) hermitage was located and the three start off on their journey from Ayodhya. For a full understanding of this half-part of the verse, it would be desirable to quote it in full as also some of the connected subsequent verses which are as follows:

Adhyardhayojanam gatva sarayva dakshina tate
Rameti madhuram vanim Visvamitro bhyabhashata
I. 21.9
Grihana vatsa salilam ma bhutkalasya paryayah
Mantragramam grihana tvam balamatibalam tatha
I. 21.10
na sramo na jvaro va te na rupasya viparyayah
na cha suptam pramattam va dharshayishyanti nairritah I. 21.11.
Tato Ramo jalam sprishtva prahrishtavadanah suchih
Pratijagraha te vidye maharsherbhavavitatmanah
Vidyasamudito Ramah susubhe bhurivikramah
I. 21.18
Gurukaryani sarvani niyujya Kusikatmaje
ushustam rajanim tatra saryvam susukham trayah
I. 21.19.

From Ayodhya, the entire journey up to the confluence of the Sarayu with the Ganga appears to have been undertaken along the right bank of the Sarayu, on which bank Ayodhya itself was situated. After having covered a distance of 1.5 *yojanas* Visvamitra asked Rama to take some water in his hand from the Sarayu (on whose right bank they were already moving) so that the former might impart to the latter the *mantras* called *Bala* and *Atibala* which would protect him from all evils (verses 9-11). Thereupon Rama touched the water and took the *mantras* from Visvamitra. Finally, they all spent the night on the bank of the Sarayu (verses 18-19).

In the above verses there is not the slightest mention that Ayodhya itself was located at a distance of 1.5 *yojanas* from the Sarayu. Thus, to draw such an inference from these simple narrative verses is wholly unwarranted. Had the poet said that Visvamitra saw or reached the Sarayu after having travelled 1.5 *yojanas* the position would have been quite different. In fact, when the poet wants to say after having travelled such a distance so and so saw such and such river or place, he does use a word like *dadarsa* as for example, in the *Uttarakanda* verse quoted by Joshi, to which we now proceed.

From the above mentioned verse of the *Uttarakanda*, viz. *Adhyardha joyanam gatva nadim paschanmukhasritam Sarayum punyasalilam dadarsa Raghunandanah* VII. 100.1, Joshi makes two deductions, viz. that (1) since Rama saw (*dadarsa*) the Sarayu after having travelled 1.5 *yojanas* Ayodhya was located that distance away from that river; and that (2) the river was flowing in a westerly direction (*paschanmukhasritam*).

In this case also, as in the previous one, it is the context that gives the correct answer. The occasion this time was the *mahaprasthana* of Rama, i.e. his final departure from this world. For this purpose, after having performed certain rituals and being followed by a host of persons, he left Ayodhya and came to a point on the Sarayu where the river flowed in a westerly direction (*paschanmukhasritam*). It is evident that such a point where the river flowed westwards was deliberately chosen for the *mahaprasthana*, for otherwise the normal general direction of the flow of Sarayu, or for the matter of all the rivers in the central (i.e. non-sub-Himalayan) part of eastern U.P., is from west to east. In one of the verses in this very *sarga*, the *spot* where the *mahaprasthana* took place is called Goprataram'.

Tathoktavati devese gopratiaramupagatah/Bhejire Sarayum sarve harshapurnasruviklavah VII. 100.20. Even today the local tradition is that it was the Guptar-Ghat (the first component of which is evidently a distorted form of Gopratara of the *Ramayana* text) that Rama made his *mahaprasthana*.

The Guptar-Ghat is about 7 or 8 kilometres west of Ayodhya and the river has many horseshoe bends in this region on account of which the water flows in all sorts of directions, including the westerly one (cf. Survey of India sheet No. 63J/NW).

To think that the Sarayu, during the days of the *Ramayana* episode, was flowing all along in a westerly direction does not seem to be justified. It is quite contrary to the present day geographic data which do not seem to have been much different in the past. Had the Sarayu flowed all along towards the west, the total geography would have been quite different. The reference in the text to a point where the Sarayu was specifically flowing in a westerly direction would only strengthen the view that the spot was particularly chosen for the purpose of the *mahaprasthana* and therefore it could have very well been 1.5 *yojanas* away from Ayodhya proper as the Gopratara (Guptar) Ghat is.

The third point made by Joshi is that according to the *Ramayana* the Sarayu joined the Ganga but it now joins the Rapti (ancient Achiravati) and *not* the Ganga. In the first place, this had no bearing whatsover on the location of Ayodhya, and thus one wonders why Joshi has brought in this point. Be that as it may, the interesting point is that even today the Sarayu (also called the Ghagra—a fact accepted by even Joshi in his paper) does join the Ganga. The confluence is near Chapra, which can be verified by reference to any Survey of India map. (The Rapti is only a midway tributary of the Ghagra, before the latter itself joins the Ganga.)

From the foregoing it would be amply clear that all the three objections raised by Joshi against the identification of the site known today as Ayodhya with the place of the same name mentioned in the *Ramayana* of Valmiki are invalid.

On the other hand, there is ample evidence in the *Valmiki Ramayana* itself to show that Ayodhya was located on the bank of the Sarayu. For example, while the following verse

Kosalo nama muditah sphito janapado mahan
Nivishtah Sarayutire prabhute dhanadhyanyavan
I.5.5.

mentions that the kingdom of Kosala was located on

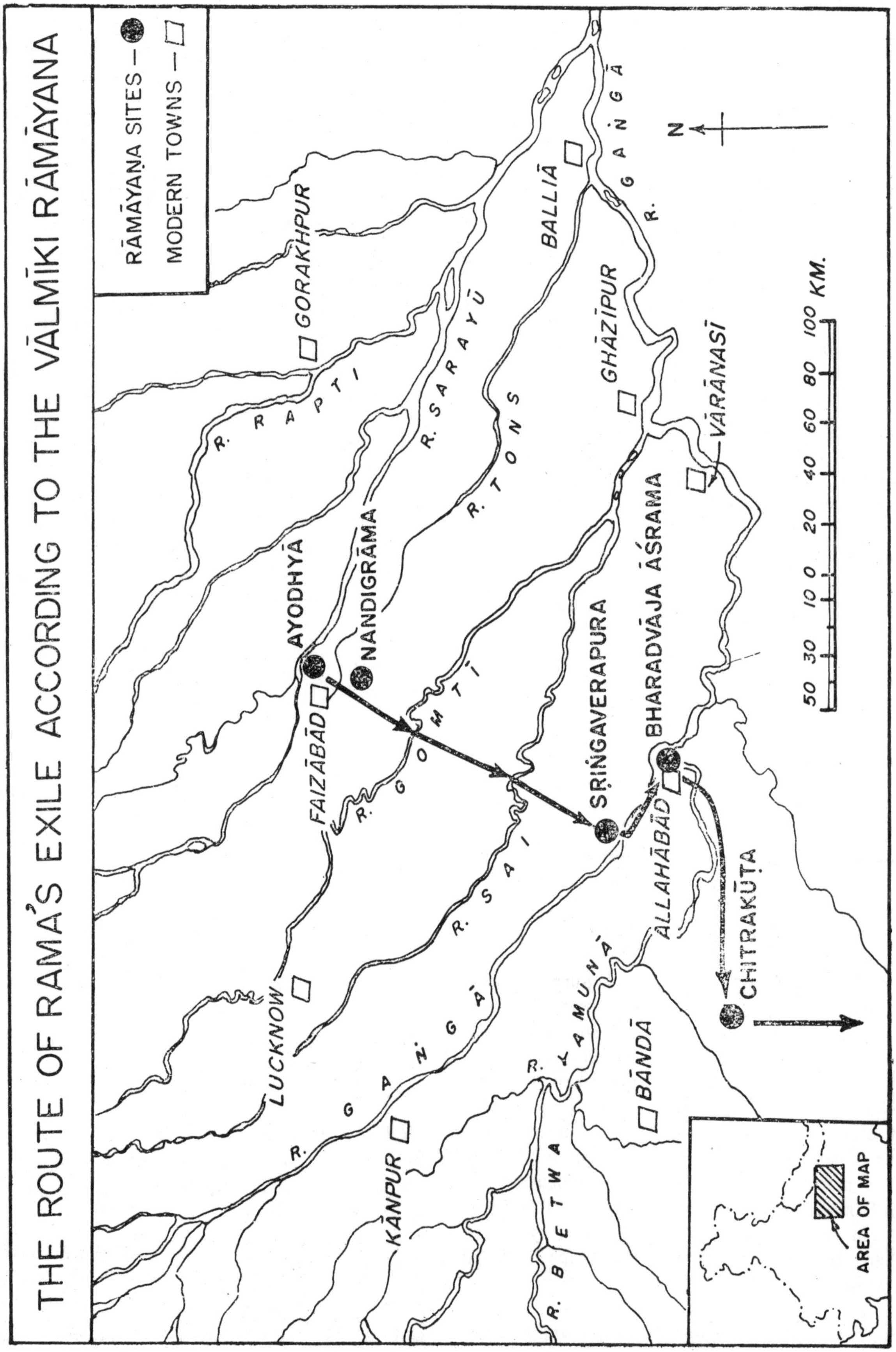
THE ROUTE OF RAMA'S EXILE ACCORDING TO THE VĀLMĪKI RĀMĀYAṆA
RĀMĀYAṆA SITES —
MODERN TOWNS —
AYODHYĀ
NANDIGRĀMA
FAIZĀBĀD
SṚṄGAVERAPURA
BHARADVĀJA ĀŚRAMA
ALLAHĀBĀD
CHITRAKŪṬA
LUCKNOW
KĀNPUR
BĀNDĀ
GHĀZĪPUR
BALLIĀ
GORAKHPUR
VĀRĀṆASĪ
R. RAPTI
R. SARAYŪ
R. TONS
R. GOMTĪ
R. SAI
R. GAṄGĀ
R. YAMUNĀ
R. BETWA
R. GAṄGĀ
N
50 30 10 0 20 40 60 80 100 KM.
AREA OF MAP

the bank of the Sarayu, the undermentioned two verses,

Kailasaparvate Rama manasa nirmitam sarah
Brahmana narasardula tenedam manasam sarah I, 23.7
Tasmasusrava sarasah sayodhyamupaguhate
Sarahpravritta Sarayupunya brahmasaraschyuta 1.23.8.

clearly state that Ayodhya (the capital of Kosala) was not merely situated on the bank of the Sarayu but was girlded or embraced by it. The term used in verse 8 is *upaguhate* the import of which is unmistakable. In fact, the Survey of India map already referred to above (Sheet No. 63J/NW) clearly shows that the Sarayu embraces Ayodhya from three sides: it first runs along its western fringes, then along the northern and finally passes on touching a part of the town on the eastern side. Can there be a better concordance between the textual description of about two thousand years ago and a map drawn in the present century?

We may now pass on to another issue raised by Joshi. He refers to the Buddhist text *Samyutta-Nikaya*[7] wherein it is stated '*ekam samayam Bhagava Ayojjhayam viharati gangaya nadiya tire.* According to Joshi, this statement shows that Ayodhya was situated on the bank of Ganga. Many scholars have rightly held that the word *ganga* has been used here in a generic sense signifying a sacred river and not as a proper noun implying the particular river called the Ganga. In this context, the present writer would like to record a small episode which indicates that even today the term *ganga* is used in a general sense for sacred rivers. Along with a few colleagues from the Institute as well as the Archaeological Survey of India, the present writer was exploring in 1981 the banks of the Mandakini near Chitrakuta in order to find out the antiquity of the site[8] On a high level of the slopy surface of the river bank, he saw a villager attending some vegetable crop. When he enquired of the villager how he (the villager) was able to water the crop, the latter replied that he brought the water all the way up from the *ganga.* The writer was baffled for a while by the word *ganga,* for he knew that the Ganga was far away at Allahabad, but his curiosity was soon satisfied when the villager pointed out to the river (Mandakini) flowing down below. It is thus clear that the term *ganga* has the generic meaning as well.

But Joshi can come up and say that the present usage of the word *ganga* in the general sense of a sacred river ought not to be projected back to the time of the *Samyutta-Nikaya.* It is, therefore, necessary to refer back and find out if the word *ganga* was used in it onl for the particular river called the Ganga or it was used in that text also in the generic sense.

Attention in this context may be drawn to *Darukhandha* 1 of *Asivisavaggo* or *Salayatana-Samyuttam* in *Samyutta-Nikaya* itself, where the opening sentence runs as follows :

'*Ekam samayam Bhagva Kosambiyam viharati Gangaya nadiya tire*'[9] ("Once upon a time the Lord was moving around in Kausambi on the bank of the river Ganga").

All scholars of ancient Indian history and archaeology including Joshi himself, know full well that Kausambi, which the Buddha did visit, stands on the bank of the Yamuna and not of the Ganga. There can possibly be two alternative explanations for this sort of statement in the *Samyutta-Nikaya.* We have either to say that the authors of the text did not have a correct knowledge of the geography of the country they are dealing with, or to accept that the authors used the term *ganga* in a generic sense for any river. While the present writer would prefer the second explanation, he would leave Joshi to choose either. If Joshi chooses the first one and admits that the authors of the *Samyutta-Nikaya* did not have a correct knowledge of the geography of the country, then he should also admit that the statement in that text that Ayodhya stood on the bank of the Ganga cannot be deemed as correct. On the other hand, if he chooses the second alternative, then the textual statement in question, viz. '*Ekam samayam Bhagava Ayojjhayam viharati Gangaya nadiya tire*' would only imply that Ayodhya was situated on the bank of a 'river' and not of the particular river called 'the Ganga.'

The geographical details relating even to the exile of Rama fully vouchsafe that Ayodhya was not on the bank of the Ganga. Briefly, these are as follows :

Accompanied by Sita and Lakshmana, Rama left Ayodhya in a chariot driven by Sumantra. The lamenting citizens of Ayodhya followed him upto the River Tamasa :

Evam vikrosatam dvijatinam nivartane
Dadrise tamasa tatra varayantiva Raghavam II. 40.30.

Rama spent the night on the bank of the Tamasa and early next morning left the camp, leaving the citizens behind. He then crossed the Tamasa:

Tam syandanamadhishthaya Raghavah saparichchhadah
Sighragamam akulavartam Tamasamatarannadim II. 41.27

Rama then proceeded southwards and successively crossed the Vedasruti, now known as the Besui, the Gomti going by the same name today and the Syandika now called the Sai.

Tate vedasrutim nama Sivavarivaham nadim
Uttirayabhumukhah prayagastyadhyushitam disam
II. 43.8

Gatva tu suchiram kalam tatah sitajalam nadim
Gomatim goyutanupamataratsagaramgamam II.43.9
Gomatim chapyatikramya Raghavah sighragairhayaih
Mayurahamsabhirutam tatara syandikam nadim
II. 43.10.

Moving further south, Rama reached Sringaverapura where he saw the sacred Ganga;

Visalam Kosalan ramyan yatva Lakshmanapurvajah
Asasada mahabahuh Sringaverapuram prati II. 44.1.
Tatra tripathagam divyam Sivotoyamasaivalam
Dadarsa Raghavo Gangam punyarishinivesitam
II. 44.2

At Sringaverapura, the Nishada Chief, Guha, welcomed the trio, viz. Rama, Sita and Lakshmana and later helped them ferry across the Ganga. Sumantra returned with the chariot back to Ayodhya.

Tatra raja Guho nama Ramasyatmasamah sakha
Nishadajatyo balavan sthapatischeti visrutah II.44.9
Tamaratah samparishavajya Guho Raghavamabravit
Yathayodhya tathedam te Rama kim karavani te
II. 44.12

Svagatam te mahabaho taveyamakhila mahi
Vayam preshya bhavan bharta sadhu rajyam prasadhi nah
II. 44.14
Anujnaya Sumantram cha sabalam chiva tam Guham
Asthaya navam Ramastu chodayamasa navikan
II. 46.65

Tatha sambhashamana sa Sita Gangamaninidita
Dakshina dakshinam tiram Kshiprameyabhyupagamat
II. 46.74

Having crossed the Ganga, the trio proceeded to the confluence of the Ganga and Yamuna where they met the sage Bharadvaja at his hermitage. On being so advised by the sage, they crossed the Yamuna and moved on to Chitrakuta.

Dhanvinau tausukham gatva lambamane divakare
Ganga-Yamunavoh sandhau prapaturnilayam muneh
II. 48.8

Ramastvashramamasadya trasayanmrigapakshinah
Gatva muhurtamadhvanam Bharadvajamupagamat
II. 48.9

Ratryam tu tasyam vyushtayam Bharadvajoabravididam
Madhumulaphalopetam Chitrakutam vrajeti ha
II.48.34

Athasadya tu Kalindim Sighrastrotasamapagam
Tatrayutam plavam kritya taratamsumatim nadim
II. 49.3

Tatastau padacharena gachchhantau saha Sitaya
Ramayamasedatuh Sailam Chitrakutam manoraman
II. 50.11

From the foregoing discussion it would be amply clear to Joshi and others sharing his view that Ayodhya was not situated on the bank of the Ganga but on the bank of the Sarayu and, as the *Valmiki Ramayana* itself states the township was girdled by that river (*sayodhyamupaguhate*)—a fact which holds good even today. Since no other township on the bank of the Sarayu except the one near Faizabad in Uttar Pradesh is known as Ayodhya, there is no reason for not accepting it as the Ayodhya of the *Valmiki Ramayana*.

At the end, the present writer would like to thank Joshi for having raised and revived certain issues because it is only through such debates that the truth utlimately emerges.

REFERENCES

1. Joshi, M.C., Archaeology and Indian Traditon—Some observations, *Puratattva*, No. 8, 1975-76, pp. 98-102.

2. Lal, B.B., Was Ayodhya a Mythical City? *Puratattva*, No. 10, 1978-79 pp. 45-49.

3. Joshi, M.C., Ayodhya: Mythical and Real, *Puratattva*, No. 11, 1979-80, pp. 107-09.

4. Vijanani, Yogendra, *Mahayoga Vijnana*, Vijnana Bhavana, Rishikesh, 1972.

5. Joshi, *op. cit.*, 1979-80.

6. Joshi all through refers to the Gorakhpur edition, Vikram Samvat 2017 whereas the present writer refers to critical edition published by the Oriental Institute, Baroda. See Bhatt G.H. (Ed.) *The Balakanda* (The First Book of the Valmiki Ramayana) Oriental Institute of Baroda, 1960. Shah, U.P. (Ed.), The Uttarakanda (Seventh Book of the Valmiki Ramayana) Oriental Institute, Baroda 1975; and Vaidya, P.L. (Ed.) *The Ayodhyakanda* (The Second Book of the Valmiki Ramayana), Oriental Institute of Baroda, 1962.

7. Feer, M. Leon (Ed.) *Samyutta Nikaya* III, Pali Text Society, London, 1960, (Originally printed in 1890).

8. The exploration yielded the NBP Ware.

9. Freer, *op. cit.*

18

A New Gupta Inscription from Kausambi

B.C. Shukla

In the month of October 1982, I came to know about a newly discovered inscription from Kausambi during my talks with Shri J.C. Tandon, a famous antiquarian of Allahabad. He not only showed me the inscription but also kindly supplied its photographs.

The inscription is engraved on a slab of sandstone measuring 54 X 40 cm. Unfortunately, it is broken at many points, as a result of which some lines and letters are missing. Two Buddha figures are shown on either flanks of the slab. The figure on the right is seated on a lotus pedestal in *Bhumisparsamudra*. According to Buddhist tradition, this posture marks the event at Bodhagaya where Gautama Buddha is believed to have invoked the earth as witness after his victory over *Mara*.[1] The head is completely defaced, but for the traces of curly hair, a popular style of the Gupta period. The upper garment or *chivara* resting on the left portion of the body is also visible. The figure on the left flank is also seated on lotus pedestal. The fingers of the right hand are placed over those of left hand symbolizing the turning of wheel or *Dharmachakra-pravartana*.[2] There is a small stupa symbol just below the left figure. The right part of the slab below the figure of Buddha is completely broken. In the middle of the slab between the two figures, some traces of pedestal of the main image (which is not there) may also be seen. It appears that the main image rested on it. It may also be taken to have contained the pedestal of the *Dharmachakra*. Here it may be pointed out that a similar slab of sandstone with Buddha figures, *Dharmachakra* and the inscription of Kumargupta I was discovered from Mankuwar,[3] a place in Karachhana subdivision of Allahabad District. It is stated in the inscription that the Buddha image was installed in Gupta era 129 during the reign of Kumargupta I.

The present inscription is engraved in two parts. The upper part of the inscription has three lines and thirty-nine letters, whereas the lower one has seven lines and seventeen letters only. The upper part is almost well-preserved and barring a few letters it is easily readable. But the lower portion of the inscription is damaged to such an extent that it is difficult to form any idea of the text. The script being Brahmi is read from left to right. The language is Sanskrit. The upper part of the inscription is as follows :

1. *Siddham ye dharma hetuprabhava hetustesham tathagato*
2. *hyavadat tesha nchayo nirodhoh evam va*
3. *di mahasramana.*[4]

Translation of the text[5]

1. Of all the things that proceed from a cause, the Buddha had told the cause.
2. And tells too how such shall come to its end. Such
3. is the word of *Mahasraman*

The lower inscription may be read as follows :

1. *De dhamoyam*
2. *Mata pitro*
3. *pi-guru*
4. *tra da* (?)
5. .. .. ..
6. *so gu*
7. *ptasya*

Orthography

The inscription is interesting and reveals some important tendencies from the palaeographic point of view. The dental *sa* has been rendered with a cerebral *sa*[5] and cerebral *sa* has been altered by palatal *sa*.[7] The palatal *sa* has also been written as dental *sa*.[8]

The tops of most of the letters are ornamented with triangular hooks but some are shown with a small horizontal line.[9] This shows the inter-mixing of different styles of the writing of Gupta Brahmi letters.[10]

The medial signs used in this record are also noteworthy. The sign *a* in the *va* of the first line has been shown by an oblique stroke with triangular hooked end touching the top of the letter. But in *va* of the second line and in *ha* of the third line, this sign is shown by a small vertical stroke touching the tops of the letters. The sign *'U'* in the letter *Gu* of the third line of the inscription in the lower part is raised upward parallelly upto the top of the letter *Ga*. This type of medial sign is rare in a Gupta inscription. However, in the Mankuwar inscription dated Gupta era 129, such an instance is met with.[11] The addition of *r* in the *pra* of the first line is shown is proportionately longer and ornamental. This tendency prominently occurs from the time of Kumargupta I.

Historical analysis

Unfortunately, no personal name is available in the record, hence it is very difficult to deduce any positive historical result. But the script is itself a definite clue to assign the record to the Gupta period. However, the only remaining word of the last line of the lower inscription, i.e. *ptasya* may be taken as *Guptasta* suggesting the reign of some Gupta ruler. The fragmentary text of the record reveals that the Buddhist formulae was inscribed on the slab either on the occasion of the installation of Buddha image or on the occasion of the donation by some one to the Buddhist church. It is a well-known fact that the depiction of Buddha figures in different postures with Buddhist formulae was much popular in Gupta and post Gupta period.[12] A large number of seals have been reported from Sahjiki Dheri,[13] Sanchi,[14] Bhita,[15] Rajghat,[16] Mirpur khas,[17] etc. showing almost the same style of depicting Buddha figures and the formulae. The records of Chandragupta II[18] (Sanchi Ins. G.E. 93), Kumargupta I[19] (Mankuwar Ins. G.E. 129), Budhagupta[20] (Saranath Ins. G.E. 157) and Vainyagupta[21] (Gunaighar Ins. G.E. 188) clearly reveal the nature and purpose of donations given to Buddhist churches.

Since, neither the name of the king nor that of the donee is available in the record in question, we have to depend mainly on indirect evidences for relating the record to a particular king. The letters are very close to those of the Mankuwar inscription of Kumargupta I. Significantly enough, the stone slab of Mankuwar also bears the Buddha figures in *Bhumisparsa* and *Dharma chakra pravartana* postures in the same way as depicted on the present stone slab of Kausambi. Moreover, the distance between Mankuwar and Kausambi is hardly 35 kilometres. The above considerations may be taken to indicate that the record in question probably belonged to the reign of Kumargupta I. Although we can exclude the alternative possibility of its being an inscription of the time of Vainyagupta on the basis of the easterly distribution of all the records referring to him. But in view of the discovery of the records of Buddhagupta from Eran[22] and Mathura,[23] and other places this argument cannot be used to exclude Buddhagupta as well. As an alternative possibility, the record may also be assigned to the reign of Buddhagupta too, as even palaeography cannot be a guide for such narrow distinction in time.

REFERENCES

1. Bhattacharya, B. *The Indian Buddhist Iconography*, Calcutta 1958, pp. 433 and 435.
2. Pramod Chandra, *Stone sculptures in the Allahabad Museum*, p. 176.
3. *Archaeological Survey of India Report* (abbrev. ASIR) Calcutta, 1880, vol. X, pp. 6 and f.
4. This formulae was first told by Assaji to Sariputta Upatissa. See *Vinayapitaka* I, p. 40.
5. This is based on the translation of late V.S. Agrawal. See his *Saranath*, Delhi 1957, p. 26
6. Of line 1 *Shiddham* for *Siddham*.
7. Of line 1 *tesam* for *tesham*
8. Of line 3 *Sramanah* for *Sramanah*
9. For horizontal line on the top see, the letter *Da* in the third line.
10. Hornele has made two divisions of Gupta Brahmi, i.e. Eastern and Western, on the basis of the letter *Sa*. See, *JRASB* Vol. LX, p. 81 for details see Buhler, *Indian Palaeography* (Hindi, Varanasi) 1965, p. 217.
11. *ASIR*, Vol. X, p. 7, plate IV.
12. All the specimens bearing the Buddha figures and formulae have come from Gupta and post-Gupta times. It was perhaps to propagate and popularise this religion when it was already on the way to decline. See Thaplyal, K.K., *Studies in Ancient Indian Seals*, Lucknow 1972, p. 219.
13. Archaeological Survey of India—Annual Report (abbrev. ASIAR) 1910-11, p. 31.
14. Thaplyal, *op. cit.*, p. 217.
15. *Ibid.*, p. 217.
16. *Ibid.*, p. 217.
17. *ASIAR* 1909-10, p. 88.
18. *Corpus Inscriptionum, Indicarum* (abbrev. CII) Vol. III, pp. 31-32.
19. *ASIR*, vol. X, p. 7.
20. Sircar, D.C., *Select Inscriptions*, Calcutta, 1942, p. 323.
21. *Ibid.*, pp. 331-35 and Upadhyay, V., *Gupta Abhilekh*
22. *CII*, Vol. III, pp. 88-90.
23. *Hindustan*, dated 17th November 1982, p. 5.

19

Coins and Small Finds of Indian Origin in Ai-Khanum (Afghanistan)

O. Guillaume

Two volumes concerning the excavations in the Graeco-Bactrian city of Ai-Khanum in Afghanistan have recently been published, one being devoted to the coins except those found in hoards,[1] the other dealing with the small finds collected in the temple.[2] Furthermore, another volume devoted to the small finds outside the temple is to be published shortly.[3]

On the occasion of the publication of these works—all of which are, unfortunately, presently available only in French—it seems appropriate to take a quick look of the coins and small finds from the Ai-Khanum excavation, which provide confirmation of the existence of relations between Hellenized Bactria and India in the 3rd century B.C. and during the first half of the 2nd century B.C.

It is known that in the 3rd century B.C. the Hindu Kush range constituted the border running between Hellenized Bactria to the north and the Indian Maurya empire to the south. The treaty signed in 303 B.C. by king Selecus I and the Maurya king Chandragupta had confirmed the latter's sway over Arachosia and the Paropamisadae (southern half of Afghanistan).

The geo-political state of affairs underwent a change at the beginning of the 2nd century B.C. The Graeco-Bactrian kings (mainly Demetrius) crossed the Hindu Kush and overran N.W. India (approximately as far as the present day India—Pakistan border). Despite the fact that these kings were definitely ousted from Bactria by nomadic invaders about 145 B.C., they continued to rule over their Indian conquests for nearly a century.

1. Numismatics.

That there was contact with India is demonstrated by the discovery, on the one hand, of a series of six coins of king Agathocles and, on the other, of numerous punch-marked coins.

(a) *The Indian coins of Agathocles*[4]

These are drachms (therefore made of silver), square in shape, struck on the Indian standard with bilingual legend in Greek and Brahmi ('of king Agathocles'). The devices are, on the obverse, Balaram depicted as 'ploughman' (sankarashana) with wing plough and, on the reverse, Vasudeva-Krishna with wheel (*chakra*) and conch shell (*sankha*).

These Agathocles coins, which, according to P. Bernard, date back to 180-170 B.C., are nearly the oldest depictions of Indian deities we have and as such constitute noteworthy evidence about the nature of the Bhagavata religion, first form of Vaishnavism (this is to be related to the Garuda column erected at Besnagar, near Sanchi, about 115-110 B.C. by a certain Heliodorus, ambassador of king Antialcidas of Taxila).

(b) *The punch-marked coins*

More than 700 coins of this sort have been found at Ai-Khanum; 677 clustered in a hoard discovered in 1970.[5] Six symbols are shown on each of these coins, 5 being on the obverse, 1 on the reverse. The most common symbol on the reverse (found on over 550 coins) is in all likelihood the mark of the Taxila mint: a dot flanked by two crescents and by two elements difficult to identify (arrows, stylized fish?). According to P. Bernard, the above mentioned hoard would have been buried about 170 B.C.

2. Small Finds

There is no doubt that almost all the small finds are purely the products of Hellenistic craftsmanship. Nevertheless, as we shall see, Indian influence is not entirely absent:

(a) It is reasonable to suppose that particular raw materials required for jewellery-making were imported from India: shell-fish, semi-precious stones such as cornelian, agate, onyx and perhaps some of the ivory carved at Ai-Khanum. However, as far as ivory is concerned we know that there were elephants at 'Ai-Khanum as shown by the discovery of two elephants, hook (*ankusa*) made of iron or bronze (Pl. 19. I). The elephants used in the Seleucid and Graeco-Bactrian armies originated, as we know, in India.

(b) However, India was not just important as a basic supplier of raw materials. Some ivory or shell finds from Ai-Khanum are quite possibly linked to Indian artistic tradition :

—A wingless ivory sphinx (Pl. 19. II) which H.P. Francfort links to similar representations found at Bharhut, Pitalkhora, Mathura, Amaravati and Begram;

—A nude female ivory figurine (Pl. 19. III) wearing a double necklace interesecting just beneath the bust. According to H.P. Francfort, Indian origin for this piece of ornament cannot be ruled out. However, Syro-Mesopatamian or Iranian origin should not be dismissed either;

—A nude female ivory figurine (Pl. 19. IV) with movable arms. Here again, the find may have originated in India. Dolls of this sort have actually been found at Champa in Bihar (6th—5th centuries B.C.) as well as at Taxila;

—The most extra-ordinary find is undoubtedly a disc made of shell.[6] Only half of this disc (diam. 2 cm) is preserved (Pl. 19. V). It is made of assembled small shell plaques in which bits of stained glass were inlaid. Enough remains to give us an idea of the motif depicted. A frieze runs right around the edge of the disc showing flowery branches alternating with animals (peacock, deer), buildings and some people. The main scene, occupying the central part of the disc, apparently depicted a retinue of riders escorting the procession of an important personage in a park. In fact, the remains of two groups of individuals underneath parasols can be made out along with the shoes of a horse team, some riders, some moulded columns and various plants.

This find indeed would appear to be Indian in origin. It is known that the making of jewellery using shells is a tradition which can be traced back to the Indus civilization. There is no doubt that the idea of motif came from India. Similar moulded columns are found in figurative representations at Bharhut, Sanchi, Bodh Gaya, etc., similar plant motifs at Begram; as for the peacock, it is a common motiff on Maurya coin punches and at Bharhut, Sanchi, etc.

This work of art, dating back to the second quarter of the second century B.C. attests to the high level of artistic achievement reached under the Sunga dynasty.

The Agathocles coins, the punch-marked coins and the shell disc all date back to 180—150 B.C. (the other discussed cannot be dated as accurately). This period is in fact the only one during which the Greek kings reigned over Bactria and India at the same time. This no doubt explains why P. Bernard takes the view that these Indian coins and disc do not reflect steady commercial exchange between Bactria and India but rather should be seen as the fruit of raids or as the result of tribute raised by Bactrian kings throughout the Indian territories. However, this will remain an open question until such time as we have a better understanding of craftsmanship under the Maurya and Sunga kings.

REFERENCES

1. Bernard, P., Fouilles d' Ai-Khanoum IV Les Monnaies hors tresors, *MDAFA*, XXVIII, Paris 1985.

2. Francfurt, H.P. Fouilles d' Ai-Khanoum III, le sanctuaire du temple a niches indentees Les trouvailles, *MDAFA*, XXVII Paris, 1984

3. Guillaume O. and Rougeulle A., pending publication, Fouilles d' Ai-Khanoum, Les petits objects (hors temple et tresorerie du palais), *MDAFA*, Paris.

4. Audouin R. and Bernard, P. "Tresor de monnaises indiennes et indo-greques d' Ai-Khanoum (Afghanistan), II les monnaies indo-greques" *Revue Numismatique*,[16] 1974, pp. 6-41.

5. Audouin, R. and Bernard, P., 'Tresor de monnaies indnnies et indo-greques d' Ai-Khanoum (Afghanistan), I les monnaies indiennes, *Revue Numismatique*, 15, 1973, pp. 238-89.

6. Bernarda nd others, Campagnede fouille 1978 a Ai-Khanoum (Afghanistan), *BEFEO*, LXVIII 1980, p. 1-104.

20

Three Saucer-Type Coins from Varanasi

Haldhar Pathak

I am reporting here three cup-shaped coins in which two are of double-obverse marks and the third is of single-obverse marks, I have already reported two double-obverse type of coins.[1]

These types of coins are only known in silver, and they are called cup-shaped or saucer-like coins because they look like shallow cups or saucers. This variety of five coins were first published in 1941.[2] After some time some more coins have come to light.[3] Blanks of these coins were prepared by flattening thin globules of specified weight and were ultimately impressed on one side with individual punches in a heated state. In this way of punching the side that received punch impression became somewhat concave in appearance. Majority of these coins bear four broad symbols.

Dr. Lahiri opines[4] that cup-shaped coins were three denominational currency. They were full, one sixth and one twelth pieces respectively weighing forty-eight, eight and four *ratti* coins, They are considerably thicker in fabric and are having four broad symbols in which two are constant, similar in design, comparatively big in size and always uniform in dimension while the other two are always found in the smaller dimension. The bigger symbols (A) has at its centre a small circle with dots, the other smaller symbols found only on the coins of lower denomination does not have that circle. In this way a formula having been framed as ABXX' Lahiri opines that the few other marks which are found on these coins were impressed by the banker, traders, and others through whose hands they passed during circulation.[5]

Eight *ratti* pieces which are flat, thin and smaller in size due to small flan bears two broad symbols A-B. Where as four *ratti* pieces are having smaller flan bear only one broad ornamental symbol with a dotted circle at the centre ('A').[6]

In this way three varieties of coins are reported but out of three, two coins are double-obverse and are of different weights. Due to double-punching two coins became some what flat. A number of silver punched-marked coins are found with the obverse group of marks stamped on both faces. On them, the group of marks on one face is older and more worn than that of the other. This shows that when the older side of obverse marks became somewhat worn out after some time they were restruck with the other set of obverse marks. Thus, these coins were re-issued by the authorities having later set of obverse marks.[7] E.H.C. Walsh first noticed double-obverse type of coins in Paila Hoard. The Paila Hoard of coins were of local series of the punch-marked coins whereas Big Bhir mound coins were of the Imperial series.[8] Sixty-four coins of Big Bhir mound were found of the double-obverse group. The older obverse symbol group was either so much jumbled with the minute Schroff-marks or had become flat due to repunching on the other side or had already become very much worn, while they were repunched. E.H.C. Walsh recognised one or two symbols on older side and P.L. Gupta recognised 25 symbols on older side.[9] Thereafter P.L. Gupta found two double-obverse coins in Raichur Hoard and 96 in the Amravati Hoard.[10] On the Amravati hoard of coins the reverse side is smaller than the coins found in Bhir Mound Hoard. Hence he could identify the older reverse on 58 coins only but not in all the cases all the five symbols.[11] Other hoards might be having such coins: but they have not yet been brought to light.

The importance of the double-obverse punched-marked coins in the study of these coins lies in the fact that they determine chronology to the coins of various symbol groups. P.L. Gupta has drawn attention to the fact and its importance but I am not aware if any work on the chronology on the basis of the double-obverse coins have been studied by any scholar. The cup-shaped double-obverse type of coins is not yet published. n think that these coins are very rare and belong to thie Kashi Mahajanpada period. These three coins arehas the collection of Shri J.S. Mishra, A.E.C. and he kindly permitted me to publish it. I am thankful to him.

Description of the coins

1st Coin: Shape: Oval Size: 3 × 2.5 cm.
Weight: 4.7 gm. (72.85 grain).

Older obverse

(1) Two big flowers in the middle having seven petals; in each petal prominent dots are present. In the right side of the flowers three petals of lower side are damaged.

(2) Two circular ponds, one pond is between the two flowers and the other below its side, each having five small fishes arranged in a circle.

(3) Two solar symbols, one is on the upper side and other is touching the left side of flower.

(4) Two trees are above the two flowers, the right side of the tree is having six branches and the left side of the tree is attached with big flowers.

(5) A circle having a small ball between the two flowers.

Reverse (new obverse)

(1) Two solar symbols, one on the upper side and the other is below side.

(2) Three bundles of flower buds, in one bundle of flower buds the upper portions are touching each other. The bundles of flowers which are four to six in number are arranged in a circle. These arrangements of symbols are never seen on any type of the coins found in Amravati, Taxila and Palia Hoards.

(3) In crescent a pellet—new type of symbols

(4) Five small trees are present.

2nd Coin: Shape: Oval Size: 2.5×2.5 cm.
Weight: 4.5 gm (68.75 gr.)..

Older obverse

(1) Two shader chakra in which three are the double-snak hood and the other three are single hoods (new types of symbols)

(2) Two double trees are present, in each big tree a small tree is installed. (New type of syambols).

(3) A solar symbol

Reverse

(1) A solar symbol

(2) Indradhwaja

(3) Trees

3rd Coin: Shape: Oval Size: 2.5×3 cm.
Weight: 4.8 gram (74.4 grain)

Obverse

(1) Two solar symbols

(2) Two big flowers

(3) Two shader chakra in which three are the double snake hood and the other three are single hoods.

Reverse

Blank

REFERENCES

1. *Journal of the Numismatic Society of India* (JNSI) Vol. XL, 1, pp. 8-11.
2. *Ibid.*, Vol. III, pp. 51-52 and V, pp. 13-16.
3. *Ibid.*, XXXIX, pp. 9 ff.
4. *Ibid.*, Vol, XXXV, p. 11.
5. *Ibid.*
6. *Ibid.*, Vol. XL, pp. 8-11.
7. *Ibid.*, Vol. II., pp. 15 ff.
8. *Punch-marked coins from Taxila*, Memoirs of the Archaeological Survey of India, No. 59 pp. 10-12, 37-39.
9. *JNSI.*, Vol. XI, pp. 845-46, 149-50.
10. *Punch-marked coins in the Andhra Pradesh Museum.*
11. *Amravati Hoard of Silver coins*, op. 112-116.

Book Reviews

J.N. Pal, **Archaeology of Southern Uttar Pradesh (Ceramic Industries of North Vindhyas)**, pp. 190, Plates 8, Figures 26, Swabha Prakashan Allahabad 1986. Price 250/-.

Amongst younger archaeologists, Dr. J.N. Pal's is a well known name. He has now come out with a very welcome book on the archaeology of southern Uttar Pradesh (U.P.). Though he starts with an Early Palaeolithic background, the main periods dealt with in the book range from Mesolithic to the Early Historic periods. The geographical area covered by the book extends from the Bundelkhand to the Baghelkhand regions of UP between 23°52' and 26°30' N and 78°08' and 83°33' E, an expanse of about 80,000 sq. kms. As the book was originally conceived as a Ph.D. thesis, it has naturally the constraints of a thesis format.

It is refreshing to see the data on ecology, climate and physiology of the areas. He gives some idea of the forest produce of the region too. Dr. Pal has had the distinction of working with the Allahabad University team, under the dynamic leadership of Prof. G.R. Sharma. Thus his firsthand experience of a variety of sites, of different periods, has imbued the book with authenticity and widest of perspective. For the first time readable summaries of the archaeological assemblages of the sites like Morhana Pahar, Baghaikhor, Lekhahia, Chopani Mando, Koldihava, Mahagara, Indari, etc. have become available. The author also discusses the numerous C^{14} dates of the sites of the southern U.P. Tables on C^{14} dates and site details are especially useful. Koldihva had given three C^{14} dates of 5000-6000 B.C. range—but the author believes that these dates do not belong to the Neolithic strata of the site, though Prof. G.R. Sharma always claimed high antiquity for Koldihva Neolithic on the basis of precisely these early C^{14} dates. The author seems to believe, though he does not make it explicit, that the Neolithic of this area could be mid-second millennium B.C., rather than earlier. A more controlled sample collection may provide the right answers. The megalithic culture represented by Kotia, Kakoria, etc. is also insecurely C^{14} dated and needs to be covered with further dates.

The third Chapter has the enigmatic title of 'Mesolithic Ceramic Industry'. This naturally sounds a bit anachronistic. Mesolithic is generally considered to be a bridge between Neolithic and the earlier Stone Age Industries and is basically a late phase of Stone Age, devoid of metal and ceramic artifacts. Mesolithic ceramic industry thus sounds a contradiction in terms. This sort of situation arises because in India we tend to associate neolithic only with polished stone axes. Neolithic culture basically is a sedentary way of life where pottery alone has a role to play. Therefore, it may be better to call these cultures Neolithic rather than Mesolithic. Pottery may be used as an indicator of settled life pattern. The pottery tables provide useful statistics of different wares in each layer—such frequency distribution is rare in Indian publication and hence most welcome. Some percentages are given to the third place of decimals, indicating more accuracy than warranted. The line drawings of the pottery are generally of good quality though the same thing cannot be said of the plates. In fact, the getup, format, printing of the book is of very good quality, only the plates produce a jarring note. Though at places the author indulges in hyper-diffusionist hypotheses, on the whole the book has been written in a very objective style. It gives a large body of data about these little known southern UP cultures in a very lucid and readable style. Thus the book is not only valuable for students and teachers but also for the general lay readers. Dr. Pal deserves the thanks of the archaeological community for bringing out this timely and small volume on the archaeology of Baghelkhand and Bundelkhand. Dr. Pal has done an excellent job, and his book is much better than other books on the archaeology of U.P.

D.P. AGRAWAL

* * *

K.M. Varma, **Amaravati and the Beginnings of stucco Modelling in India**, published by proddu, Santiniketan **(1985), pp. 82.**

Dr K.M. Varma is a well-established author known for his in depth studies on Indian art and for his strong grip on literary, especially the Sanskrit sources. In his latest book under review, Varma advances arguments to show that the art of stucco modelling was first practised in India at Amaravati and not in Gandhara as is normally believed. He critically analyses the available evidence and traces the tradition of the use of stucco to the period of Harappan civilization.

Dr Varma's small book has about twenty-three sub-headings under which he discusses besides a general introduction, meaning of the sord wtucco, its antiquity in India, beginning of stucco modelling, antiquity of Amaravati, stucco in Amaravati and elsewhere, theory of Gandhara association of stucco modelling, Amaravati stucco sculptures and other similar figures from Andhra sites and the technique of Amaravati stucco and their importance in Indian art. It also contains three plates illustrating Amaravati stucco sculptures, useful bibliography and an index.

Defining stucco Dr Varma says that it is termed as *sudha* in ancient Sanskrit literature but then he writes that *sudha* is used sometimes to mean slaked lime for white-washing walls which according to him is technically an incorrect usage, and in ancient technical literature it is never used with a such a meaning. However Varma's contention creates difficulty in tracing the origin of a word like *saudha*, i.e. a palace (literally) coated with lime plaster or covered with lime wash (*sudha subhram saudham*), which has been very commonly used in ancient Sanskrit texts. In our view *sudha* seems to stand for stucco and lime plaster as well as lime-wash.

On the tradition of embellishing the stupas partly with stone slabs and partly with ornate designs on plaster in Andhradesa, Varma strongly contradicts the opinion of Longhurst and Ramachandran who regarded it to be the contribution of Gandharan Buddhists. He, on the other hand, regards it to be of Amaravati origin although we feel that chances of the emergence of the plaster ornamentation were more in western Indian Rock-cut caves where perhaps aesthetically it was found essential to cover the rough and porus surfaces of the colconic trap, whether sculptured or plain, with a coat of white plaster which was also painted. Yet one cannot deny some Hellenistic impact on the art of Amaravati in the motifs like garland-bearers or other art centres of Andhra and in Deccan. Another important point raised by Dr Varma is that the *navatala* system of measuring human body, which according to him began around 1000 B.C., was evolved or at least systematized and perfected at Amaravati. He also admits that this system was already known in Greece around the fifth-fourth century B.C. from where Romans borrowed it. Yet, he says that there is no reason to believe that Amaravati artists got it from the Graeco-Roman traditions and he proves his contention by stating that the *navatala* system was hardly known to Gandharan sculptors who were otherwise so close to Hellenistic wofld.

Dr Varma stylistically dates the fragments of Amaravati sculptures in stucco, discovered nearly a century back by Alexander Rea, to the first century A.D. and calls them pre-Gandharan in character and thereby stresses his postulate that stucco modelling started in India at Amaravati. But an assessment of his three illustrations—two human and a lion figure—suggests for them a date not earlier than the second century A.D. especially, in view of the *kapardin* like knotted hair on a head (fig. 1), sharp facial traits and a cap like head-dress uncommon in Andhra sculptures in the other (fig. 2) and stylized features of lion (fig. 3). It appears that the idea of independent image in stucco is basically outside the Indian context for it could not have been subjected to daily rituals and therefore, its use initially was possibly to serve some sort of a decorative purpose. So far as the emergence of the art of stucco modelling at Amaravati is concerned Dr K.M. Varma does not deny the probability that the Roman contacts with India might have inspired the Amaravati sculptors to make use of stucco as a medium for figure sculpture. He further feels that it was only the idea that seems to have been borrowed from the Romans by Andhra artists and there was no direct influence. We have no comments to offer on these inferences. However, we may like to add that hollow kaolin figurines (terracottas) available in the excavations in the levels associated with early centuries of Christian era in Deccan and elsewhere also seem to have an outside source as far as the technique is concerned. On the whole Dr Varma's book in itself is a well written text with thought provoking contents and remarkable precision. He is also to be thanked for its fine production.

M.C. Joshi

* * *

Amarendra Nath. **Buddhist Images and Narratives;** pages XI+120; plates 16; published by Books and Books, C4A/20A, Janakpuri, New Delhi. Price Rs. 254.

Edsin-gol! Whoever has heard of this! Yet, here an young Indian archaeologist, Amarendra Nath, has written an attractive book, *Buddhist Images And Narratives* on the finds from an archaeological site called

Khara Khoto on the bank of Edsin-gol River in inner Mongolia. It is gratifying to note that young archaeologists, especially Indian, have turned their eyes towards archaeological sites washed by unknown rivers, unknown even to editorial boards of standard atlases and encyclopaedias, when focussing attention on sites in well and little known river valleys of the Indian subcontinent is the *a la mode*. Incidentally this is the first book to appear on the finds of Sir Aurel Stein.

The site, we learn, was discovered in 1908 by a Russian Explorer, Col. Kozlov. Sir Aurel Stein toured the Edsin-gol delta in 1914 and brought his finds to India. The finds now form part of the Central Asian Collection of the National Museum, New Delhi.

The author has planned the book very well, devoting special attention to the ratio or proportion of space to importance of the topic, a ratio more often ignored by scholars. In the first twenty seven pages, called backdrop by him, he has dealt with factors like setting, historical perspective, the route favoured by explorers, earlier works on the subject, etc. Thus he has acquanted the reader with information required for a clear comprehension of what follows. Then he proceeds to three topics, Buddha and Bodhisattvas, Female Divinities and Male Divinities, assigning a Chapter with an average of nineteen pages to each. Lastly he takes up the narratives, which get almost the same space as the first chapter. What precise planning?

This passion of the author for mathematical accuracy is reflected in the treatment of his subject. As a scholar he is bound by certain conventions, i.e. he has to describe the finds, compare the finds with similar finds discovered at other sites, probe literary sources and finally offer his conclusion. He has meticulously adhered to this. For instance, take his treatment of Mahamayuri in the chapter titled Female Divinities. Two scholars, Alice Getty and A.K. Gordon have thrown much light on the forms of Buddhist divinities and variations in their forms in other regions. But their description on the 'Queen of Magic Art', one of the forms of Mahamayuri, is rather sketchy. Our author has not only tallied his woodcut of Mahamayuri with those referred to by Getty and Gordon, but also compared it with another woodcut representation from Tibet. Further he has delved into Buddhist scriptures like the *Sadhanamala Nispannayogavali*, etc. to give authenticity to his views. Consequently the reader never feels bored.

Authors generally leave the note and reference portion either to their students or assistants. This author is an exception. He leaves nothing more to desire or find fault with in this respect.

The publishers have lavished care in the production of this book. The dust-jacket is pleasing, the message about the book and the author kindles the curiosity of the reader, as it should. But they have followed the dicta of their fellow publishers in propitiating the printer's devil and editor by giving them full liberty to appear wherever they like. Not fair.

A very well written book, worthy of emulation by aspiring authors; other Edsin-gols are waiting.

S.P. GUPTA

* * *

D.K. Chakrabarti & S.J. Hasan, **The Antiquities of Kangra**, Munshi Ram Manohar Lal Publisherr Pvt. Ltd., New Delhi 1984, pp. 86; Plate 26, price not stated.

The *Antiquities of Kangra* is a useful consolidation of studies about finds of archaeological significance, both prehistoric and historic including artistic, numismatic and epigraphical. It also incorporates the results of the explorations undertaken by the authors in 1980. It is a useful guide to (a) morphology of the rock strata, whether quartzite, granite or gneiss, which occur erratically in the Shivalik hills at other comparable sites. This would also enable the verification of the explanation for erratic morphology of rock strata as due either to glacial action or the formation of Sikhov Cones. (b) the status of stone tool industry: the significance of Ror (along with the polished implements from Haripur Guler area) as marking the change from paleolithic to neolithic culture. In this context there is need for more detailed description of the stone tools discovered at Ror, although this has been done elsewhere by G.C. Mohapatra, the excavator of the site. (c) status of the iron industry :

(i) the types of ores—haematite, magnetite, linonite, laterite—available locally and mine sites;

(ii) the technique of fabrication of sponge iron and of welding and bonding instead of fusion;

(iii) the fabrication equipment and facilities to appreciate how far the iron industry was local, the level of technology and that the solitary piece of iron knife .and an iron arrow-head (page 86 was not imported from outside the area.

I would, however, like to point out that chapter 2, Prehistory, though it contains valuable material, is expressed in a manner that it can be understood only by those who are familiar with prehistorical archaeological studies.

The concluding chapter emphasises the importance of Kangra studies in the main stream of Indian history. It highlights the fact that the prehistoric and early historic finds are fragmentary and meagre; and that there is an intriguing hiatus between the early historical and the medieval periods at the present stage of our knowledge.

Y. KRISHAN

* * *

Gregory L. Possehl, **Kulli,** Carolina Academic Press, Durham. USA, (1986), pp. 168+XII. 25 figures and II plates, Price not mentionted.

The book deals primarily with the problem of trade between the Indus Valley and Mesopotamia, both in the light of Mesopotamian texts and the archaeological remains located in the Euphrates—Indus Divide, covering much of southern Iran and southern Baluchistan. It has, therefore, far larger a canvas to cover than merely the sites of Kulli culture, although Kulli has been used as the pivot. The book has been divided into five chapters, grouped in two parts, followed by Conclusions, two appendices, notes, tables and bibliography. The first three chapters (Part I) deal with the material remains located at Kulli and Mehi as well as Nindowari, Niai Buthi, etc. all in southern Baluchistan. This part also mentions eighty odd sites of Kulli culture-complex known so far. Finally, it reflects upon the relationship between the highland sites of Kulli Culture and the lowland sites of the Harappan Culture with the central idea that Kulli may have played the middle man's role in the Indus-Mesopotamian trade.

Chapter 4 deals with subjects like Economic Relationship of southern Baluchistan and Sind with south-west Asia during the third millennium, in the light of material remains located at sites like Tepe Yahya and Shahr-i Sokhta in Iran and sites located in Persian Gulf islands, supposed to be Dilmun region of cuneiform texts.

Chapter 5 deals with the age old problem of the Indus Urbanization, but exclusively in the light of Mesopotamian trade with the Indus.

The author concludes that Mesopotamian interests in the Indus arose as the direct consequence of the disputes that often arose between the rulers of Mesopotamia and Iran over imports, repeatedly hampering the royal and temple projects which the Mesopotamians used to undertake in their cities.

A lot of theoretical approaches to ancient trade have been discussed although, understandably, C.C. Lamberg-Karlovsky and his writings in the light of Tepe Yahya's reports have been discussed in great detail. The author has taken note of all the recent relevant publications including Shashi Asthana's *Pre-Harappan Cultures of India and the Borderlands* (New Delhi 1985) and the unpublished works of Jim Shaffer, such as 'The Harappan External Trade: A critical Assessment' and 'The Indus Valley, Baluchistan and Helman Traditions: Neolithic to Bronze Age' and of M.R. Mughal such as *The Early Harappan Period in the Greater Indus Valley*. However, one significant omission has been the paper entitled 'Indus-Mesopotamian Trade: Nature of the trade, and a structural Analysis of the operative System', published in the *Essays in Indian Protohistory* (New Delhi 1979), since here a fresh model of Indus-Mesopotamian trade was presented by an Asian author.

It is a very well argued thesis which has not only republished all relevant material on the Kulli complex but which has also picked up issues which have been engaging all serious scholars of the Indus Civilization. But we doubt if the hint that the roots of the Indus urbanization may lie in the Indus-Mesopotamian trade will be acceptable to scholars at this stage of our knowledge.

The author, like many of us in India, also feels that a significant lacuna still exists in our knowledge regarding the transition from the so-called Early Harappan to Mature Harappan.

The book has been beautifully produced although the plates at the end could present enlarged pictures, at least double of their sizes, for better view (it was possible even though these were copied from Aurel Stein's old publications). We however recommend it for all serious students and researchers of the Indus studies.

—S.P. GUPPTA

* * *

A.K. Singh, **Trans-Himalayan Wall Paintings,** Agam Kala Prakashan, New Delhi, 1985. pp. 192+viii. Photographs 126, including seven in colour. One map. Price: Rs. 400.

The book, a Ph.D. thesis, is divided into eight chapters with a couple of appendices. It deals with the 11th-13th century works of art—paintings and stucco—primarily in the Buddhist monasteries and temples located in Ladakh, Lahul, Spiti and Kinnaur, such as Alchi, Mongyu, Tabo, Nako and Charang. These were known to art historians earlier also, but Alchi alone was studied in great detail. That Dr. Singh revisited all of them again, restudied them, separated the old from the new as well as the repainted ones, is indeed a commendable exercise by a young scholar with very little financial support from our universities—we sometimes collected small sums of money at Delhi to finance his journeys which he undertook during the period of his studies. Dr. Singh has gathered here a lot of information on the subject—both on styles and iconography—and this can be utilized as a base-work for long-term projects. Once Shri M.N. Deshpande had also done some very useful work in the monasteries of Lahul and Spiti valleys but it has as yet not been published. Profs. Tucci, Snellgrove and their students worked earlier in trans-Himalayan region and their publications are also available, but good research work by Indian students has started only with the work of Dr. Singh.

Unfortunately, such a good work has been published by one who very often publishes good things in worst blocks and full of proof mistakes.

—S.P. GUPTA

The Collection

(Copper Hoard Implements in the National Museum)

1. 65.256 Harpoon
Shahabad, Distt. Hardoi
33.5 x 7.2 cm.

2. 65.267 Flat celt
Shahabad, Distt. Hardoi
16.3 x 9.3 cm.

3. 65.258 Flat celt
Shahabad, Distt. Hardoi
14 x 7 cm.

4. 65.259 Bar celt
Shahabad, Distt. Hardoi
19.2 x 5 cm.

5. 66.28 Antennae sword
Shahabad, Distt. Hardoi
37.8 x 8 cm.

6. 66.29 Harpoon
Shahabad, Distt. Hardoi
36 x 6.1 cm.

7. 66.30 Flat celt
Shahabad, Distt. Hardoi
20.3 x 15.2 cm.

8. 66.31 Flat celt
Shahabad, Distt. Hardoi
10.6 x 7 cm.

Shahabad, Distt. Hardoi
10.6 x 7 cm.

9. 66.188 Anthropomarphic figure
Chandausi, Distt. Moradabad
42 x 38 cm.

10. 67.138 Harpoon
Shahabad, Distt. Hardoi
19 x 4.2 cm.

11. 67.139 Antennae sword
Shahabad, Distt. Hardoi
26.2 x 4.5 cm.

12. 67.140 Harpoon
Shahabad, Distt. Hardoi
35.7 x 6.8 cm.

13. 70.60 Antennae sword
Modhera, Distt. Mahasana
L.50 cm.

14. 70.61 Antennae sword
Modhera, Distt. Mahasana
L.46. 05 cm.

15. 70.62 Antennae sword
Modhera, Distt. Mahasana
L.32.5 cm.

16. 70.63 Antennae sword
Modhera, Distt. Mahasana
L.52.05 cm.

17. 71.219 Flat celt
Shahabad, Hardoi
10.5 x 5.7 cm.

18. 71.220 Flat celt
Shahabad, Hardoi
11.5 x 7 cm.

19. 71.221 Flat celt
Shahabad, Hardoi
14 x 5.5 cm.

20. 71.222 Flat celt
Shahabad, Distt. Hardoi
6.5 x 4.5 cm.

21. 71.223 Flat celt
Shahabad, Distt. Hardoi
5 x 5.5 cm.

22. 75.152 Antennae sword (broken three pieces)
Shahabad, Distt. Hardoi
L.56 cm.

23. 75.153 Hatchet or *Parasu*
Shahabad, Distt. Hardoi
13.5 cm.

24. 75.154 Flat celt (with an engraved leaf)
Shahabad, Distt. Hardoi
14.8 cm.

25. 75.155 Flat celt
Shahabad, Distt. Hardoi
11 x 5.3 cm.

26. 75.156 Flat celt (rectangular)
Shahabad, Distt. Hardoi
15.1 x 9 cm.

27. 75.157 Shouldered Celt
Shahabad, Distt. Hardoi
15.6 x 12.5 cm.

28. 75.158 Flat celt
Shahabad, Distt. Hardoi
17.1 x 11 cm.

29. 75.159 Flat celt
Shahabad, Distt. Hardoi
15.8 x 7.8 cm.

30. 84.387 Harpoon
Uttar Pradesh
32.5 x 1 cm.

31. 84.388 Harpoon
Uttar Pradesh
39.5 x 6 cm.

32. 85.20 Shouldered axe
Uttar Pradesh
18.5 x 16.1 cm.

33. 85.21 Flat celt
Uttar Pradesh
12.7 x 8.4 cm.

34. 85.171 Antennae sword (in four parts)
Shahabad, Distt. Hardoi
49 x 6.7 cm.

35. 85.172 Antennae sword
Shahabad, Distt. Hardoi
33 x 4 cm.

36. 85.173 Antennae sword
Shahabad, Distt. Hardoi

37. 85.174 Antennae sword (fragmentary)
Shahabad, Distt. Hardoi
16.7 x 4.4 cm.

38. 85.175 Antennae sword (fragmentary)
Shahabad, Distt. Hardoi
11.2 x 3.2 cm.

39. 85.176 Spearhead (tang missing)
Shahabad, Distt. Hardoi
27 x 5.2 cm.

40. 85.177 Harpoon
Shahabad, Distt. Hardoi
25 x 6 cm.

41. 85.178/1 Splayed axe
Shahabad, Distt. Hardoi
14 x 12.2 cm.

42. 85.178/2 Flat celt
Shahabad, Distt. Hardoi
1.56 x 10.8 cm.

43. 85.178/3 Splayed axe
Shahabad, Distt. Hardoi
17.8 x 15 cm.

44. 85.179/1 Shouldered celt
Shahabad, Distt. Hardoi
11.7 x 12.6 cm.

45. 85.179/2 Shouldered celt
Shahabad, Distt. Hardoi
12 x 11 cm.

46. 85.180/1 Tanged Weed-Chisel (*Khurpi*)
Shahabad, Distt. Hardoi
20.9 x 6.5 cm.

47. 85.180/1 Tanged Weed Chisel .*Khurpi*)
Shahabad, Distt. Hardoi
20.9 x 6.5 cm.

48. 85.181/2 Tanged Weed-Chisel
Shahabad, Distt. Hardoi
20 x 6.2 cm.

49. 85.182 Spearhead
Shahabad, Distt. Hardoi
19.9 x 1.8 cm.

50. 85.183 Splayed axe (two fragments)
Shahabad, Distt. Hardoi
(i) 5.7 x 7.6 cm.
(ii) 10 x 10.4 cm.

51. 86.2 Harpoon
Amroha, Moradabad
35 x 4.5 cm.

52. 86.3 Flat celt
Amroha, Moradabad
16.4 x 13.6 cm.

53. 86.4 Flat celt
Amroha, Moradabad
24 x 5.4 cm.

54. 86.5 Harpoon
Uttar Pradesh
31.5 x 6.5 cm.

55. 86.6 Flat celt
Uttar Pradesh
12.5 x 8.5 cm.

56. 86.59/1 Lugged axe
Mohamadabad, near Sitapur
13 x 11 cm.

57. 86.59/2 Shouldered celt
Kanpur
15.7 x 13.8 cm.

58. 86.59/3 Shouldered celt
Shahabad, Hardoi
20 x 16.3 cm.

59. 86.59/4 Shouldered celt
Kanpur
13.3 x 11.5 cm.

60. 86.59/5 Flat celt
Unnao
16.5 x 11.2 cm.

61. 86.59/6 Flat celt
Shahabad, Hardoi
19 x 13.8 cm.

62. 86.59/7 Flat celt (fragmentary)
Kanpur
14 x 8.5 cm.

63. 86.59/8 Flat celt (fragmentary)
Shahabad, Hardoi
11 x 9.6 cm.

64. 86.59/9 Flat celt
Shahabad, Hardoi
13.2 x 9.8 cm.

65. 86.59/10 Flat celt
Shahabad, Hardoi
14.5 x 8.8 cm.

66. 86.59/11 Flat celt
Unnao
9.2 x 8 cm.

67. 86.59/12 Flat celt (broken)
Kanpur
7.6 x 4 cm.

68. 86.59/13 Flat celt (fragmentary)
Kanpur
10.7 x 7.9 cm.

69. 86.59/14 Flat celt
Shahabad, Hardoi
12.6 x 7.7 cm.

70. 86.59/15 Flat celt (fragmentary)
Shahabad, Hardoi
8.5 x 8.2 cm.

71. 86.59/16 Flat celt (fragmentary)
Unnao
8.9 x 7.5 cm.

72. 86.59/17 Flat celt (fragmentary)
Kanpur
5.5 x 5.9 cm.

73. 86.59/18 Flat celt
Kanpur
18.7 x 7.6 cm.

74. 86.59/19 Flat celt (fragmentary)
Unnao
10. x 6.1 cm.

75. 86.59/20 Flat celt
Unnao
15.3 x 7.4 cm.

76. 86.59/21 Flat celt
Shahabad, Hardoi
12.8 x 6.5 cm.

77. 86.59/22 Flat celt
Shahabad, Hardoi
5 x 4.4 cm.

78. 86.59/23 Flat celt
Kanpur
7.5 x 5.2 cm.

79. 86.59/24 Flat celt
Kanpur
12.5 x 10.1 cm.

80. 86.59/25 Flat celt
Shahabad, Hardoi
8.7 x 13 cm.

81. 86.59/26 Flat celt
Shahabad, Hardoi
10.8 x 8.8 cm.

82. 86.59/27 Flat celt
Sitapur
18 x 6 cm.

83. 86.59/28 Chisel
Sitapur
12.2 x 4 cm.

84. 86.59/29 Chisel
Shahabad, Hardoi
12.2 x 4 cm.

85. 86.59/30 Chisel
Sitapur
13.3 x 2.9 cm.

86. 86.59/31 Tanged Weed-Chisel (Kharpi)
Shahabad, Hardoi
23.6 x 5 cm.

87. 86.59/32 Harpoon
Kanpur
26 x 7.5 cm.

88. 86.59/33 Harpoon
Shahabad, Hardoi
16 x 3.6 cm.

89. 86.59/34 Spearhead
Kanpur
39.8 x 6.1 cm.

90. 86.59/35 Spearhead
Kanpur
24 x 6 cm.

91. 86.59/36 Spearhead (fragmentary)
Unnao
6.7 x 3.5 cm.

92. 86.59/37 Spearhead (fragmentary)
Shahabad, Hardoi
6.4 x 3.1 cm.

93. 86.59/38 Spearhead (fragmentary)
Shahabad, Hardoi
5.8 x 3.8 cm.

PLATES

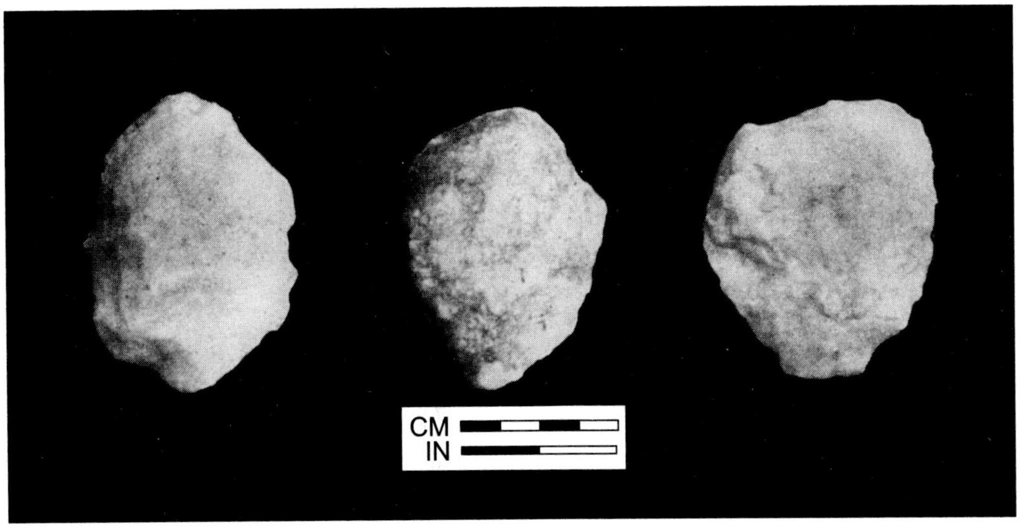

Plate-4.I

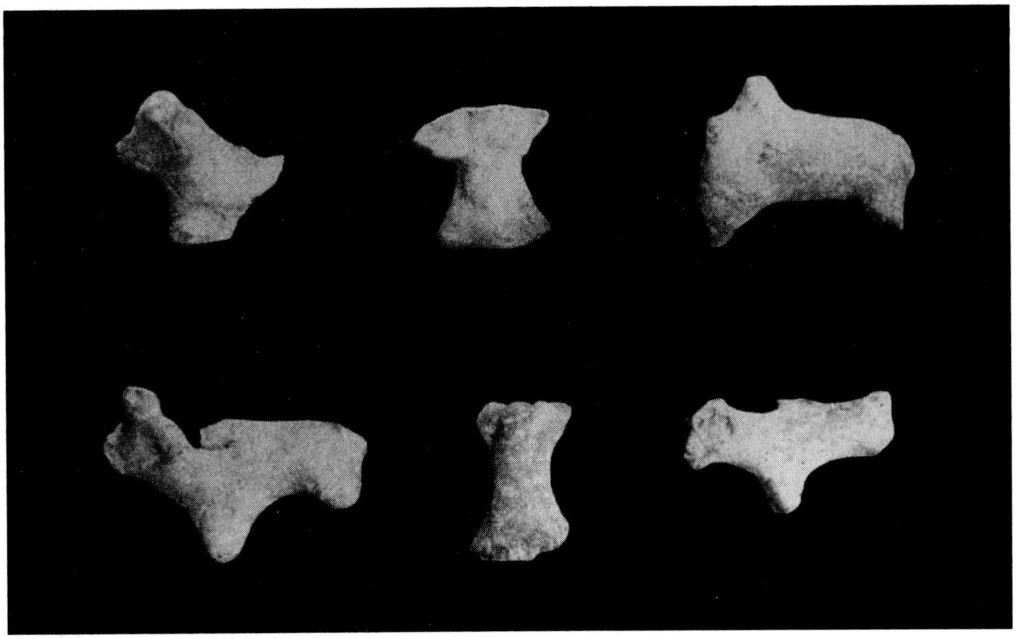

Plate-4.II

Plate-6.I

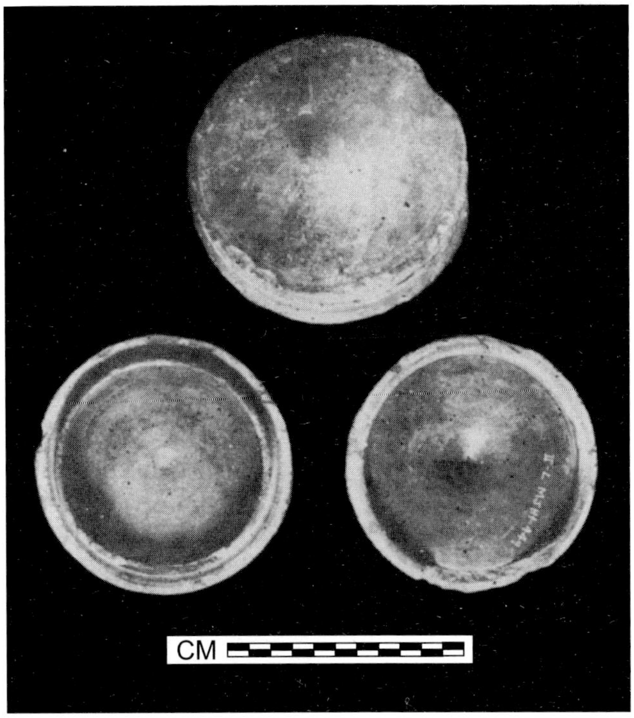

Plate-6.II

Plate-6.III

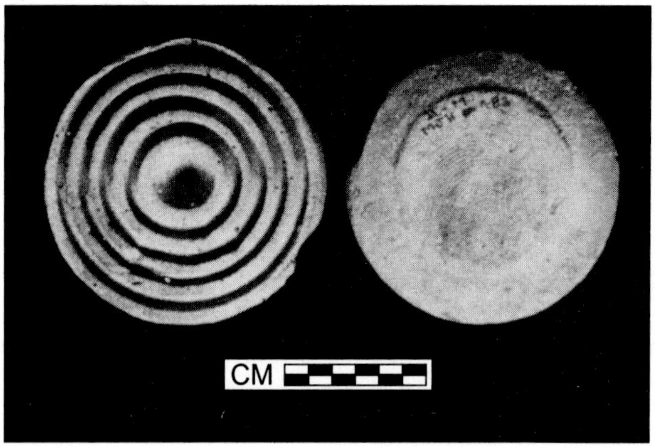

Plate-6.IV

Plate-6.V

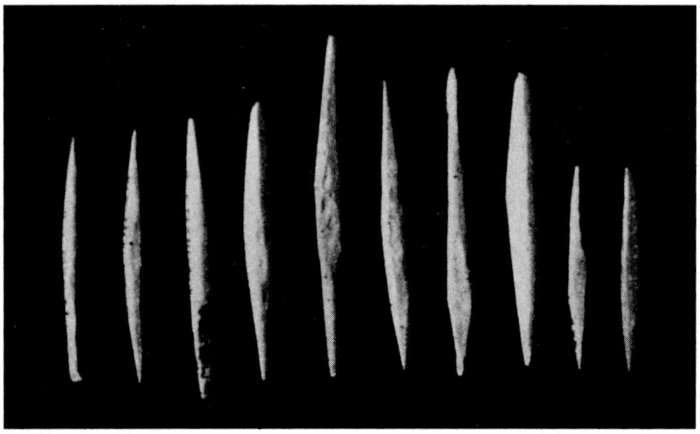

Plate-6.VI

Plate-6.VII

Plate-6.VIII

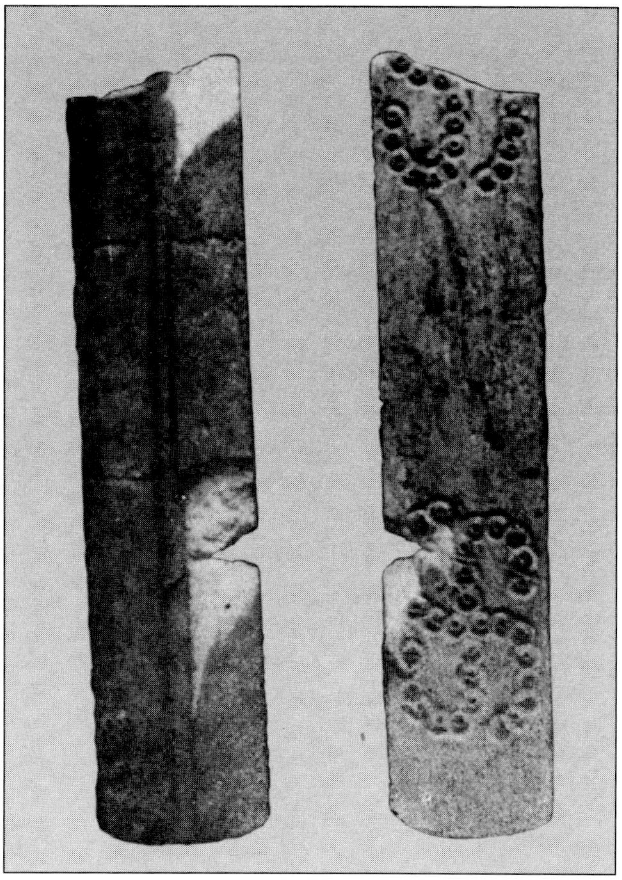

Plate-6.IX

Plate-8.I

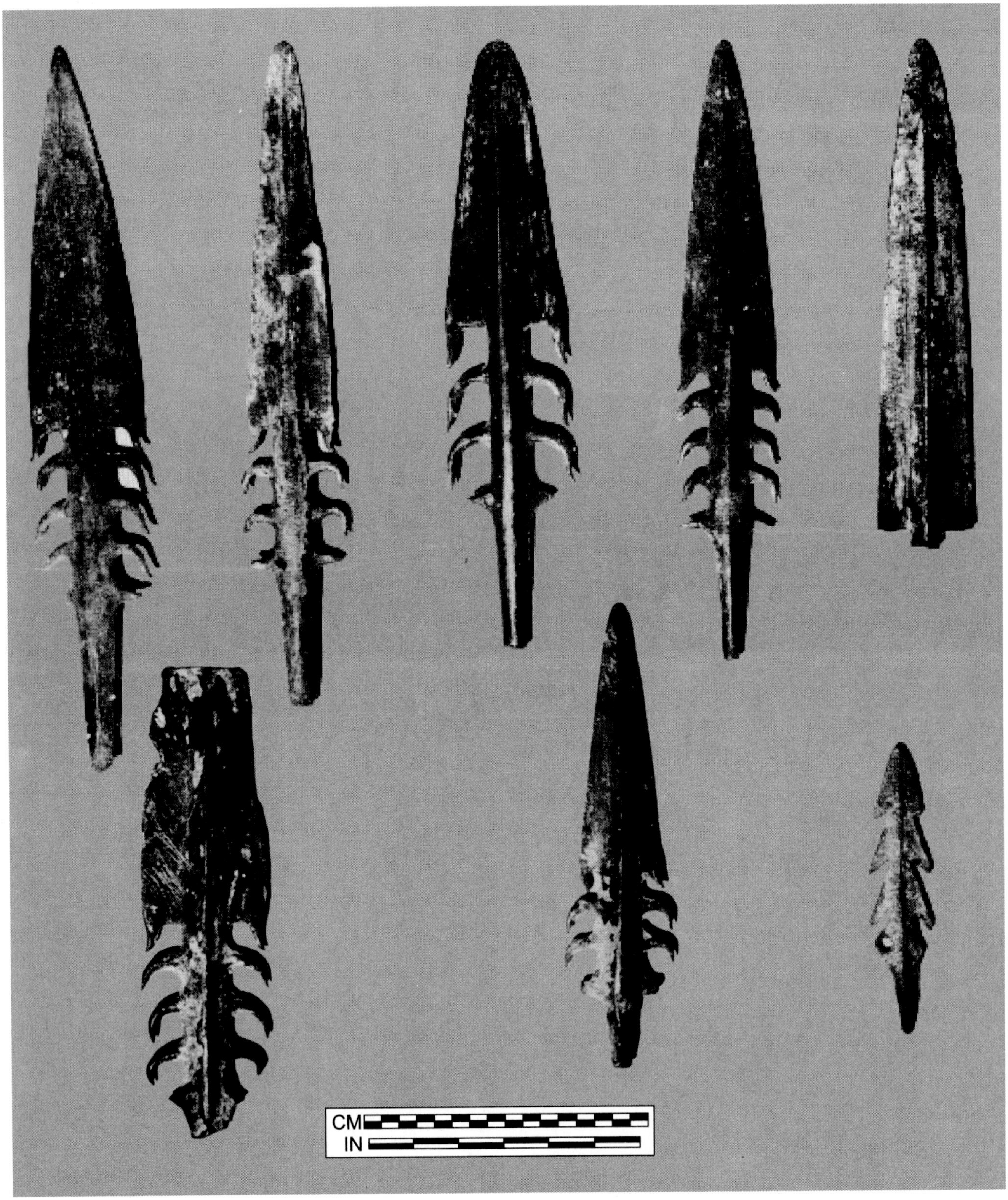

Plate-10.I

Plate-10.II

Plate-10.III

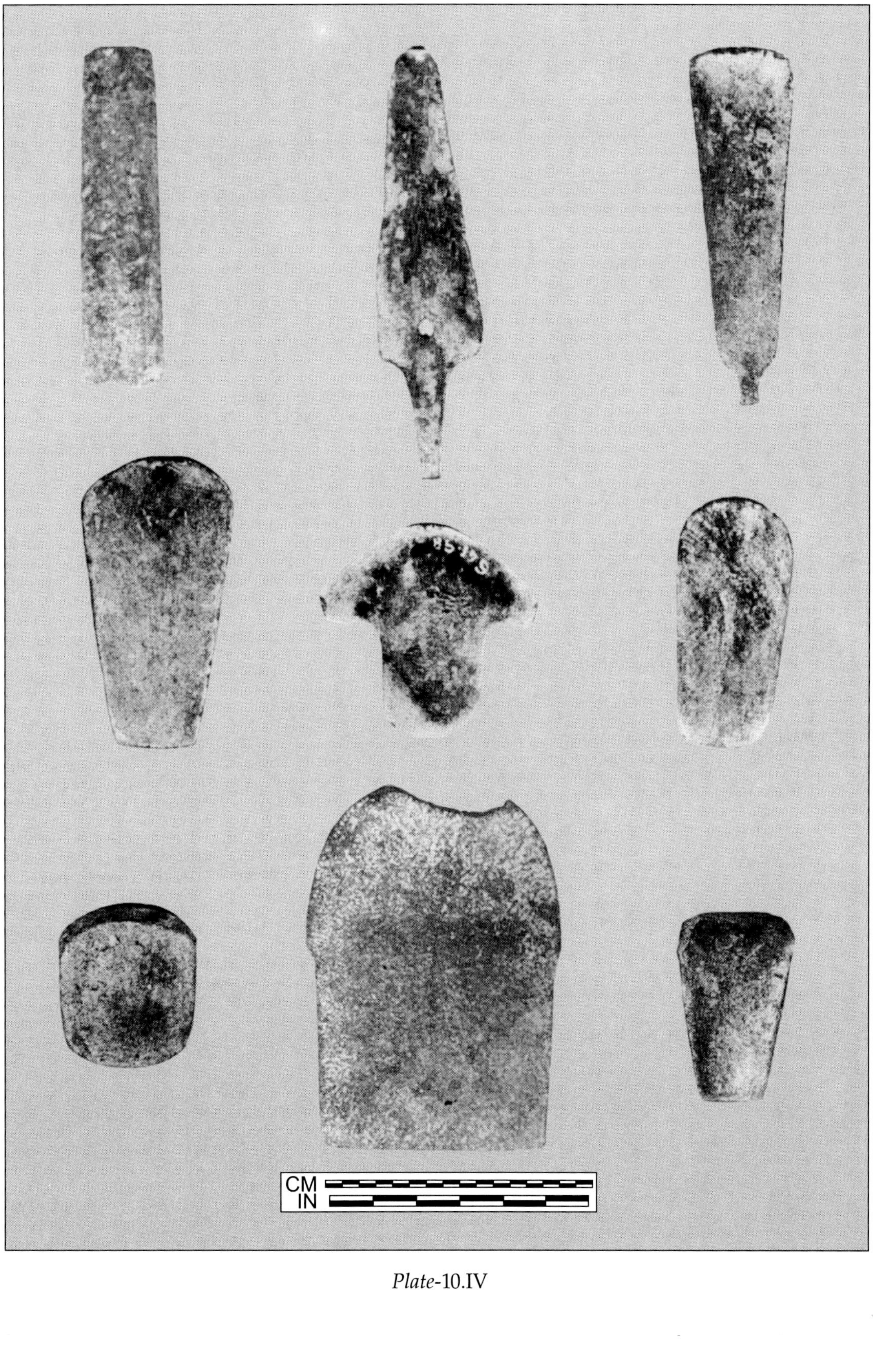

Plate-10.IV

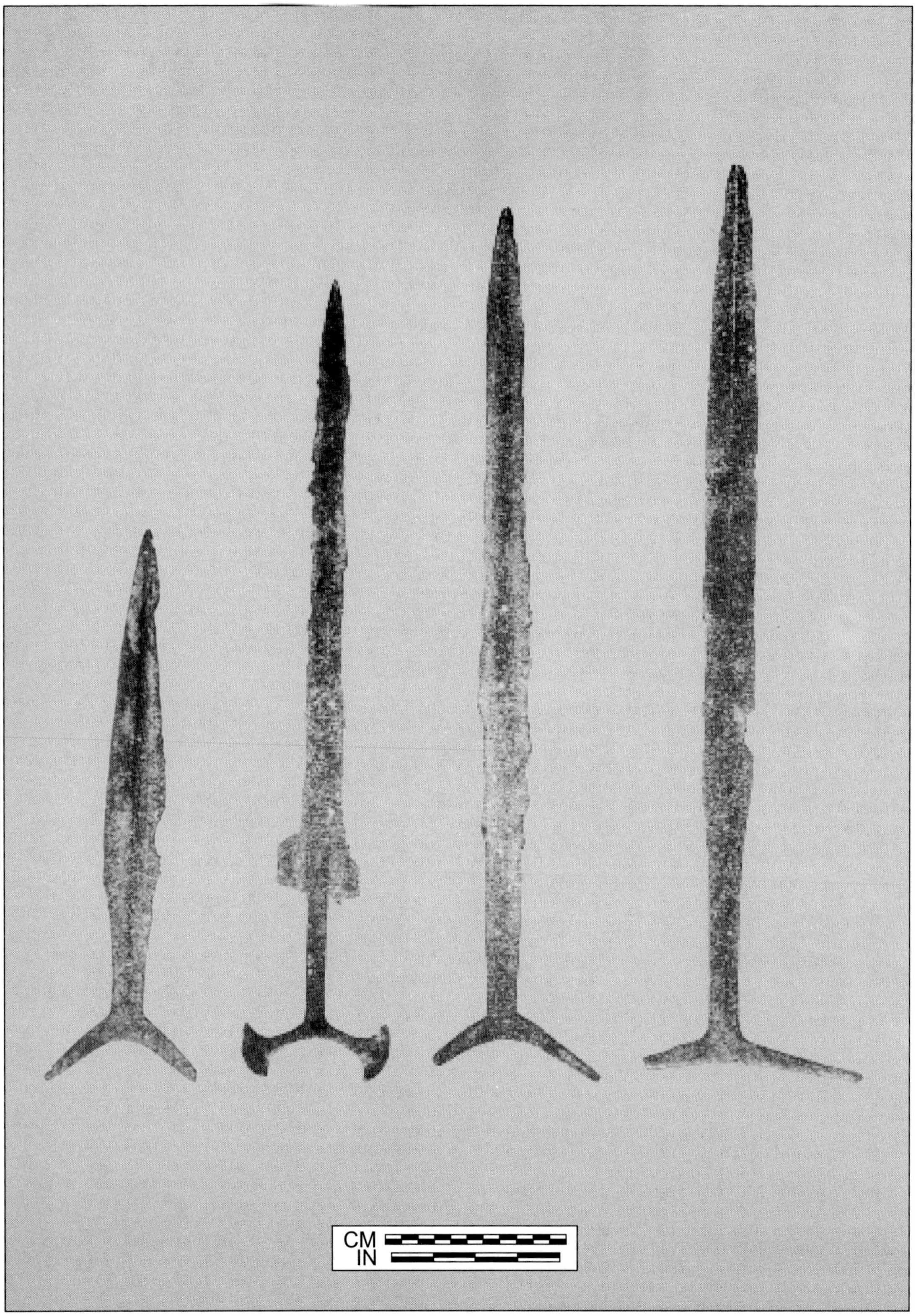

Plate-10.V

Plate-10.VI

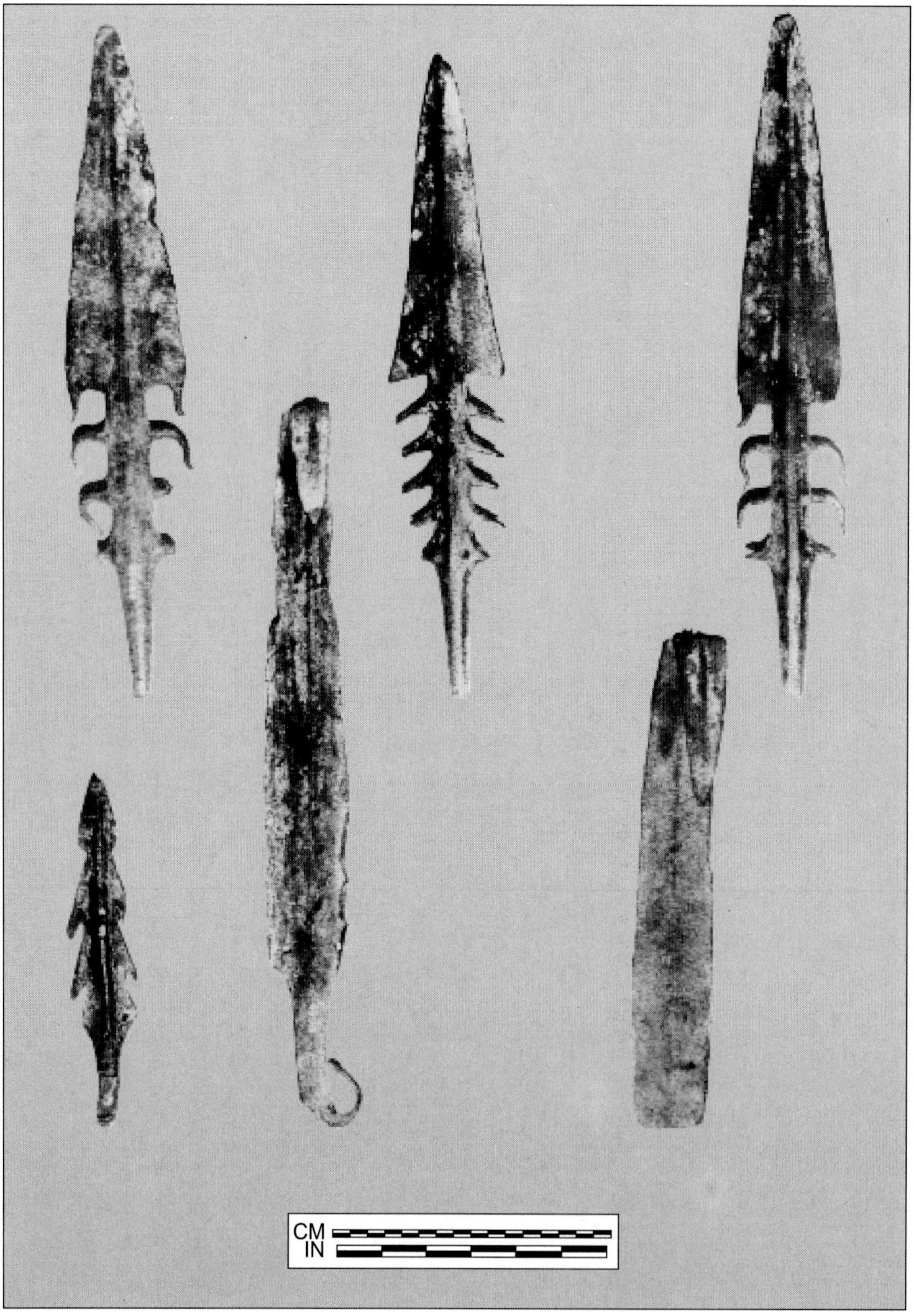

Plate-10.VII

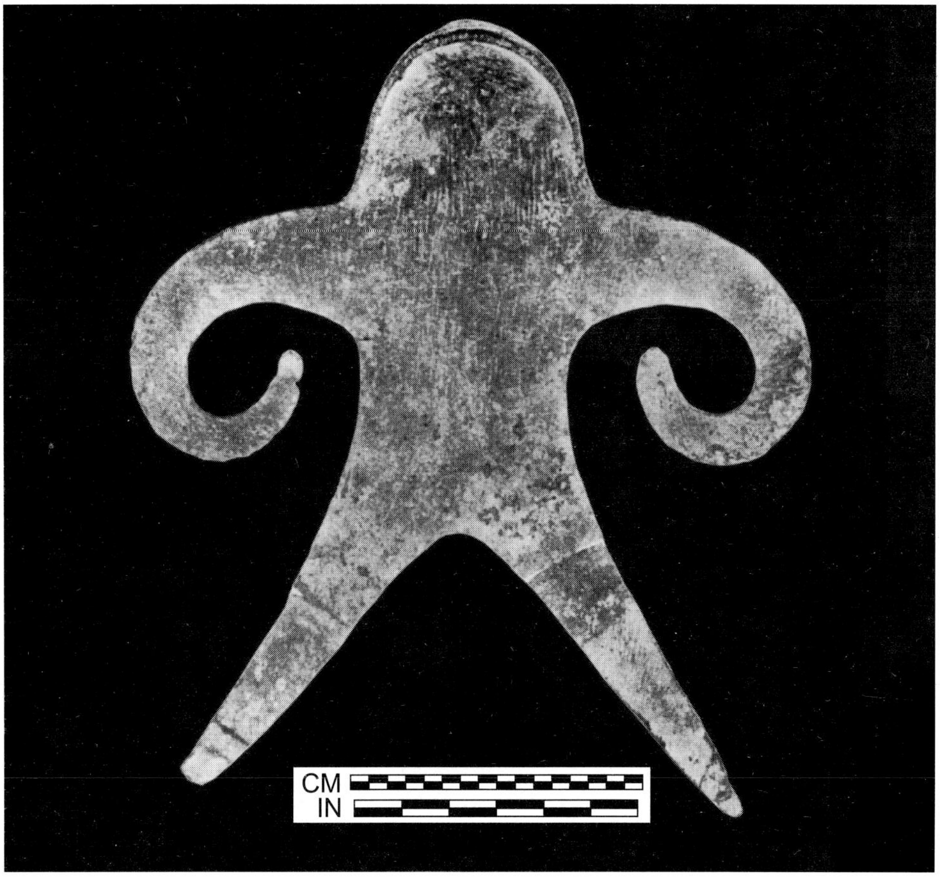

Plate-10.VIII

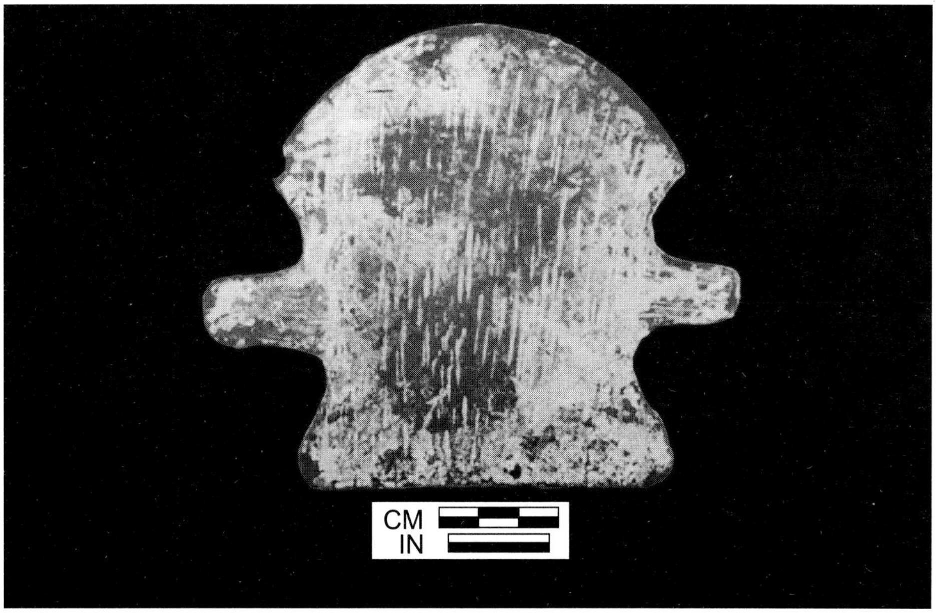

Plate-10.IX

Plate-10.X

Plate-10.XI

Plate-11.I

Plate-11.II

Plate-11.III

Plate-11.IV

Plate-11.V

Plate-11.VI

Plate-11.VII

Plate-11.VIII

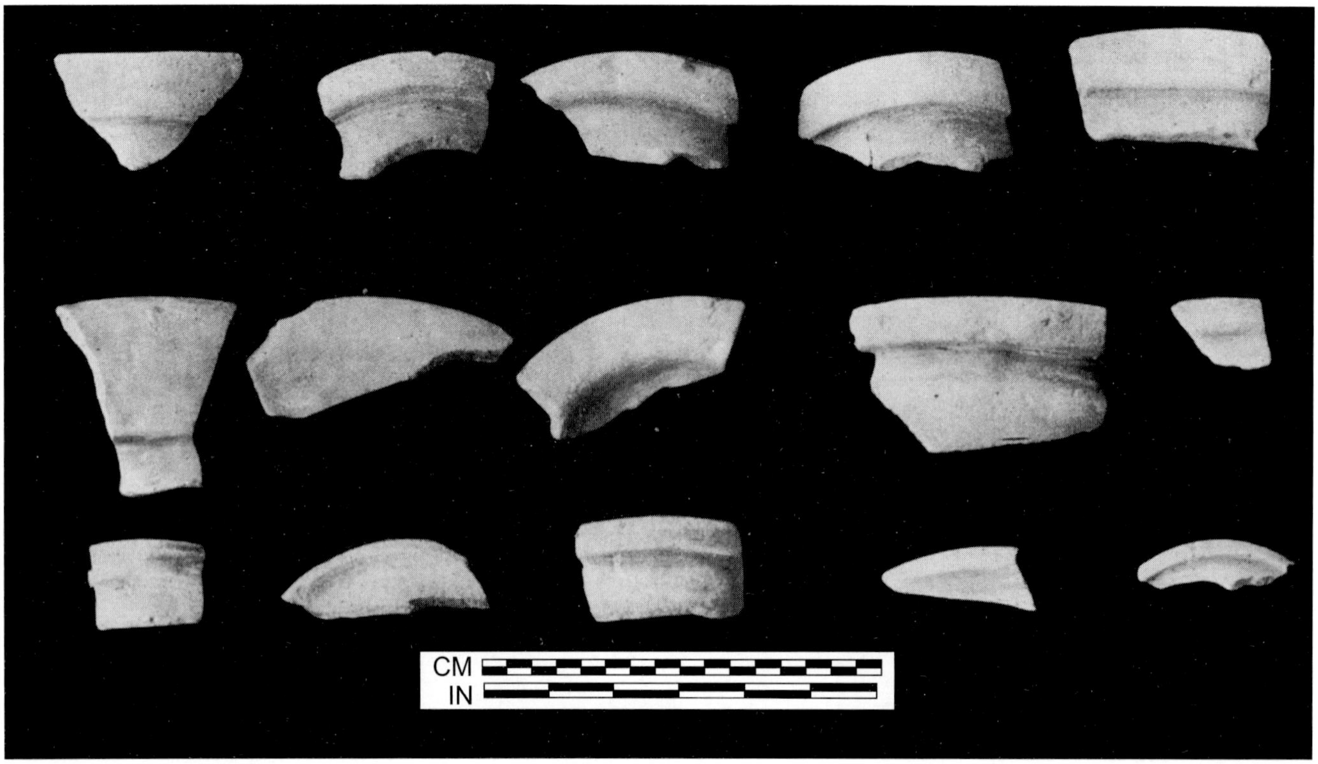

Plate-16.I

Plate-16.II

Plate-16.III

Plate-16.IV

Plate-16.V

Plate-16.VI

Plate-16.VIII

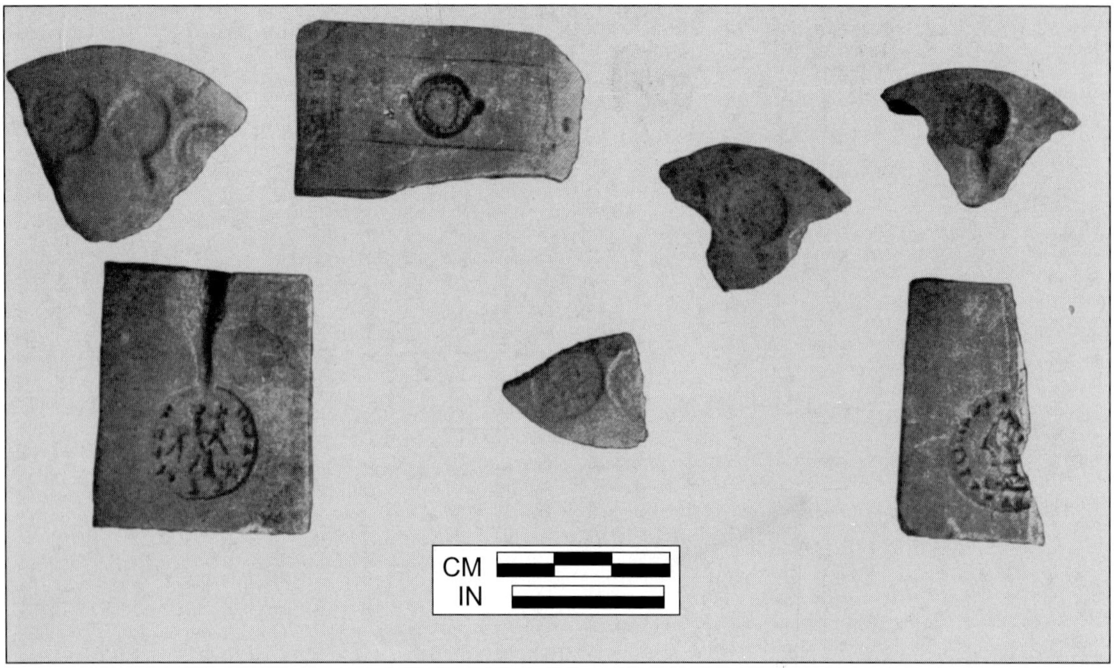

Plate-16.IX

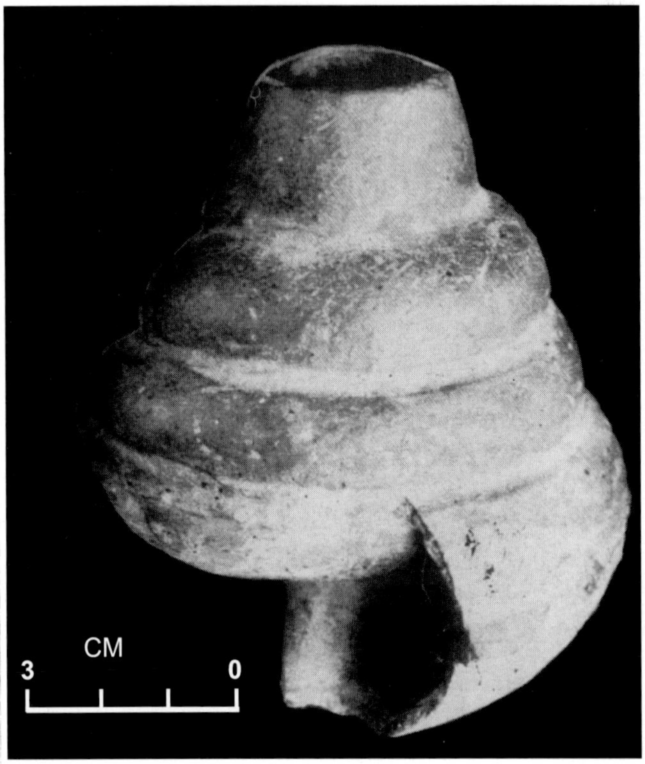

Plate-16.X

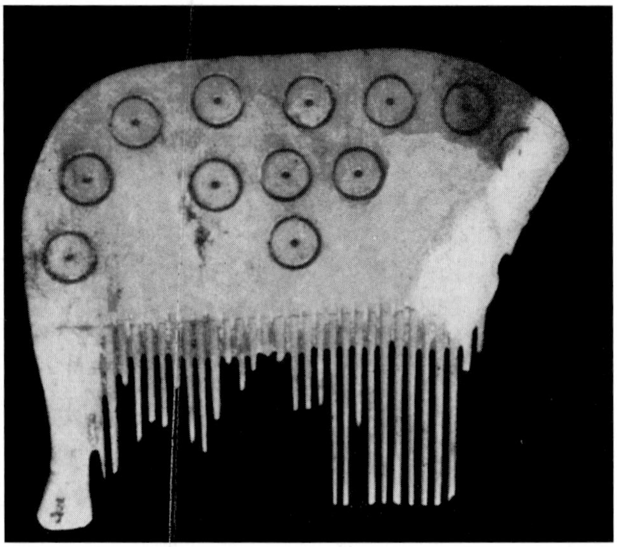

Plate-16.XI

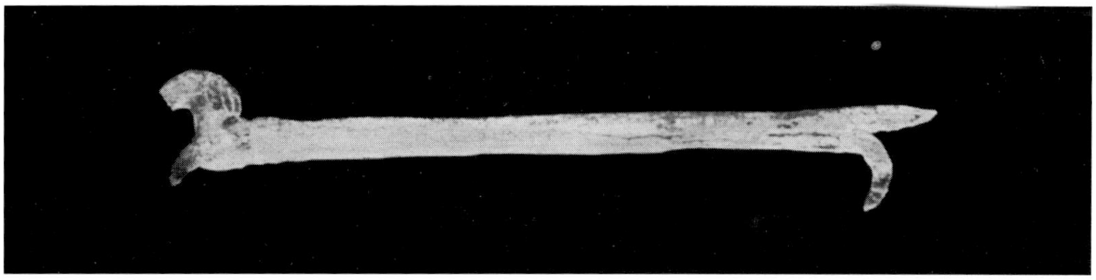

Plate-19.I

Plate-19.II

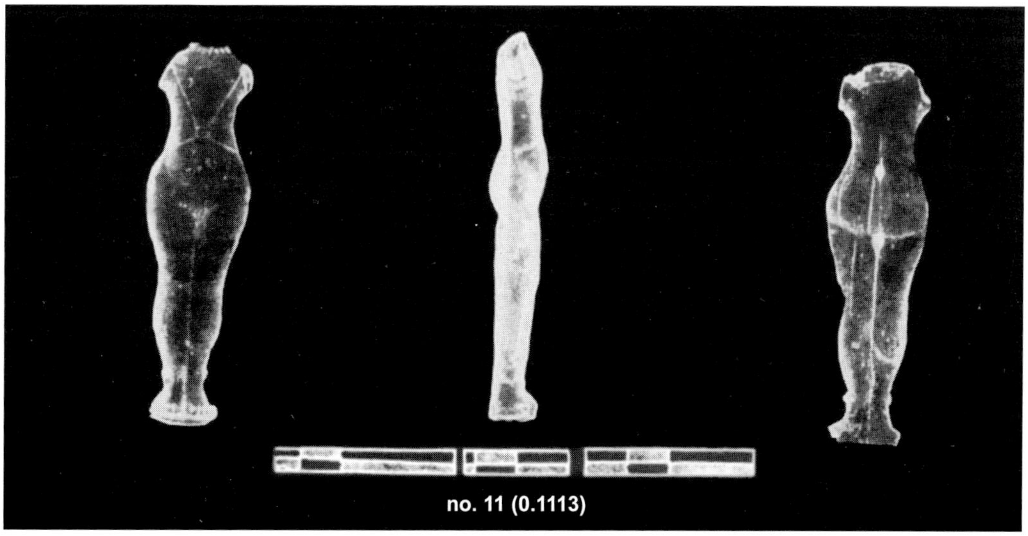

Plate-19.III

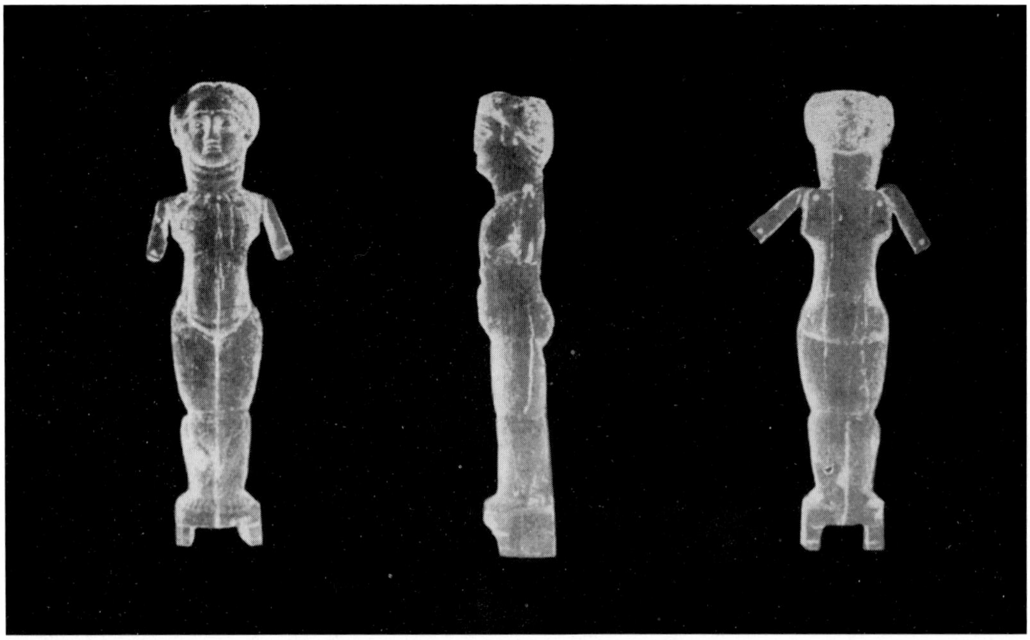

Plate-19.IV

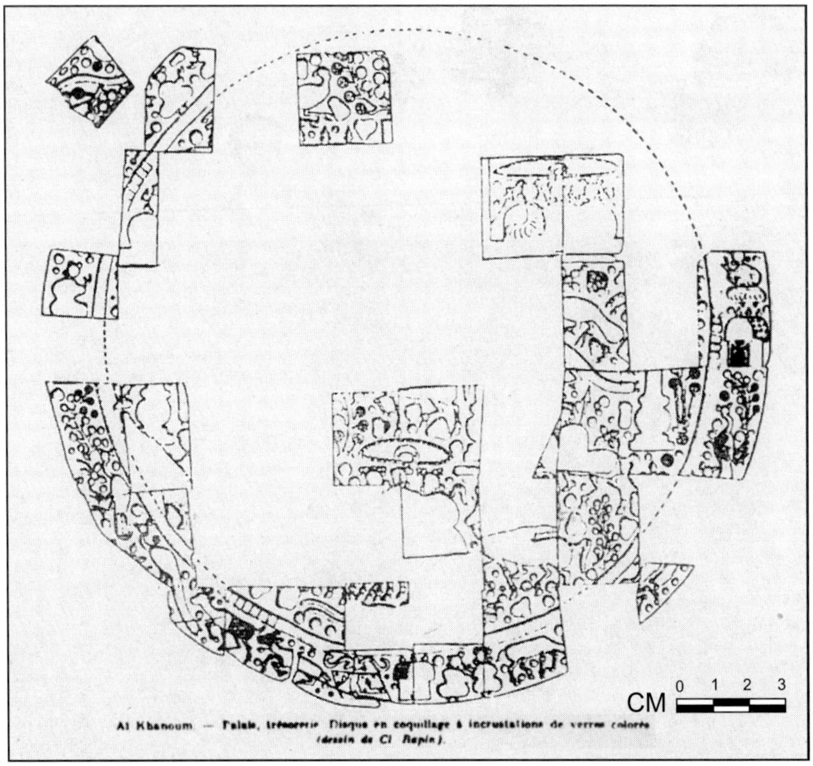

Plate-19.V